MW00558825

MASTODONS, MANSIONS, AND ANTEBELLUM GHOSTS

A Sketchbook of Voices Rising Up from Florida's Red Hills

Rose Knox and Graham Schorb

Mastodons, Mansions, and Antebellum Ghosts: A Sketchbook of Voices Rising Up from Florida's Red Hills

Copyright © 2020 by Rose Knox and Graham Schorb

ISBN: 978-1-949810-07-3

The Florida Historical Society Press
435 Brevard Avenue
Cocoa, FL 32922
http://myfloridahistory.org/fhspress

PRESS

Dedication

For Anna Sophia and Julia Rose-Marie, my grandchildren: "Remember the days of old, consider the years of many generations; ask thy father, and he will show thee; thy elders, and they will tell thee." From *The Song of Moses*, Deuteronomy 32:7.

May the wisdom of the ages and the wisdom of the storyteller bless your lives.

"The memory is a living thing—it too is in transit. But during its moment, all that is remembered joins, and lives—the old and the young, the past and the present, the living and the dead." Eudora Welty

Acknowledgments

Artistic Contributions: Theodore Morris and Patrick Elliott

Photography: State Library and Archives of Florida and Madison County Photographic Collection. Other photographs, unless otherwise cited, are courtesy of Graham Schorb.

We owe our gratitude to the following people: the staff at the Florida Historical Society for preparing the manuscript for publication: Dr. Ben Brotemarkle, Executive Director of the Florida Historical Society; copy editor, Christine Gallaway; and Jon White for creating the cover; North Florida College (formerly North Florida Community College) librarians and staff: Lynn Wyche, Hope Johnson, Jhan Reichert, and Katie Miller for their support in fulfilling our research requests. Further appreciation goes to many talented artists who over the years have become our friends and who have graciously contributed their works for this Red Hills project. They are listed as follows: Robert Patrick Elliott, noted artist and our friend, for his depiction of an ancient hunter with sloth, (along with many other regional illustrations) and his generous hospitality in touring us through his studio in Tallahassee; Pat and his wife Holly also provided an entire library from their personal collection and willingly gave them to us for our regional research; Theodore Morris, preeminent painter of *Florida's Lost Tribes* and of *Florida & Caribbean Native People* fame, for his American Indian artistic renderings, his interview responses, and the time he allowed us to spend in his art studio when he lived in St. Augustine; Lisa Dunbar, the senior curator at the Museum of Florida History, for helpful information about the inscription on a Spanish church bell found in a Madison County lake; Teenie Cave and Jim Sale at the Madison Treasures Museum for information and leads concerning the Mammy grave in Oakridge Cemetery and for the "Mammy in Life" photo from the E. Bailey Brinson family archives, and for their assistance with the Madison County Photographic Collection and the State Library and Archives of Florida for use of the sketch of the Clifton mansion once located in Lovett; Jim Sale for setting up the space in the museum for a video recording interview with history Professor Jason Welch, a Civil War re enactor; Graham Schorb for his technical support with the Jason Welch interview; Mary Lu Phiel and

Teenie Cave for information on Benjamin F. Wardlaw and the Smith mansion; Dee Counts and the Jefferson Historical Society for historical maps and area informational leads; and to my teachers, mentors, and friends the late Frances Sanders, who taught me to value antebellum history and the fine art of storytelling; and to the late Joe Akerman, author/professor who urged me to understand my own sense of place; to his wife, Princess, for her Southern hospitality; to Leland and Beverly Moore and to Jim and Kathy Sale, for their prayers and friendship; Graham Schorb, my husband, for his well-planned trips into the Red Hills, and for his faith in this work; to my students for their patience with my never-ending fascination about local history and the idea of the importance of teaching sense of place; to my Mother and Father, the late Charles Samuel Knox Senior and Lunita Parrish Knox, for giving their five children freedom during childhood to explore the wonders found in the public library, and for their cemetery outings in the Oakridge Cemetery after Sunday School and church.

Table of Contents

American Mastodon. Courtesy of Patrick Elliott

Preface

"Southerners in each generation have fallen in love with and hated with a passion the places in which they live. They have written about these places. They have sung about them. They have painted them. They have given these places to the world as a common artistic property. These artists help us understand what William Faulkner meant when he remarked that early in his life he realized he could write for a lifetime and never fully exhaust his 'little postage stamp of native soil.'"[1]

It is true that each generation has "fallen in love" but may also hate "with a passion" the place where they live. The idea of place is recorded in a person's memory, but it, too, is still kept alive in songs, stories, artwork, poetry, and legends of a region, and the extent of this supply is always inexhaustible. What sort of distant echoes of the past might be heard if their voices lifted themselves up, rising above these Red Hills of Florida? "And what are the Red Hills?" you may ask. The term "Red Hills" describes a place in Middle Florida; many native-born individuals feel connected to and long for this land of our upbringing. That personal sense of place is the little postage stamp of soil where I happened to be raised. Let me begin by defining the actual geological place: the sloping hill-regions of northern Florida that have since been named the Red Hills span in width about twenty-five miles. Those hills cover the northernmost sections of several counties that go by the names of Madison, Jefferson, Leon, Jackson, and Gadsden. This compilation only covers Madison, Jefferson, and Leon counties, however.

Let me first confess I was not born in the Red Hills, missing the mark by a few miles. Up a tad further north of Madison's Red Hills is the town of Valdosta, Georgia, which is situated on the Florida line. Valdosta was the nearest place with a state-of-the-art maternity ward back in the 1950s and '60s. It was likewise a short distance from the town named Madison located in Florida. That is the reason our Mother would see fit to deliver her five children at Pineview General Hospital, even though she and our Father ended up raising us in the Red Hills of northern Florida. Mother was raised in Howell, Georgia, and our

Daddy was from Atlanta. They'd met and later married in 1946 in Atlanta, at the Central Presbyterian Church. Our Father then settled with his wife, coming to the area of the Red Hills to sell his wares to regional drug stores, working as a representative for the Columbia Drug Company.

Let me return for a moment to the idea of sense of place. When I was a child, there were no courses taught in elementary, middle, or high school about regional history and of how the very geology of the area had drawn people to the Red Hills for thousands of years. Over time it became more apparent, the more I read, that the Red Hills region was a special place indeed, and through coming to some understanding about the stories of the people, hearing their voices and their perceptions, I started to be aware of what a sense of place truly means. William R. Ferris can further remind us of Faulkner's notions about a place when he says, "Each of you carries within yourself a 'postage stamp of native soil,' a 'sense of place' that defines you. It is the memory of this place that nurtures you with identity and special strength, that provides what the Bible terms 'the peace that passeth understanding.' And it is to this place that each of us goes to find the clearest, deepest identity of ourselves."[2]

I never consciously understood that sort of identity until I was older; yet the nurturing of sense of place, it is evident now, began early for me and my siblings, because during our childhood Mother and Father were prone to tour their children around in a graveyard! That activity was an old remnant from back when people of the South were inclined to visit graveyards and many even enjoyed picnicking in a cemetery. But it was the memory of that hometown graveyard, consequently, that served as the catalyst to how this book eventually unfolded.

How it started with us:

The First Presbyterian Church of Madison was where Daddy was a Sunday school teacher and deacon. The Knox family would be dressed to the nines and all seven of us were regular members, filling up a whole pew. After Sunday meeting each week, our Mother would set out a grand dinner, and then our family had an odd sort of pastime that happened after that Sunday banquet. Since a pioneer cemetery was situated just across the highway from our home, members of the Knox clan, on any given Sunday, could be seen, sometimes one or two of us, or at times, all seven of us, wandering around in what people still today call the "white section" of one of the oldest graveyards in Florida.

Even before my brother and I had learned to read, our parents would take us by the hand, leading us to certain "interesting" graves. Mother would often proceed about other parts of the cemetery, going to particular stones, reading names, dates, and inscriptions out loud, while Charles and I toddled around, playing near the etched tombs. Mama was also sure to point out in one section "the babies that poor woman buried." There would then follow some detailed narrative from Mama about their lives, and a plague, even though it was impossible for her to have ever known any of them! Those early outings were most-probably the initial source of my interest about the subject of the American South and the event that first planted the idea of sense of place.

While the cemetery is being discussed, I wanted to say that although the title of this work has ghosts in it, and there are chapters on the supernatural, I have approached the idea of "haints" from an historical perspective, keeping the oral tradition alive, in much the same way as a folklorist would. It is additionally important to understand that death in the Celtic tradition has been a preoccupation which manifested itself in ancestor worship and their belief system that the burial place was either a porthole to the next world or the place where the deceased continued a ghostly life. Even the tradition of putting flowers on the graves of the departed seems to still be almost an instinctive perpetuation of the ancient Celtic practice of revering and placating the dead. As for the African belief, there are many oral stories about ghosts and magic in that tradition, too.

After I was grown and when I was a beginning teacher, I was invited to serve as a chaperone on a Kids' Culture Club tour hosted by Mrs. Frances Sanders, a fellow teacher at Madison Middle School. The adventure in the graveyard was to continue with her! One grave plot always of curiosity to Frances Sanders was where a few prominent citizens are now reposed, their big tombs a testament to the affluence of that family. But in the back corner of that same family plot, near an ornate wrought-iron fence, was a smaller marker, with the words "Mammy: Faithful Servant of the Livingston Family" inscribed. Those captivating stories of the people were still alive in that cemetery, she was to remind me! And much later when I began working at the local college, I was sometimes known to walk students up to the same nearby Oak Ridge Cemetery. We'd congregate at the end of the "black section," sitting under the shade of mossy oaks. Sometimes students would take turns reading Whitman and Crane, there at the particular plot that cradles tombs lined up in a regimental row of unnamed (white)

American Civil War soldiers. I wanted my students to understand that a graveyard is full of stories; I hoped the tour might also help them try to begin to understand and define their own sense of place.

Not only the cemetery, but the antebellum mansion that we always had to pass on the highway on our way to town was a place that was inundated with ever more stories during our growing up. In addition, those notions of such places that consumed that small-town world of ours seemed to somehow deal with life, death, glory, and decay. Other words that dominated the world around us were the colors of white and black; of integration and segregation. These were also the very themes and settings I'd later come to recognize and to identify with in graduate school, while studying the works of people like Faulkner, O'Connor, Crews, and Welty.

In putting together regional stories, I was to come across ways to present the Red Hills. Some of those ideas show up as anecdotes, historical summaries, and haunting legends, but they might offer you clarity and identity, as they did me. Not only the written text, but the State Library and Archives of Florida, along with several pre-eminent Florida artists, also gave me their permission to use images that might offer more insight. It is my hope then that the visuals will add more understanding to the writing, and with differing ways of presenting people and places, perhaps this sketch—for that is all it truly is, a sketch—will help give a bit more clarity to how things "used to be" around these parts, telling the accounts from several perspectives by using various mediums. Let me also take the time to apologize if some sections seem redundant. That is what happens when someone is a little obsessed with particular topics!

What you are about to read goes back to an idea of understanding the impact of sense of place on someone. I'm not an historian, archeologist, or folklorist, but I am native to the Red Hills, and I do like listening, reading, and writing. And listening to stories and having mentors was very important. I want to thank the following folks because through them my own sense of place was born and nurtured: my Mother, Lunita Parrish Knox; my fourth-grade teacher, Mrs. Frances Sanders; Professors Joe Akerman, Louis [Coach] Thompson, and Mark Cherry! Books, like Rick Bragg's *All Over but the Shoutin'*, Joe Akerman's *Jacob Summerlin: King of Crackers*, Patrick Smith's *A Land Remembered*, Alex Haley's *Roots*—and the romanticized thinking in *Gone with the Wind*—had further inspired me by showing a way to frame some of my own perspectives. Living constantly around natural-born storytellers, the children of my family and the townfolk I hung around with couldn't help but absorb tales of times gone by. Because of that exposure to the storytelling tradition, gradually I'd come to early impressions (as was mentioned previously, when in the early 1960s, I was still just toddling around); but what I would come to know much later was that the stories of a place are a treasure, and a rich history that was known to be forever swirling around in the American South! Thus, my hometown of Madison, located in the Red Hills, and the people who founded it—and some who are buried in that same cemetery I used to toddle around in—did, in due course, form the backdrop of my upbringing. It is indeed the place that does carry inside of me a postage stamp of native soil, a sense of place, and it defines me. It is the memory of this place that has also nurtured me with identity and special strength. And Ferris was right when he said. "It is to this place that each of us goes to find the clearest, deepest identity of ourselves." I hope you will enjoy reading this compilation about a place they call the Red Hills, and the place where the bones of my Mother and Father are buried, in that same old Oak Ridge Cemetery. It is the place I still call home; and the place that has always helped me to "find" that "clearest, deepest identity."

Before we'd learned to read our Mother would take us by the hand, quietly leading us to certain "interesting" graves. Courtesy of Graham Schorb

"Each of you carries within yourself a 'postage stamp of native soil,' a 'sense of place' that defines you. It is the memory of this place that nurtures you with identity and special strength, that provides what the Bible terms 'the peace that passeth understanding.'" William R. Ferris. The Knox Clan is pictured from left to right, on the patio of our home in Livingston Spring Acres/Back Row–Charles Samuel Knox Senior (our Daddy), Mary Kay Knox, Carol Anne Knox, Linda Suzanne Knox (Sue). Front row–Charles Samuel Knox Junior, Leslie Rose Knox. Courtesy of Carol Knox Froude

Rose Knox and Graham Schorb

Endnotes

1. William R. Ferris, "1966 Speech to the Commonwealth Club of San Francisco," *Humanities* 19.1 (January/February 1998).

2. Ferris, "1966 Speech."

Voices Rising Up

The voices of the Red Hills echo across this land! They are varied and many. For a keen listener those voices resound still, into modern times. Near ancient spring beds and tannic or crystal-clear rivers, they sing out. Hear the Paleolithic Indians as they ready themselves for a perilous hunt. Thirteen thousand years ago they gathered around campfires, perhaps discussing strategies to kill dangerous game. Listen for the last desperate cry of the mastodon as a sharp spear point mortally wounds the beast and it tumbles into a deep limestone crevasse.

Today the underwater archeological record remains as a testament of that long-ago time and lives to remind us of those tales. The stories found in the skeletal record speak of the ancient ones; they hunted camels, tiny horses, giant sloths, mighty cats, and huge flesh-eating birds, among other creatures of that Paleolithic era. These ancient ones continued hunting many kinds of game, including the megafauna, until many of the age-old creatures disappeared in a mass extinction. That race of hunters lived on.

Thousands of years passed. Eventually their descendants learned to plant and, as an agricultural people, they established villages along the embankments of lakes, rivers, and ponds of these Red Hills and established extensive trading routes. But their voices were silenced by the brutal blade of the Spanish, and their populations were ultimately ravished by European diseases and enslavement. Nonetheless, the tales of that time remain and are found in towering ceremonial mounds where the people once conducted their spiritual rituals and buried their dead. Relics crafted in stone—of effigies in the form of people and beasts—and human skeletons are what are left; but those remnants speak to us of family, of faith in deities, of an aesthetic spirit, and of special knowledge of planting, harvesting, and storing food, bounty enough to sustain tens of thousands of people.

As time ticked by, more of the voices echoed through the land, resounding amid these sloping hills. The voice of the friar in his quest to convert these natives rings still. A line of Spanish mission sites once existed in a chain from St. Augustine, stretching to the land of the Apalachee—this time spanning from the 1500s to the 1700s. Spanish and British would fight for the territory we call northern Florida; blood would be spilled as all suffered, including the first peoples of this sloping region. The reconstructed mission of San Luis in the land of the Apalachee is a living history museum that speaks of that way of life and the eventual destruction of the original site.

Thousands upon thousands of suns would set over these hills as time crept forward. In the 1800s, the cry of the Seminole survives in swampy domains, places like Gum Swamp, where vigilante justice of settlers against natives was meted out. An acute observer might likewise hear the lament as violence against encroaching settlers was common, and the time of suffering and travail for the native race, too, cries out in sorrow. For the natives lost their ancestral hunting grounds and the wars against the Seminole all but destroyed that ancestral way of life. For the women and children of the early pioneers, including the antebellum planters, they too saw privation and endured hardships as their mansions, those opulent homes, were set ablaze by a displaced and angered native people. The aristocrat's children were trapped in the flames. There is an old graveyard on Old Dirt Road in Tallahassee where the wife and children of one prominent planter had to bury his loved ones.

It was in the early 1800s that those wealthy planters from Georgia, North Carolina, South Carolina, and Virginia, among other states, flocked here after the agricultural lands they or their forefathers had farmed were no longer fit for planting. Imagine hordes of people— Africans and those of European descent—streaming in with ox-driven carts, forging a way, the planters determined to get to the land of the Red Hills where the soil was said to be as rich for farming in Middle Florida as that of the Black Belt of the Mississippi Delta! Thousands of enslaved Africans labored from dusk until dawn in the cotton fields of Madison, Jefferson, and Leon Counties. Planters relied on area waterways like the St. Marks and the Suwannee to float bales by the ton to commercial destinations like New York City and Liverpool, England.

Narratives of the former enslaved individuals were also recorded after Freedom came, after the South fell in a horrific Civil War. In the aftermath emerged a ravished southern landscape, and an entire society found itself in the midst of social upheaval. Planters had left to fight in the War; women were forced to take charge of the plantation.

Some enslaved persons escaped. Those once-enslaved peoples can retell history in their own honest voices, thanks to the Federal Writers' Project. Tales of the enslaved and their plantation experiences still survive. And the lore and superstition of the encroaching immigrants and of the African followed these migrating peoples, reminding us that some believed in strange tales of ghosts, haints, and sprightly happenings. These folkloric stories survive today, lurking in antebellum mansions and in old pioneer cemeteries of the American South. So listen carefully if you ever are driving down highways or back roads of northern Florida, because in swampy or coastal regions, river corridors, forested areas, and sloping hills, there is an ongoing story being told.

The voices of the Red Hills are indeed today alive and well; they are rising up! Lend an ear, and you shall hear.

Madison County

Rose Knox and Graham Schorb

Travel Notes

The Red Hills: A Rich History

"During the height of antebellum agricultural production, it is estimated that there were nearly fifty thousand plantations in the slaveholding states of the South."[1]

The Red Hills is a region which harbors many stories of events that have taken place over thousands of years. It does not matter if you were born and raised around these parts, or if you are merely interested in the area, a keen listener can still discover those old tales. They remain lurking near springs and rivers, or inside of towering mounds that speak of a far-distant past, of mortuary burials of a long-ago race of people.

More stories emerge out of the presence of various memorials. In present-day city parks stand markers alluding to a Spanish march; one bronze sign indicates the location of a safe-haven that was used to protect Celtic pioneers against native Indian retaliations. Some towns feature exquisitely carved marble monuments in memory of the heroic—the sentinel or the slave. Cemeteries hold all kinds of stories, too—those tombs that cradle the bones of the people who once lived on sprawling, antebellum estates; they were many, and they all played different parts in the society. There was the plantation planter; the estate's overseer; a boy soldier; a hopeful maiden; a wife and mother; aristocratic children playing under moss-laden oaks; and the African slave who played the role of father, mother, craftsman, planter, and house domestic.

As far as the physical estates where lasting stories still live, only a few of the actual home estates exist today. But one writer reveals, "During the height of antebellum agricultural production, it is estimated that there were nearly fifty thousand plantations in the slaveholding states of the South."[2] The land holdings of such plantations ranged in size from the small farm with as few as twenty or so slaves to extensive farms sprawling over tens of thousands of acres. Such plantations spread from the old tobacco fields in Virginia and Maryland, on down to the watery coastal rice fields found in South Carolina and Georgia, through the huge cotton belt of Mississippi, Alabama, north Florida, and other states, and on over to the acres in Louisiana and Texas, where sugarcane, not cotton, was king.

Collectively these family-owned plantations, fueled by their huge slave labor force that comprised several million individuals, birthed a thriving agricultural economy in the American South that has yet to be replicated. These plantations, and the people who lived there, also created a diversely rich culture of class, color, and conflict which inundated the entire South. Those conflicts linger today, as television viewers see how terrible violence erupts under shadows of stone monuments; the argument is about the past: how it should be remembered, how it should be forgotten, how it should be dealth with. Remembering and forgeting are enduring themes told by various narrators in intellectual works of the American South.

Such estates and their inhabitants sculpted from wild, forested, or extensive fields an entirely new social environment that created a unique, significant legacy. It has been proclaimed by many that these estates of the Old South and the people who commingled there offered to the future the most incredible architectural relics ever created by an agrarian people!

Therefore, to better understand the antebellum era, it is important to learn about the stories of the planters, the slaves, and the happenings on these landed estates, for they, according to the author of *Lost Plantations of the South*, serve to "Collectively represent the South—the good and the bad—and ultimately they reflect upon us and how we as a society deal with our own intricate, complicated past."[3]

The stately Clifton mansion was once located near the crossroads of 150 and 146 in the Hamburg area. The house was a large, two-story residence. Six columns graced the front porch. Extensive gardens were said to have sprawled over six acres, surrounding the mansion. The Mays family owned the home up until the 1880s, although it was not occupied by them for all of that time. The Clifton Mansion looks much like the Lane family house, which is still standing near the Florida-Georgia line. James (Jim) Sale, a Madison resident, told me that the Lane House was his great-great-grandfather's home. His grandfather built it in Clyattville, Georgia. Jim's great-great-grandfather's name was Benjamin Franklin Lane, and as of December of 2017, Jim's 85-year-old aunt, Susie Lane, still lived in the Lane House. The house is the oldest house in Lowndes County and much resembles the Clifton Mansion of Madison County, which is no longer standing. Courtesy of the Madison County Photographic Collection and the State Library and Archives of Florida

Rose Knox and Graham Schorb

Endnotes

1. Marc R. Matrana, *Lost Plantations of the South* (Jackson: University Press of Mississippi, 2009).

2. Matrana, *Lost Plantations.*

3. Matrana, *Lost Plantations.*

Early Peoples of North Florida

"I live on land that has not surrendered the last of its wildness. It keeps secrets, and those secrets prompt us to pay attention, to look for more. This is how we first engaged with the world, and we still do it. We are hungry to know. Wild land and wild animals taught us about themselves, but they also helped make us who we are: resourceful, persistent, with a knack for imagining what we have not seen. Most of the time we catch mere glimpses, and from them we surmise a whole."[1]

If a soul were to journey back through time to the landscape of 12,000 years ago—at the pinnacle of the last Ice Age—they would be astounded at the creatures living at that time in what is today called Florida. There were giant ground sloths, saber-toothed cats, dire wolves, huge tortoises, enormous beavers, and great herds of roaming mastodons and mammoths—extinct relatives of the elephant. People often speculate as to why such magnificent animal populations are no longer walking the earth. The debate continues, with several theories being posited. One is the idea of drastic environmental changes that resulted in a scarcity of food for such creatures, but another factor often considered is that human beings hunted them to extinction. Peter Ward, a professor of geological sciences, illustrates the human factor premise when he writes, "Very recently in the geological past, a great catastrophe took place. That . . . caused a great number of large mammals and birds to go extinct in very short order. I believe that this great catastrophe . . . removed from our Earth in a mass extinction, all of the mammoths, mastodons, ground sloths, saber-toothed tigers, among many other creatures, and that this episode that has so robbed the Earth . . . was a catastrophe aided, or even largely caused by the influence of humankind."[2]

Imagine a group of strong men standing in an ancient landscape, deliberately sharpening stones. Their faces are serious, for they are familiar with what the future holds, and they also have a profound knowing that a sharp spear point could very well save them from death. The time has come for a big kill, and the men must somehow

Rose Knox and Graham Schorb

prepare themselves, physically and psychologically, for what soon awaits them on the next group hunt. They are already dressed in skins of wild beasts like the saber-tooth cat, so they've been called to find, to somehow summon, such bravery before. That kind of ancient cat was capable of ripping to shreds a human being in an instant. So going up against an angry sloth, one fighting for its life, they must once again somehow forego human fear and find the courage within to come against a giant beast. If their hunt is successful the men and others in the community will use what the sloth has provided to sustain them for a time—until the next hunt comes. And that is what Susan Hand Shetterly means when she says, "Wild land and wild animals taught us about themselves, but they also helped make us who we are: resourceful, persistent, with a knack for imagining what we have not seen."[3]

The ancient hunting ones were once in this place that is today called Florida. Long before the place was named as Madison, Jefferson, or Leon, the primeval creatures and the people who hunted them lived there. But what might the peninsula have looked like 12,000 years ago? The landmass then was roughly twice the size of what it currently is, and the shoreline of the Gulf of Mexico was more than one hundred miles west of today's present location. The region was much drier during that particular period, and many present-day watery places, like rivers, lakes, and springs, had not even been formed yet. Such was the landscape where the ancients, the Paleo-Indians, lived, hunting big game like the mastodon, the mammoth, the saber-toothed cat, and the sloth. A giant ground sloth, such as the one depicted here by artist Patrick Elliott, would have weighed three to four tons, and its claws would have been big, sharp, and quite dangerous to hunters. The great sloths went extinct around 12,000 years ago, but they once roamed in what is today North and South America.[4]

Though there is still much debate as to exactly how those peoples ultimately made it to North America and on into what is now called Florida, the most accepted theory among many archeologists and anthropologists to date is that they travelled from eastern Asia during the Pleistocene epoch, the Great Ice Age.[5] Back then the sea levels were much lower, and experts guess the people were able to make it across a land bridge. These hunter-gatherers soon colonized the Americas. What archeologists do know about these ancient gatherers comes from former watering holes found within deep springs, places like Wakulla Springs and the Page-Ladson site on the Aucilla River. Near those watering holes, the ancients left behind ample evidence of the way they lived out their lives.[6] Some rivers in north Florida, like the Ichetucknee, still harbor the old stories of the hunters' daily survival, because the Paleo-Indian camps found by archeologists' underwater investigations have turned up bone and stone weapons, tools, and spear points. That is true of many rivers in and around the Red Hills. Also discovered near such worked-stone pieces are the skeletal remains of the various kinds of animals that roamed in the region during the last Ice Age. Amazingly enough, some of the bones, such as skeletons from beasts like the mastodon, still show the actual butchering patterns made by natives even after all this time. Other bones discovered have been those of bison, horses, camels, rabbits, raccoons, deer, and the giant land tortoise.[7]

Paleolithic man was not only an adept hunter but an artist. During the Paleolithic period prehistoric men carved sophisticated tools of great complexity and created artful paintings and effigies. In caves all over the world, stone-age people were expressing themselves by carving woolly mammoths or painting bison, horses, and other Paleolithic creatures in the caves of France. Early carvings have also been discovered around the world, in effigies of women or stick figures or animal forms. Such artifacts of a similar sort have been discovered by Florida archaeologists in the mounds of northern Florida.[8]

The ancients, long ago, walked the terrain of the Red Hills region and were hunters of these great beasts. What must their lives have really been like? Modern-day people can only imagine! Places like the Florida Museum of History in Tallahassee can help visitors in trying to recreate for the imagination such ancient scenes. The museum features displays of ancient artistic backdrops, replicas, and even one life-size skeletal mastodon.

Artist Patrick Elliott depicts the intensity of an ancient hunt as he shows early Indians cooperating in a group kill, as they surround a giant sloth. The Paleo-Indians of the last Ice Age hunted the saber-tooth cat, the mammoth, and the giant land tortoise, making the best of the bounty from their natural environment. Those resources provided them with food, along with a means to make clothing and tools. Underwater archaeological investigations of regional Florida rivers and springs have revealed skeletal remains of such beasts, as well as many stone tools made by early hunters. Courtesy of Patrick Elliott of Tallahassee, Florida

Endnotes

1. Susan Hand Shetterly, *Settled in the Wild: Notes from the Edge of Town* (Chapel Hill, NC: Algonquin Books, 2010).

2. Peter D. Ward, *The Call of Distant Mammoths: Why the Ice Age Mammals Disappeared* (New York: Springer-Verlag Publishers, 1997).

3. Shetterly, *Settled in the Wild.*

4. Mary Pope Osborne and Natalie Pope Boyce, *Sabertooths and the Ice Age* (New York: Random House, 2005).

5. Jerald T. Milanich, *Florida Indians and the Invasion from Europe* (Gainesville: University Press of Florida, 1995).

6. Theodore Morris, *Florida's Lost Tribes* (Gainesville: University Press of Florida, 2004).

7. William R. Ervin, *Let Us Alone* (W and S Ervin Publishing Company, 1983).

8. Clark F. Howell, *Early Man* (New York: Time Life Books, 1965).

Rose Knox and Graham Schorb

Travel Notes

Paleolithic Giants

"Four million years before man, the age of the great mammals had begun. The greatest of the animals, the teeth of which have been found in Florida, began in that early time in Africa as a small river beast that wandered where rivers led, growing big ivory tusks and a nose slowly elongating and becoming flexible. . . . Millions of years later this first of the great beasts, with trunks and ivory tusks, the elephant kind, had developed many forms. There were the mastodons, bigger than elephants, some with pairs of upper and lower tusks, and the mammoths."[1]

Scientists today wonder how the creatures of the last Ice Age finally disappeared, and debates continue about such mass extinctions. Historically speaking, the word "mammoth" is derived from behemoth, meaning "huge animal," and was first used by Russian scientists in the early eighteenth century. The word mammoth eventually became common in the English language by the early 1800s, and was used to describe any object or animal with huge proportions. Regarding such great beasts, one Native American legend, originating out of what is today the state of Kentucky, contends that long ago there lived a herd of huge creatures. They came from a place called Big Bone Lick, and the beasts began to destroy all the animals living there, like elk, buffalo, and deer. When the Great Spirit Man who lived in the sky saw what was transpiring, he became enraged. The God then came down to Earth, took a seat on a neighboring mountain, and soon began hurling lightning bolts into the herd of invading mammoths. All of the fearsome beasts were killed except for one massive bull. Not slowed down, however, by a gaping wound he had incurred in his side, the bull leapt over the Ohio River and the Great Lakes and raced away northward. According to Indian folklore, the bull still holds dominion over that ice-encrusted region.[2]

Far from that legendary "ice-encrusted" region, many prehistoric animals have been discovered in rivers and springs of northern Florida, including the American mastodon. Like the creatures found in the Aucilla River, not far from Tallahassee, a Paleolithic beast and other ancient bones were discovered in another local spring. A find was made in 1850 that proved to be a pivotal sighting at Wakulla Springs, located sixteen miles south of Tallahassee. That was when a young woman from North Carolina spotted in the spring huge tusks and giant bones. Sara Smith had indeed discovered something that would intrigue people even to this day![3]

Such a find is a feast for the imagination; how many thousands of years had those skeletal remains of a mastodon rested on the spring's bottom? And what human eyes had seen the creature when it was alive and walking around? It would not be until 1930 that the entire skeletal structure of the ancient mammal would finally be brought up from watery depths. Once the bones were reassembled, the mastodon was ready to be displayed for the public, and in 1977 the skeleton was placed at the entrance of the Museum of Florida History located in Tallahassee, where it still stands today. The impressive, foraging beast of ancient times once stood eight feet eleven inches high at the shoulder and it is an extraordinary sight to see such a huge skeleton.[4]

The north Florida region at that time soon gained the attention of the archeological community, because discovery of the mastodon in the spring meant that mankind may have also established a presence in the area. Other waterways likewise told an ancient story. From the Ichetucknee River, for example, artifacts crafted from ivory were discovered in 1941, and such artifacts revealed how the domain had once supported the needs of a community of ancient game hunters! Further exploration took place in 1954 when graduate students studying at Florida State University went in, using scuba gear. In those underwater explorations many species were found, including Paleolithic skeletal remains of deer, sloth, mastodon, and mammoth, all extinct mammals of the last Ice Age. With that find, six hundred bone points, a vast variety of them, were also pulled from the Ichetucknee River.[5]

Regarding the disappearance of the mastodon and the mammoth from the Earth, several theories remain. "Perhaps no single explanation can account for the extinction of the mammoth and mastodons. It may have been . . . a combination of factors."[6] Those factors could have been weather changes, over-hunting by humans, or some epidemic disease that caused a mass extinction. Scientists today are studying the elephant to make assumptions and to also try to save the endangered elephant herds of the world.[7]

Joseph Campbell attempts to reveal the mindset of what these great beasts meant to the hunter. He said, "Out there, somewhere beyond the visible plain of existence, was the animal master who held over human beings the power of life and death. . . . The beasts were seen as envoys from that other world, a magical wonderful accord growing between the hunter and the hunted . . . [a] cycle of death, burial, and resurrection . . . [it appeared in] . . . their art and oral literature and gave form to the impulse we now call religion . . . these people didn't think of animals the way we do, as some subspecies. [Rather] Animals are equals . . . The animal has powers that the human doesn't have."[8]

Theodore Morris paints an ancient hunter in pursuit of a Paleolithic beast, in what is today north Florida. Several skeletal mammoth remains have been recovered from areas in the Red Hills. Joseph Campbell attempts to reveal the mindset of what these great beasts meant to the hunter. He said, "Out there, somewhere beyond the visible plain of existence, was the animal master who held over human beings the power of life and death. . . . The beasts were seen as envoys from that other world, a magical wonderful accord growing between the hunter and the hunted . . . [a] cycle of death, burial, and resurrection . . . [it appeared in] . . . their art and oral literature and gave form to the impulse we now call religion." Courtesy of Theodore Morris

Endnotes

1. Marjory Stoneman Douglas, *The Everglades: River of Grass,* 50th anniv. ed. (Sarasota, FL: Pineapple Press, 1998).

2. James Cross Giblin, *The Mystery of the Mammoth Bones* (New York: Harper-Collins, 1999).

3. "Lanier, Florida: Its Scenery, Climate," Tallahassee *Floridian and Journal,* 25 May 1850.

4. Herman Gunter, "Once Roamed Land of Sunshine," *Florida Highways,* August 1941, 13, 35.

5. Gunter, "Once Roamed Land of Sunshine."

6. Giblin, *Mystery of the Mammoth Bones.*

7. Giblin, *Mystery of the Mammoth Bones.*

8. Joseph Campbell, *The Power of Myth with Bill Moyers,* Betty Sue Flowers, ed., (New York: Doubleday, 1988).

Rose Knox and Graham Schorb

Travel Notes

Distinctions between Mastodons, Mammoths, and Elephants

American mastodons stood eight to ten feet tall and weighed four to five tons, and paleontologists surmise they lived 2 million to 10,000 years ago. American mastodon molars had a few rounded domes used for crushing bark, leaves, and twigs in a forested landscape.[1] "Of the mastodons, mammoths, and elephants, mastodons evolved first. The most obvious visual differences between mastodons and mammoths are in their teeth, skulls, and body designs. While individual teeth of mastodons have cone-shaped grinding surfaces, the eating surfaces of the mammoth teeth are formed of ridges, like those of modern elephants. Mammoth skulls were domed while mastodon skulls were low-browed. And while mammoths were considerably taller, mastodons had proportionally longer and more massive bodies."[2]

Woolly mammoths ranged across frozen lands in places like Siberia. The tooth of a woolly mammoth had many sharp ridges—up to twenty-six pairs—perfect for grinding grass on frigid plains. The woolly mammoth stood nine to eleven feet tall, weighed four to six tons, and lived, paleontologists believe, from 250,000 to 10,000 years ago.[3]

Columbian mammoths, also called Imperial mammoths, stood thirteen feet tall, weighed ten tons, and lived 100,000 to 10, 000 years ago, according to the paleontological record. Plentiful food sources in warmer regions helped the Columbian mammoth grow taller and weigh more than the woolly mammoth and the American mastodon. Their teeth had fewer ridges spaced farther apart, because their diet included a variety of plants, in addition to grass.[4]

The following quotation sums up the mammoths' existence on earth: "The ancestry of the mammoths can be traced back through time to about fifty-five million years ago. The last dinosaurs had become extinct about ten million years before the emergence of a group of mammals we know as the Proboscideans, which soon evolved protruding tusks and extended, trunk-like noses. Some fifty million years later, the first mammoths arose from this ancestral line. Although they were related to modern elephants, mammoths were not their ancestors but came from a separate branch of the family tree."[5]

African elephants stand ten to eleven feet tall, weigh four to six tons, and still live to the present day. The fate of the elephant is in question, however. They are a threatened species because of habitat loss and ivory poachers. They represent the last remaining members of the once-prolific Proboscidean species that included mastodons and mammoths. The earliest Proboscideans lived 50 million years ago and were small elephant-like creatures. Scientists today are studying elephants in an effort to unlock clues to how mammoths and mastodons might have existed, perhaps in large herds with a communal spirit.[6]

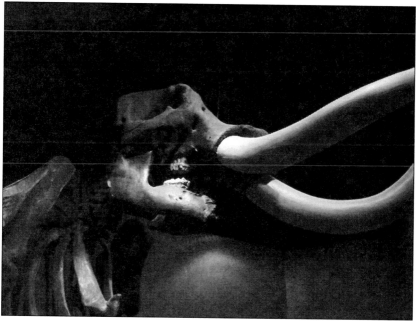

When visiting the Museum of Florida History in Tallahassee, I was awed as I stood under this Paleolithic beast, the mastodon that was "resurrected" from Wakulla Springs back in 1930. Bones and tusks were first spotted in 1850. Courtesy of Graham Schorb

Mammoths and mastodons were so abundant that their teeth are the most commonly found mammalian fossil remains in the state of Florida. Although the Pleistocene is generally termed the Ice Age, the ice cap did not reach as far south as Florida, and the woolly mammoth was never a resident of the peninsula. The remains of the Imperial and Columbian mammoths are among the most common fossil finds in Florida. Text and sketch Courtesy of the State Library and Archives of Florida/Image of Pleistocene mammoths Courtesy of Andrew R. Janson 1956

Columbian mammoths, also called Imperial mammoths, stood thirteen feet tall, weighed ten tons, and lived 100,000 to 10, 000 years ago, according to the paleontological record. Plentiful food sources in warmer regions helped the Columbian mammoth grow taller and weigh more than the woolly mammoth and the American mastodon. Their teeth had fewer ridges spaced farther apart, because their diet included a variety of plants, in addition to grass. According to the book, *Mammoths: Giants of the Ice Age*, "The first mammoths walked and browsed in the tropical woodlands of Africa, but later migrated into Europe and Siberia and eventually reached North America." Columbian mammoth is courtesy of Patrick Elliott

Rose Knox and Graham Schorb

Endnotes

1. Cheryl Bardoe, *Mammoths and Mastodons: Titans of the Ice Age* (New York: Abrams Books for Young Readers) in association with the Field Museum, Chicago, 2010.

2. Ian M. Lange, *Ice Age Mammals of North America: A Guide to the Big, Hairy, and the Bizarre* (Missoula, MT: Mountain Press, 2002).

3. Bardoe, *Mammoths and Mastodons*.

4. Bardoe, *Mammoths and Mastodons*.

5. Adrian Lister and Paul Bahn, *Mammoths: Giants of the Ice Age* (London: Marshall Publishing, 2000).

6. Bardoe, *Mammoths and Mastodons*.

Timucua Natives: People of the Red Hills

The wise ones living among the rolling hills have always paid close attention to all things around them. They own a deep wisdom born of living generation after generation, over thousands and thousands of years, in close connection to the earth—and they are sure to teach their children about these important signs. The sun, the stars, and the moon all help to guide them in their planning and in their planting of seeds, and likewise in their hunting of wild game. From the clues hinted at by Nature, they know exactly when certain kinds of animals are on the move. Keen awareness thus tells them when is the best time to hunt or to trap. And that is the reason why the wise ones of the Red Hills pay close attention, always alert, forever seeking wisdom from the forest, the fields, and the sky; they keep passing that age-old knowledge of existence down to their young ones.

Try to envision a scene that may have transpired hundreds of years ago in the Red Hills. Picture a father as he stands confidently dressed in a handsomely crafted panther-warrior headdress. Colorful feathers and artistic tattoos adorn his chiseled physique as he lovingly holds a toddler in the paternal posture of his protective love. The child grips a tiny bow in one hand, a toy that was perhaps crafted by the doting father. Or imagine a little baby girl as her mother sings sweet serenades. The mother is soothing her child while she is busy weaving clothing with the other women, making garments out of Spanish moss. She also wears pretty jewelry on her wrists and around her neck, and those pieces have been created from bone and from wood. From time to time, she mindfully glances down at her infant, and the mother's soft, satisfied giggles drift across the village. Another, quite older, woman, perhaps the grandmother, pauses for a few moments to marvel at the child; she suspends a red bird's feather over the baby, making the baby smile with glee, as she reaches her tiny hand out, trying to clutch the brightly colored, dangling object. Such scenarios might have taken place not too far from a gentle, sloping hill or beside a winding river's shoreline. In the distance, for as far as the human eye can perceive, and just beyond the village of thatched homes, are growing rows and rows of various crops of corn, beans, and tubers. The archeological record of thriving native peoples can offer only a few ideas of the highly sophisticated ways of Indian tribes that were at one time thriving and worshiping in what is today called Florida. Many archeological investigations have upturned old relics, clues that record such human existence. Towering mounds are still visible in several areas of the Red Hills, and those manmade vestiges can speak silently about the spiritual and societal history of the first peoples and the timeworn wisdom they needed for survival.

Some historians and archeologists believe that as many as twelve million Native Americans lived and worshipped on the North American continent as far back as 14,000 years ago. Later tribes, those original ancestors of the ancient race they call the Paleo-Indians, eventually evolved through time as distinct cultures with their own sophisticated spiritual beliefs. They also possessed conceptual knowledge of language and of symbols. One confederation living in regions of the Red Hills has been named Timucua. These Indians, today referred to by archeologists as the "Lost Tribes of Florida," once had a complex societal structure, complete with religious observances and superior agricultural techniques, and the people were all operating within an economic system. When the European explorers initially arrived on what is now the Florida peninsula, there existed thirteen major Native American Confederations. Today they are called the Apalachee, Timucua, Guale, Pensacola, Potano, Ocale, Tobobaga, Mayaimi, Ais, Jeaga, Calusa, Tequesta, and the Matecumbe.

The largest of these confederations was the Timucua. They lived in the northeastern portion of Florida, and their population has been estimated by some archeologists at about 200,000. These indigenous peoples lived in the vicinity west of the Aucilla River, all the way over to the Gulf Coast, near what is present-day Tampa Bay. Eastward, they occupied areas to Cape Canaveral and northward into Southern Georgia. The Timucua were a sophisticated agricultural people, surviving by farming and also by hunting game. Major crop yields were of beans, maize, and tubers, with other sorts of vegetables and fruit supplementing their diet. Tobacco was also harvested, and the Timucua used the tobacco plant as an herb in their ceremonial gatherings. As hunters, they were adept. The men of the tribe were known to pursue many types of animals, including bear, deer, alligator, and bison; they also depended on the trapping of small game for subsistence.

The Timucua were also known to value aesthetics, and liked to adorn themselves by painting art on their bodies and decorating themselves with tattoos. The men and women wore jewelry, ornaments crafted from shell and from bone; some men even decorated themselves by wearing earrings made from the bladders of fish. Animal hides were also used for clothing, and the Timucua were known to make cloth from fibers of plants, such as Spanish moss.[1] As explorers and settlers began invading the Red Hills, the Timucua were eventually converted to Christianity. But in due time they were ultimately killed off by European epidemics, and by the year 1763, only one Timucuan Indian was still living.[2]

The Timucua Confederation was a part of what has officially been termed the Mississippian Mound-Builder societies, and evidence of their ceremonial mounds is widespread in central and north Florida even today, though many of the ancient mounds have since been destroyed—demolished to make way for modern Florida development, like roadways.[3] Driving around in the Red Hills, visitors can seek out mounds. One such mound not too far from my hometown, and about fourteen miles east of Tallahassee, is situated on Highway 90 near Lake Miccosukee, just outside of the city of Tallahassee. The official name for the mound park is Letchworth-Love Mounds Archaeological State Park.

To sum it up, the indigenous peoples of what would eventually be named La Florida by the Spanish would, in the long run, suffer seriously from interaction with Europeans and also with those peoples brought over later from Africa. The impact of such encroachment, by the middle of the seventeenth century, was devastating, for disease and enslavement had almost entirely decimated coastal indigenous populations. Native American groups in the interior fared slightly better, though in the long term, they too would experience the dire impact of ecological and environmental change brought about by the arrival of Europeans and, later, Africans. The Europeans would later rely on African slave labor following the decimation of Florida's indigenous Indians. Consequently, in just 350 years of outside invasion, through disease, war, starvation, and forced exile, only 250,000 natives remained by 1850.[4]

Marjory Stoneman Douglas describes the decimation of an entire race of people in a poetic, tragic way when she vividly illustrates what happened to the natives further south. She writes, "They were ravaged by . . . diseases, by yellow fever and smallpox and measles, all of which killed them off like flies. Their dismembered bones were heaped in mass burials of as many as five hundred at a time, only hastily covered with scattered earth at the tops of burial mounds, slowly piled higher, far beyond the once populated lagoons. The ashes of [their] villages were scattered."[5]

Suggested reading: Miles Harvey, *Painter in a Savage Land* (New York: Random House, 2008).

Try to envision a father as he stands confidently dressed in an intricately crafted panther-warrior headdress. Feathers and tattoos adorn a chiseled physique as he lovingly holds a toddler in the posture of protective love. The child grips a tiny bow in one hand, a toy that was perhaps crafted by the doting father. Courtesy of Theodore Morris

Rose Knox and Graham Schorb

Endnotes

1. William R. Ervin, *Let Us Alone* (W and S Ervin Publishing Company, 1983).

2. Theodore Morris, *Florida's Lost Tribes* (Gainesville: University Press of Florida, 2004).

3. William R. Ervin, *Let Us Alone.*

4. Ervin, *Let Us Alone.*

5. Marjory Stoneman Douglas, *The Everglades: River of Grass,* 50th anniv. ed. (Sarasota: Pineapple Press, 1998).

Spanish Arrive and Convert Native Americans

"After the salvation of my soul, there is nothing I desire more than to be in Florida, to end my days saving souls." Pedro Menéndez de Avilés, 7 September 1574.

The words of a Spanish leader can show the zeal and dedication the European men espoused in their efforts to bring the Catholic belief system to the Indians of Florida. The missionary period happened during what has been termed the Reconquista of Spain. Religious conversion would be one of the most vital aids in influencing Spain's North American colonization.[1] Governmental Spanish forces in charge also knew the power of conversion. In fact, so determined was Spain's authority to take over new lands and to make converts of the native tribes, these powerful political entities were willing to fund very costly expeditions.

For example, a few of the Spanish accounts reveal specifics about such voyages. One of the expeditions to Florida held up to 500 soldiers, 1,000 servants, and 240 horses, using a fleet of 11 ships. On some of the vessels sailed traveling men, women, and children. The people onboard played various roles: monks, soldiers, laborers, and colonists, and they all were coming to the New World for different reasons. In addition, these ships were well stocked with supplies of all kinds and enough food to get them through a long voyage and a bit beyond—to this "new" land.[2]

In many regions of the New World the missionaries served as all-important emissaries and those who had first-hand contact; these men were able to build human relationships with the Native tribes. As a direct result, the religious men were successful in establishing extensive communities that created a strong foothold for Spain out in the wilds of Florida.[3] Such work by the Church would, in turn, serve the goals and purposes of military leaders, religious zealots, and colonists alike, by trying to "tame" the Florida Native American tribes through religious conversion.[4] John E. Worth, in his anthropological studies and excavations, once wrote about the power of conversion, revealing, ". . . Subjugation would be accomplished not by the sword, but with the cross."[5] And there were many thousands to convert. When Ponce de Leon first came to the New World, for instance, in 1513 there were hundreds of thousands of indigenous peoples already living in La Florida. According to archaeologist Jerald T. Milanich ". . . the sum of their respective populations has been estimated at about 350,000: 50,000 Apalachee in the eastern panhandle, 150,000 Timucua speakers in northern peninsular Florida (with more in southern Georgia), and another 150,000 people in central and southern Florida and the western panhandle."[6]

Later, in the year 1539, another Spaniard, Hernando de Soto, entered Florida's west coast. Traveling with him on that voyage were Spanish priests. Eventually they were to come into contact with the culturally established Indians, the Timucuans and the Apalachees. The clerics were to meet with terrible resistance, for these ancient tribes were already a spiritual people, worshipping the sun and the moon. Like many ancient societies all over the world, they performed sacred rituals which they believed would help their community bring in good crops. One ritual has thus been described. "In a ceremony enacted early each spring, a stag's skin, stuffed with choice roots and garlanded with fruits and flowers, was set up in a high tree facing the east."[7] During the ritual natives, led by their own holy men, chanted and sang their prayers and supplications to the sun, asking for a successful harvest. Because these native ancestral tribes of the Timucuan and the Apalachee of the "Red Hills" had been worshiping in such a manner for hundreds and hundreds of years, they were not interested in being converted to another faith.

What very little we know about these Native Americans comes from the Spanish. As the priests traveled with de Soto's army, they wrote in their dairies particulars about the lives of the indigenous Natives then living and thriving in what is today north Florida. One journal, as quoted in a modern work titled *The Spanish Missions of Florida,* revealed that, "Almost every act of the Indian was attended by prayer, accompanied or not by feasts and dances." By the late 1550s, because the natives had by then come to vehemently distrust the Spanish, they were willing to attack them even before any meetings of introduction ever took place. For when two cultures and two faiths collide, there can often ensue horrific violence. That was to be the case in La Florida. There are also detailed records from the priests' diaries over many decades that chronicle how and why the priests were sometimes put to death by the natives. To illustrate such violence, around the year 1558 several missionaries were killed in La Florida by the Native Americans. One priest, whom La Florida Indians had formerly come to trust, admonished their murderous acts by trying to explain the weighty, moral nature of their dire deed. In this priest's very words of reprimand, however, the awful atrocities against the Indians were mentioned by him. He implored, "These people that you have killed are not like other Spaniards, because they seek neither gold nor silver nor would they take your women or your lives. They seek only to teach you the law of the true God who is in Heaven, that you may know and worship Him, for in this consists your happiness."[8]

Therefore, the first decades of Spanish-Indian dealings in La Florida were quite violent due to the threat that incoming Europeans posed to the Natives' way of life. This included the eventual obliteration of their ancient tribal ways and their cultural and spiritual belief systems.[9] So right off, the resistance by Natives led directly to the murder of a number of Jesuit priests. Such bloodshed caused the Jesuits in Spain to quit all missionary attempts in La Florida in the year 1572. Then the first Franciscans came to Florida in 1573, but it was not until 1587 that they were able to establish missions among the Timucua and Guale coastal Indians. Later, by 1606 the Franciscan priests extended their mission efforts, and by 1633 they were well established across north Florida.[10]

Later still, by 1640 missions and trading posts had been set up at San Marcos on the Gulf of Mexico and all the way to San Luis near what is today the city of Tallahassee. Old Spanish maps can reveal the many mission sites which were established across northern Florida. In some of the missions, Native Americans were converted to the Christian faith and were treated well by the priests; however, there are also accounts of how the Natives were forced to work as slaves without pay. As a consequence of poor treatment and hard labor many Indians died of hunger and wounds from torture.[11]

The mission era of Spanish La Florida, however, came to an abrupt halt between 1702 and 1704, after a series of bloody military attacks by the British and their Creek Indian allies. During these fierce strikes, almost all of the missions except those positioned in the immediate area of St. Augustine were altogether abandoned or destroyed.[12] One such very violent British raid took place in what is today Monticello.[13] (The Mission San Pedro near Lake Sampala in what is today Madison County was also burned, according to the archeological evidence.) The destruction by the British in these particular mission raids included the burning of churches, the burning of books, and the destruction of shrines. Such horrific decimation was even questioned by a few Englishmen. During the raid leading up to the Monticello attack, for example, library books worth about $600 were burned; included in that collection were Greek and Latin Christian writings. One priest wrote ". . . and the Holy Bible itself did not escape" [the destruction].[14]

Then on January 25, 1704, one of the most ruthless British strikes to date was to transpire. Governor Moore was in charge of the English colony of South Carolina, and his men attacked a Native American town named Ayubale. That community is located south of present-day Monticello. On the Spanish side was Lieutenant John Mexia, who was in charge of commanding thirty Spanish soldiers and four hundred Apalaches. The priest, Father Parga, encouraged all of them to put up a hard fight and he offered all of them absolution. He was determined to stay with them during the upcoming attack, though the soldiers vehemently encouraged him to flee for his own safety. Though Mexia and his allies put up a strong fight, they were ultimately doomed when their ammunition ran out. Most of them were killed or taken as prisoners. Mexia, Father Parga, and another priest, Father Miranda, were a few of those captured. Known today as the Massacre of Ayubale, it has gone down in history as one of the most ruthless episodes in colonial America. After Father Parga was taken, he was burned at the stake. Later Moore's men decapitated the priest and also chopped off one of his legs. One brother, Delgado, tried to save Father Parga, but he was also eventually murdered.

Moore's men marched on with their campaign of horrors to another town named Patali. There they shot the priest and burned the town. Later, at the settlement of San Luis, one scribe told how Moore had taken almost 1,000 Apalachee prisoners whom he planned to sell into slavery. Father John de Villalba was traveling with Moore through the ruined towns. He described the destruction he saw as ". . . a scene of unparalleled horror." His account told of dead people all around him—some were burned, scalped, pierced through by stakes, and/or mutilated. One father, Mendoza, was discovered with his sacred beads and a partially melted crucifix pressed deeply into his skin. These incidents occurred in the Red Hills of north Florida.

Doug Alderson, in his work *The Great Seminole Trail*, writes, "The mission San Luis ended abruptly in 1704. British Governor James Moore . . . himself a Christian but not Spanish or Catholic, put together a small armed force . . . and more than a thousand Creek [Indian] allies and swept into the land of the Apalachee." (Many of those Creeks had invaded the area because they had been driven south by colonization in other states.) "All fourteen mission villages and numerous satellite settlements and Spanish ranches between the Aucilla and Ochlocknee Rivers were burned and their inhabitants killed, enslaved, or forced into exile. Many of the Apalachee groups who dispersed were eventually hunted down. . . . The land of Apalachee, once considered the most concentrated population . . . lay in ruins."[15]

Mission sites in and around Madison County: Around the 1630s missions were built, extending into the land of the Apalachee beyond the Aucilla River. They existed near an Indian trail which later was named the Old Spanish Trail, among other names. There were at least five missions that have been recorded in the vicinity. San Juan de Guacara was situated near the banks of the Suwannee River in today's Suwannee County. San Pedro y San Pablo de Protohiriba was built near Lake Sampala. Santa Elena de Machaba has never been discovered but may have been somewhere close to the Hixtown (sometimes spelled Hickstown) Swamp (according to old maps) in Madison County. And located west of the community of Sirman's was a mission called San Matheo de Tolapatafi. San Miguel de Asile has been located near the Aucilla River on the Jefferson County side of the river. Interestingly enough, the phonetic names of Assile, Machaba, Puturiba, and Tolapatifi were all names of Timucuan towns, and by naming the missions some record of those villages remains.

In Willis Physioc's interpretation, notice the church mission is the center of mission life. The priests made sure that the natives planted enough crops that would help sustain the whole community; notice rows of cultivated fields in the background. Courtesy of University of North Carolina Press, from the book *Spanish Missions of Georgia*

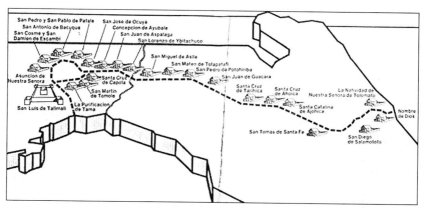

During the Spanish mission period the Spanish established many missions across the north Florida region. As in a line, these missions crossed over the Aucilla River near present-day Lamont. Courtesy of the State Library and Archives of Florida

Rose Knox and Graham Schorb

Endnotes

1. Bonnie G. McEwan, ed., *The Spanish Missions of La Florida* (Gainesville: University Press of Florida, 1993).

2. *The Spanish Missions of Florida*, compiled by WPA Florida Writers Project (New Smyrna Beach, FL: Luthers, 1940).

3. McEwan, *Spanish Missions.*

4. McEwan, *Spanish Missions.*

5. John E. Worth, *Timucuan Chiefdoms of Spanish Florida*, Volume 1: Assimilation (Gainesville: University Press of Florida, 1998).

6. Jerald T. Milanich, *Florida Indians and the Invasion from Europe* (Gainesville: University Press of Florida, 1995).

7. *The Spanish Missions of Florida,* WPA.

8. *The Spanish Missions of Florida*, WPA.

9. McEwan, *Spanish Missions.*

10. McEwan, *Spanish Missions.*

11. *The Spanish Missions of Florida*, WPA.

12. McEwan, *Spanish Missions.*

13. *The Spanish Missions of Florida*, WPA.

14. *The Spanish Missions of Florida*, WPA.

15. Doug Alderson, *The Great Seminole Trail* (Sarasota, FL: Pineapple Press, 2013).

Desoto's March: A Brief Summary

In the 1500s Hernando de Soto arrived in Tampa Bay, and traveling with him were many people from various classes. They included monks, noblemen, conquistadors, carpenters, and laborers. The expedition was comprised of not only six hundred men, but two hundred horses and several hundred boars, and aboard were also cattle and greyhounds. The greyhounds later were used to track down Native Americans. De Soto eventually made his way through the Red Hills of north Florida. Historical markers to chronicle his route are dotted along roadsides such as Highway 90, and his route is documented by other historical signs in several counties of the Red Hills.[1]

In 1539 de Soto's soldiers, after leaving what is today Madison County, came upon a village known as Ivitachuco, located near Nutall Rise in today's Jefferson County. Written diaries of his journeys show he also traversed an area between the Aucilla and Wacissa Rivers, where it was recorded he saw "lakes" that Narvaez's expedition had earlier mentioned. That "plain," it is surmised, is located a few miles above Nutall Rise. De Soto's expedition was attacked by the Apalachee Indians near those lakes and a violent scene unfolded there. Several natives were hanged, and such brutal treatment of the Natives would be the hallmark of de Soto's march. Those encounters created terrible ill will among the Native nations, who came to hate the Spanish conquistadors. It is believed his group trudged on, moving in a northwesterly direction, passing through the sloping Cody Scarp region, past what is today Chaires Crossing and into present-day Tallahassee, where he set up an encampment for several months. A general consensus contends that he celebrated Christmas there in 1539 (considered the first Christmas in America) and departed Tallahassee in 1540, traveling for four years, still on a quest for riches. He is known today for trekking through nine other states, wreaking havoc and instilling terror among the native populations.[2]

The artist George Gibbs depicts a pivotal scene when de Soto's men first arrived in the "Land of La Florida" where they began to interact with the Indians of the region. Gibbs's art reveals one heavily arrayed warrior from Europe as he is encountering scantily clad Indian braves. The artist's depictions can serve as a good social commentary of how one more-advanced society is destined to obliterate another because of progressive weaponry and war armor.

Once de Soto's army crossed over the Suwannee River, they found themselves in the land of the Uzachile, a Timucuan group who lived in the region near Lake Sampala in what is today known as Madison County. In fact, the Spanish passed through one small settlement before coming to the main village called Uzachile located near that lake. Text courtesy of Jerald Milanich in his book, *Florida Indians and the Invasion from Europe*. Image is courtesy of Grace E. King, Macmillan Publishers, George Gibbs, and the State Library and Archives of Florida

Such was the scene among the indigenous peoples of many southeastern states when they were to meet the Spanish warriors. De Soto's expedition, after leaving what is today Madison County, was attacked by the Apalachee Indians, and a violent scene unfolded near the Aucilla and Wacissa Rivers. Several natives were hanged, and such brutal treatment of the natives would be the hallmark of de Soto's march. Those encounters created terrible ill-will among the Native nations, who came to hate the Spanish conquistadors. Courtesy of State Library and Archives of Florida

Rose Knox and Graham Schorb

Endnotes

1. Eric Musgrove, *Reflections of Suwannee County*: 150th anniv. ed., 1858-2008 (Live Oak: North Florida Printing Co., 2008).

2. Musgrove, *Reflections*.

Archeological Find in Madison County:
San Pedro y San Pablo de Potohiriba

In 1972 B. Calvin Jones, an archaeologist of the State Bureau of Historic Sites and Properties, was exploring around what is today known as Madison County, not far from Lake Sampala. While searching in the vicinity, he took note of a distinct difference in the color of the dirt that had been burrowed up from the earth by a digging creature. He was convinced that a large mission named San Pedro y San Pablo de Potohiriba must be located somewhere in the near vicinity. This particular mission was a Yustega province and, according to the Spanish diaries, had been established between the years 1609 and 1655, most likely around 1617. The name of the mission indicates that there may have also been two Native American towns connected to the Spanish mission. Later B. Calvin Jones and four of his anthropology students from Florida State University traveled to Madison and began excavating the site where the "salamander's" dirt had been flung up to the surface.[1]

During the official dig, the team identified three structures that looked much like a convent, a church, and a storehouse. When they discovered the mission cemetery they guessed it held several hundred graves. Of those, only a selection of interment sites was excavated. The find revealed that the natives had not been buried in the traditional manner, and neither were there any ritualistic native artifacts buried within the tombs. Rather, the Christianized Indians were laid to rest in an extended, supine position.[2] Jones also discovered during his investigations that some graves were stacked in layers–"two and three layers deep."[3] He was not sure if these layers represented several burials or if they were perhaps disturbances from other interments intruding on top of even earlier burials.[4] Jones also further recorded details that the individuals were buried in the Christian pose, with their hands folded over their chests, and that human remains of more youthful Natives were discovered at one section, most likely revealing the interments were established according to age. Spanish mission items were discovered as well, including one broken brass bell and one brass crucifix.[5] Once Jones and his students had made measurements of the area cemetery, they found it to be approximately 120 feet long and 50 feet wide; they then took some photographs and afterwards covered up the dig, allowing the site to return to its natural state.[6]

The old Spanish writings can bring the San Pedro y San Pablo mission site to life. In the early 1600s there were about 1,000 Yustega Natives. Perhaps one important reason why the mission was built was so these Natives could grow and harvest crops and later transport those vital foodstuffs, like corn and squash, to larger, more populated, areas of European occupation. In fact, when the Spanish first made their way through north Florida, they noted the miles and miles of cultivated fields and orchards that were visible as far as the eye could see. The crops growing were corn, beans, and fruit trees, enough to sustain tens of thousands of Native Americans.[7] But in those early mission years the Indians were forced to work as slaves, hauling food crops they had planted, grown, and harvested to St. Augustine via the Old Spanish Trail. However, because the natives were so mistreated and because they continued to resent conversion methods, there arose a general revolt by the Timucuan nation of the region. To illustrate the revolt, the Yustega chief, Don Pedro, leader from San Pedro, was instigating the rebellion. (Note: The Timucua of north-central Florida were known historically as Yustega, Utina, and Potano.) To quell the Indian unrest, a group of sixty Spanish soldiers were directed over from St. Augustine to try to stomp out a potential rebellion. Their plan was set. They chose eleven Native subjects to execute. Don Pedro was more than likely one of those whom they killed. Also during the conflict, some of the established mission sites were destroyed. It should be noted, however, that by 1659 some of the structures had already been rebuilt.[8] Still more doom awaited the Yustega Natives, and several factors resulted in their waning numbers: because of bloodshed caused in their rebellion, along with infectious, deadly diseases brought over by the Europeans, their population had been tremendously reduced by the late 1600s.[9]

Evidence of such violence was later discovered by archeologist B. Calvin Jones and his students as they discovered charred wooden posts from the convent at San Pedro mission located in what is today the county of Madison, Florida. The burned remnants speak of the destruction caused by John Moore and his Creek Indian allies. Other artifacts attest to mission life west of Lake Sampala. Around the year 1840 someone, possibly an African plantation slave, was fishing in a pond. Some accounts say it was in Lake Sampala. The man had happened upon an old bell. He dug it up out of the mud. Later, when the object was studied by others, it was determined that the old mission piece was made of an alloy of copper, tin, and silver, measuring eighteen inches tall and four feet at the base. Inscribed on the bell were the words "SANTA MARIA ORA PRO NOBIS." A date of 1758 was also inscribed. On one side of the metal bell was the image of a raised cross made up of twenty-four, eight-pointed stars. Then about a year after the discovery of the bell, in a wooded area, and inside of an Indian mound, a clapper was also unearthed.[10]

For some time the Spanish mission bell was housed in Jacksonville at the Florida Historical Society Museum. Later it was on loan in Gainesville at the Florida State Museum. According to Elizabeth Sims, a Madison County historian and writer, the bell was owned by the family of T. J. and J. W. Cobb of north Florida.

Additional Note: The "salamander" that B. Calvin Jones mentions in his notes about discovering an important archaeological site in Madison County is actually called the southeastern pocket gopher. According to the *National Audubon Society Field Guide to North American Mammals*, the small mammal is active in all seasons, but it stores food in its extensive burrow system which extends from right beneath the ground surface to several feet deep. The creature relies on long claws to dig out a burrow, and it has heavy incisors to cut through root systems. As soil accumulates inside its burrow behind the pocket gopher, it turns and pushes the dirt forward using its feet and its head. Excess soil is moved in this way out of the burrow, and it creates a mound on the surface of the landscape. The mounds are quite visible, and they can number several hundred per acre of land. In Florida the pocket gophers have sometimes been called salamanders. The name is derived from the sound of southern pronunciations. For instance, someone in the South might call it a "soil mounder," and that has been heard and then translated into "salamander."[11]

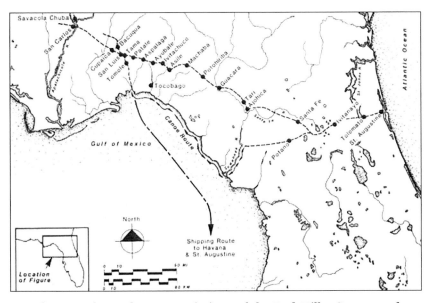

The map shows the many missions of the Red Hills. Courtesy of
State Library and Archives of Florida

When they discovered the mission cemetery they guessed it held several hundred graves. Of those, only a selection of interment sites was excavated. The find revealed that the natives had not been buried in the traditional manner, and there were no ritualistic native artifacts within the tombs. Rather the Christianized Indians were laid to rest in an extended, supine position. Photograph came from an old newspaper clipping from a Madison County paper.

Rose Knox and Graham Schorb

Endnotes

1. Beth Sims, *A History of Madison County, Florida* (Madison, FL: Jimbob Printing, 1986).

2. Sims, *History of Madison County.*

3. B. Calvin Jones, "Spanish Mission Sites Located and Test Excavated," *Archives and History News* 3:6 (1972): 1-2.

4. Bonnie G. McEwan, ed., *The Spanish Missions of La Florida* (Gainesville: University Press of Florida, 1993).

5. Sims, *History of Madison County.*

6. Sims, *History of Madison County.*

7. Susan Cerulean, Laura Newton, and Janisse Ray, eds., *Between Two Rivers: Stories from the Red Hills to the Gulf* (Tallahassee, FL: Heart of the Earth and the Red Hills Writers Project, 2004).

8. Sims, *History of Madison County.*

9. Sims, *History of Madison County.*

10. Sims, *History of Madison County.*

11. John O. Whitaker Jr., *National Audubon Society Field Guide to North American Mammals* (New York: Chanticleer Press, 1980).

Mystery of a Church Bell Found in Area Lake

"Unfortunately, nothing is known of the bell's origins or how it ended up in the lake." Lisa A. Dunbar, senior curator at the Museum of Florida History in Tallahassee.

A rare relic of Spanish origin from the Roman Catholic Church was found in a local lake. How it got there is a mystery to this day. Such a find was considered an historical treasure because very few relics from that time period are still in existence. Upon examination, the bell was found to be cast in an alloy of silver, copper, and tin. It measures four feet around the base and is eighteen inches tall. The inscription bears the words SANTA MARIA ORA PRO NOBIS and the date ANO 1758. There is a raised cross composed of twenty-four, eight-pointed stars. When found, the bell was reported to be very well preserved.

The story of how the bell was discovered shows up in a letter, which was signed by J. W. Cobb from Perry, in Taylor County, Florida.

Excerpts from his letter reveal:

> The old Spanish Bell was given to me by my Father Mr. T. J. Cobb. Judge Vann was an old friend of my Father's and let him keep the bell for me. Now in reply to the offer you make me I will except (sic) same on the account that by selling it to the Society it will be preserved for generations to come. . . . History of the bell as was told to me by my old and greatly esteemed friend Judge Perry, of Madison Co. He was a great surveyor and spent much of his life surveying for the government. As was related to me by my friend–In and about the year 1840 a man by the name of Bell was fishing in a Pond and was wadeing and came in contact with this bell–he stumbled over it and stoped (sic) and found that it was a bell–so told a few years after that the clapper was dug out of a mound in Gee

> Hammock not a great ways from where the bell was found. . . .
> (signed) J. W. Cobb, Perry, Taylor Co. Fla.

The archeological record, as well as information extracted from the diaries of the Spanish Catholic priests, can confirm that there were indeed many missions extending in a line throughout the Red Hills territory, stretching through what is today Madison County. But a note from a senior curator at a museum in Tallahassee reminded me that historians are cautious in calling it a "mission" bell. Such a religious relic found in a Madison lake is one of the few lasting reminders that Spain was intent on Christianizing the native peoples of the region, and by 1635 Florida was mostly Christianized. Yet later, in 1684, troubles set in for these thriving, established missions. A native tribe called the Yemassees brought sweeping changes when they invaded the area and ". . . plundered and ravaged all that fell in their path." Later still, in 1702 and 1703, Governor Moore of Carolina laid further waste to the mission sites of the territory. It was also during that time that fourteen hundred Native Americans of the Red Hills region were sold as slaves and taken to Savannah, Georgia. Then the last devastating invasion came in 1763 with the British occupation of Florida.[1]

Additional Note: In compiling the story of the bell, questions arose in my mind about the date that was inscribed on it. After several inquiries sent to regional experts, I received this email from Lisa A. Dunbar, senior curator at the Museum of Florida History in Tallahassee. Here is an excerpt of her email reply to my questions.

> Ms. Knox,
>
> Your request for information about the mission bell was forwarded to me. Yes, the bell does say "1758." Unfortunately, nothing is known of the bell's origins or how it ended up in the lake. Perhaps a mission was founded in this region at a later date, possibly near St. Marks. A Spanish garrison did occupy St. Marks (then named San Marcos), and a group of Apalachee later settled there, having returned from Pensacola sometime after the British raids. Whether the bell came from a mission that may have been at the Apalachee settlement, or whether it came from a ship landing at St. Marks, or if it got to the region some other way, is unknown. I am attaching an early issue of *Florida Historical Quarterly* from 1927 that has a brief article about the bell. It begins on p. 159. Jerald Milanich's book, *Laboring in the Fields of the Lord*, has more information

about the Spanish garrison at St. Marks so you may want to take a look at this book, also.

The bell has traveled quite a bit. It had been in the collection of the Florida Historical Society in the early 1900s. The Historical Society sent it to the Florida State Museum (now the Florida Museum of Natural History in Gainesville). Then it went back to the Historical Society, then to Mission San Luis, and finally to the Museum of Florida History. It is now on display in the Museum's *Forever Changed: La Florida, 1513–1821* exhibit. We call it a church bell and not specifically a mission bell because we can't be sure that it came from a mission. Hope this has been of some help to you. Unfortunately, the bell's origins are a mystery. Please let me know if you have further questions.

Lisa Dunbar

A life-size replica of a Franciscan monk is exhibited in a display called "Meeting of the Cultures" in the Museum of Florida History in Tallahassee, Florida. Graham and I toured the museum in June of 2012. Courtesy of Graham Schorb in Museum of Florida History

Endnotes

1. C. Julien Yonge, ed. and Emma Rochelle Williams, asst. ed., "The Bell of a Florida Spanish Mission," *Florida Historical Quarterly* 5:3 (Gainesville: Pepper Printing Company, January 1927).

Rose Knox and Graham Schorb

Travel Notes

Plantation Belt of Middle Florida

"The plantation belt in Middle Florida . . . was more or less an island in that its economy, social structure, and soil type differed from the remainder of the state. During these years the planter-class received unusual returns from its investments and slaves, and the cotton economy of this small and isolated region, lying between the Apalachicola and Suwannee Rivers, compared favorably with that of the Georgia Piedmont or the Black Belt of Alabama and Mississippi."[1]

The area of great interest to cotton planters was a fertile, oval strip situated in Middle Florida. Because of that special soil, large and small planters alike would bring the plantation system to the region. It was also about the same time period when "new" territories were emerging; this was so because Native American tribes were being finally forced from their ancestral lands by United States legislation, under the decrees of the Indian Removal Act. These domains were now "free" for settlement as agriculture moved south and west. Consequently, it was from Virginia, the Carolinas, and Georgia that these hopeful planters began migrating even further south and west. They arrived with their African slaves to farm the now-available lands and to grow their cotton.[2] Geologically speaking, Middle Florida is a natural topographical expanse which is part of the Upper Coastal Plains Belt that makes up the larger Piedmont domains of Georgia, the Carolinas, and Virginia and which also extends through southern Alabama and central Mississippi. This Upper Coastal Plains Belt landmass, more generally referred to as the Appalachian foothills, is mostly known for its gentle, sloping hills. Elevations there can range from two hundred to five hundred feet. The Appalachian foothills sprawl down into northern Florida, where they are called the Tallahassee Hills or, more often, the Red Hills. Their average elevation ranges around three hundred feet. These hills stretch to the east, starting from the Apalachicola River, for approximately one hundred miles, finally leveling down between the Suwannee and Withlacoochee Rivers. These same red hills are surrounded on the north by Georgia and then go on southward for about twenty to thirty miles.[3]

The hilly region of north Florida is also comprised of mostly Hawthorne layer, and covering the Hawthorne formation can be found, in places, Pleistocene marine-terrace deposits. Appearing out from the Hawthorne layer is a gray or red-colored soil which can be found under the topsoil. The topsoil is brown, gray, or reddish in hue; this is because of its makeup of two natural fertilizers, marl and lime. Over time, people traveling through the area have penned many accounts about the soil. For instance, one traveling journalist in 1850 wrote his descriptions of the soil, calling it "a dark-red color, composed of sand, clay, lime, and iron, and having an unctuous feel as though it contained fatty matter."[4] He went on to say the rich soil was ". . . the finest red land in America."[5] Soil deposits, therefore, with hues of red and gray found in the Red Hills and on old plantations in the area have given the sloping landscapes around these parts the name, "Red Hills of Florida."[6]

This "finest soil in America" lured the planter society. But in order to talk about a plantation, the term should first be described by its many varying definitions. The word in most literature refers to the beginning stages, the founding "moments" of something, such as a community or a colony established in a "new" country, as for instance in North America. More specifically a plantation can be defined as land planted by laborers, such as in the West Indies or many tropical and semitropical countries; or, in this particular case, like plantations that existed in the southern United States. A plantation can be further described as a fairly large agricultural domain, worked by free or slave labor, to extract from the land a money crop, such as rice, tobacco, sugar, coffee, or cotton, intended for trade to a distant market.[7]

Some scholars have also compared the southern plantation of the American South to that of the European Old World manor system; this was a "New World" planter society appearing on the world stage with the birth of other world markets. One writer once compared both the New World plantation and the Old World manor to each other, describing them as "relatively large landed estates based upon agricultural economics, governing numbers of people on the principle of authority."[8] Using such a definition, the old European feudal attitudes of the manor have been likewise mimicked on the plantation. Nevertheless, the old manor was quite different from the plantation because it was a self-sufficient entity, producing an assortment of necessary crops in order to sustain the immediate and local population. It was with the rise of trade and commerce, and the growth of town life in Europe, that new markets and a new way of living came into being, so the existing manor system could not compete with such change. Consequently, the plantation emerged only when these new markets and a demand for staple crops began to burgeon.

These incoming planters also knew that location was the absolute key to a growing economy. Therefore, the plantations of the New World started to flourish in areas that allowed for accessible trade, those places situated near convenient watery places—coastal areas, archipelagoes, sea-islands, or inland waterways like rivers and their tributaries. Though Madison County was landlocked, it was nevertheless located near several important rivers. The St. Marks and the Suwannee Rivers journey all the way to the Gulf of Mexico, which made it possible for area southern planters to get their cotton crop to market and later shipped to a worldwide commerce system.

There have furthermore been several distinctions made concerning the hierarchy of the planter class, and it is a fact that not all planters held the title of what has been termed the elite "planter aristocracy," often portrayed in romanticized books and movies about the American South. If anyone has ever read *Gone with the Wind* or watched the movie "North and South," the aristocratic South is presented idealistically, with some of the main characters portraying the roles of the highfalutin' upper class. Such scenes tap into the mythical South, and books and films have brought these ideas of genteel grandeur to the masses. These Red Hills "high society" folk statistically were few in number, but they were owners of hundreds of African slaves. Some accounts say that only around seventy-nine very rich planters owned the choicest soil of the Red Hills region. Such powerful men entered the realm of planting for one thing, and one thing only—to make money! Because of the influence and prestige these aristocratic men enjoyed in the financial world, they were free to import their African laborers—sheer "armies" of them—and so to impose their own rules, controls, and disciplines upon their workers. The elite planter then would often attempt to destroy an already existing society, while trying to break the spirit of his imported labor force. He accomplished his goal by reducing the workers to a state of bondage as a way to create a social order for his own personal and financial gain. To illustrate, Julia Floyd Smith, in her academic work on antebellum Florida, states, ". . . the southern frontier was not won for democracy. It was won for a slaveholding society by slave labor. . . . [We] forget the millions of blacks, exploited in a state of human bondage."[9] Also, because these men that made up the planter class had great wealth and resources before ever coming to farm in the Red Hills, some were absent from their estates altogether, traveling to the North or vacationing abroad, leaving the day-to-day management of their plantations in the hands of employed overseers. Yet much time and effort was put forth in order to start and to sustain an estate. The African people are now being recognized for the hard work and impeccable craftsmanship which they contributed in their enslaved circumstances.

Then there was what has been termed the "middle class" planter. Unlike the very rich aristocratic owner, he stayed on his estate, and along with his wife and family members contributed actively to the management of his plantation. He hired an overseer to work directly with the labor force, so he was not actively involved with the plantation workers. The middle class planter would have had thirty to forty, but maybe even up to a hundred slaves, and as his wealth increased he liked to identify himself closely with the ultra-wealthy, aristocratic class of planters.

Finally, the last plantation class would have been the small estate owner, but he should not be confused with a farmer. Rather, he was in charge of a small labor force, playing the active part as a planter, but having only a few workers. He would not have helped physically to produce crops, however.

And the last on the hierarchical list would have been the farmer. He worked alongside one or two of his laborers. As for the planters of Middle Florida, each of these types lived a life indicative of the monies that would ultimately get produced on the plantation. It is true that only a very select few lived in elegant mansions and enjoyed many fine, aristocratic luxuries, while so many others struggled to scrape by, living in log-hewn cabins and using what was in the immediate environment for their basic survival.[10]

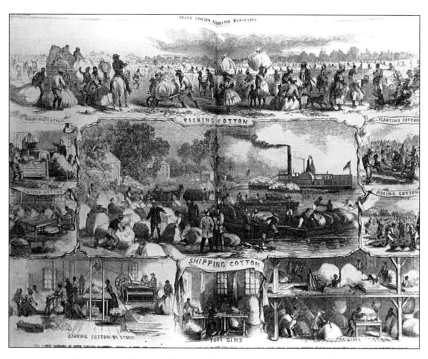

It was because of a fertile, oval strip in the Red Hills that the plantation system of the antebellum South came to fruition; and it was from Virginia, the Carolinas, and Georgia these hopeful planters began migrating even further south and west. They arrived with their African slaves to farm the "available" lands and to grow their cotton. Courtesy of State Library and Archives of Florida

A monument situated in the Four Freedoms Park in Madison, Florida, was dedicated in 1996 to the former slaves of Madison County. The picture was taken at the city park when Rose Knox's students took an historical tour. The African people in modern times are now being recognized for the hard work and impeccable craftsmanship which they contributed in their enslaved circumstances. Courtesy of Graham Schorb

Endnotes

1. Julia Floyd Smith, *Slavery and Plantation Growth in Antebellum Florida: 1821–1860* (Gainesville: University of Florida Press, 1973).

2. Smith, *Slavery and Plantation Growth.*

3. Wythe Cook, *Geology of Florida* (Tallahassee: State of Florida, Department of Conservation, 1945).

4. *The American Agriculturist* 10 [1851] (New York: Saxton and Miles, 1850–1859): 148.

5. Cook, *Geology of Florida.*

6. Cook, *Geology of Florida.*

7. Smith, *Slavery and Plantation Growth.*

8. Edgar J. Thompson, "The Plantation as a Social System in Plantation Systems of the New World," 29.

9. Smith, *Slavery and Plantation Growth.*

10. Thompson, "The Plantation as a Social System."

Rose Knox and Graham Schorb

Travel Notes

The Fertile Oval of Madison, Florida: Aristocratic Planters Flock to Rich Soil

Though there were numerous cotton plantations in Madison County, many of the twenty or so bigger plantation owners, those men out of South Carolina, farmed inside of one particular boundary positioned in central Madison. It should be noted that, back then, the county was mapped out as a much larger domain than it is today. The fertile oval, according to author Clifton Paisley, was ". . . [The area] shaped like a football on its tee, ready for the kickoff. The eastern boundary of this football was a sweeping curve that began four miles north of Madison." This particular boundary line cut through Madison, going along two state roads, one 14 and the other 360, and traveled westward all the way to the neighborhood known as Moseley Hall. The middle of the football-shaped area stretched from ". . . just to the east of Sampala Lake to a sprawling 10,000-acre swamp known as the Hixtown Swamp. That swamp is located seven miles west of the town of Madison.[1] It was William Bartram, the famed botanist, who once wrote about the same geographical domain called Middle Florida as early as the year 1773. The stretch of land is just below the thirty-first parallel of latitude between the Apalachicola and Suwannee Rivers, and the regions around these waterways were quite fertile and therefore ideal for planting and harvesting cotton crops.[2]

In a mass migration out of South Carolina and a few other states, planters flooded to Madison County starting in the late 1820s and continuing into the 1830s. Their goal was to farm the rich soil of a north Florida paradise. Quite a bit of the landscape often referred to as "hammocks of hardwood" made for the ideal environment, beneficial for a kind of cotton called "upland short staple" variety. According to one regional account, the short staple cotton made up four-fifths of the cotton grown on Madison County plantations. Later, however, another kind of cotton became quite popular. The Red Hills of Florida's financial, agricultural accounts of that time period chronicle the first introduction of a different kind of cotton to the area. "Sea Island [variety cotton] had begun by the 1840s to take over the pinelands of inland southeastern Georgia as well as some counties in northeastern Florida." It was prolific, growing east of the Suwannee River. Sea Island cotton eventually burgeoned into the crop of choice and was driven by the price that plantation owners could fetch for it at market, and that price was twice the profit for that of the upland short staple cotton variety.[3]

According to the United States census records of 1830–1860, the geographical lands offered a soil type which was different from the rest of the state of Florida. So in a generally small, central area, a thriving cotton economy came forth between 1821 and 1860, and the crop and financial yields can be compared with those of the Black Belt of Alabama and the Georgia Piedmont.[4]

In addition, according to the land records of the 1800s, between the years 1825 and 1830, 6,440 acres were distributed as part of a land grant. The following people were listed in a local history book as land owners of the Madison area, and many of the descendants of those families are still living in the region today. They were as follows:

Bellamy, Abraham
Bellamy, John
Bellamy, William
Bradley, John
Bryan, Hardy
Carter, Elizabeth
Hankins, Dennis
Hollingsworth, William
Lewis, Romeo
Lipscomb, John
Mays, Rhydon
Richardson, Samuel B.
Rushing, John G.
Searesy, J. B.
Taliaferro, John S.
Taylor, John
Thomas, David

1830 was a land-rush year; 7,580 acres were distributed to many individuals, as follows:

Bailey, William J.
Beazley, Robert
Calloway, David
Copeland Ann
Copeland, Eliza
Copeland, Henry
Copeland, James
Copeland, Robert
Dees, Matthew H.
Hadley, Samuel H.
Hadley, Simeon
Hay, Thos. B
Johnston, Geo. W.
Kerr, William
Lastinger, John
McGehee, John C.
McGuire, Peter
McIntyre, Daniel
Murat, Achille
Platt, Daniel
Ponder, Hezekiah
Ponder, Wm. G.
Roberts, Wm. T.
Sessions, Geo.
Waters, Hezekiah, M.
Wirick, Adam

(Some were absentee owners, including Lewis, Murat, the Bellamys, and Thomas Alexander.)

Elizabeth Sims, in her book, *The History of Madison County, Florida*, also lists the large-scale planters. Sixteen planters in Madison County owned 1,000 acres or more. They are as follows:

Bradley, John L. (1,400)

Bunting, Isaac (1,345)

Church, Lucius (2,200)

Hankins, Dennis (1,250)

Harrison, Richard (1,300)

Hartridge, Theodore (1,200)

Linton, Thomas J. (3,380)

Lipscomb, James (1,247)

Lipscomb, John (4,980)

Mays, Enoch G. (1,700)

Mays, Rhydon G. (1,200)

McGehee, John C. (2,450)

Mosely, William A. (1,040)

Paramore, Redding W. (4,400)

Reid, Jeremiah (1,300)

Tooke, William L. (1,000)

Of these sixteen planters, eleven were from South Carolina, two from Georgia, two from North Carolina, and one, Lucius Church, was from New Hampshire.

On an anecdotal note, it is ironic how destiny leads people to places. I happen to live in the same vicinity of the fertile soil area, not because I do much planting but because I chose to live in a wooded area dotted with spring-fed ponds—plus I like waterfowl and songbirds of many kinds! It was back in 1998 when I was finally ready to buy land and to raise my family. Ironically, like many other people before me, I ended up only a "stone's throw" from many historically important thoroughfares of the antebellum past. In shade of century-old oaks, near archaic spring-fed ponds, my child grew up, not too far from Sampala Lake and the Moseley Hall regions.

When I am riding down backroads in my hometown and see a field like this one, I am reminded of a song once sung by the country music singer, Charlie Pride. He sings "When I was a little bitty baby, my Mommy she rocked me in the cradle, In them old cotton fields back home." Historically speaking, in a mass migration out of South Carolina and a few other states, planters flooded to Madison County starting in the 1820s and continuing on into the 1830s. Their goal was to farm the rich soil of this north Florida paradise and to grow their cotton. Courtesy of Graham Schorb, 2008

Rose Knox and Graham Schorb

Endnotes

1. Clifton Paisley, *The Red Hills of Florida 1528–1865* (Tuscaloosa: University of Alabama Press, 1989).

2. William Bartram, *Travels* (New Haven, CT: Yale University Press, 1958).

3. Paisley, *Red Hills*.

4. United States Census 1830–1860.

Finding Clifton Plantation Site: Lovett

On Sunday morning, April 26, 2015, Graham and I and our two canine companions, decided to try finding the old plantation site known as Clifton. The big home was built by Richard J. Mays, back during the antebellum period. Leaving our home from the Sampala Lake area, we traveled to town through the heart of Madison. I always like taking a long look at the old Smith-Wardlaw-Goza place, because it seems to somehow still hypnotize me, like it did when I was little. As we cruise past, the story of its history, of the fearless Mrs. Smith, flashes again in my memory.

On this day there is a big "For Sale" sign that fronts the highway; I know that the local college cannot afford to maintain an antebellum mansion anymore, in this day and age of budget cuts. Somebody told me a while back, it takes thousands of dollars just to keep the mansion painted. It's sad to think the place might slip back into decline again. Those were my thoughts about it that day.

But change is, indeed, the one constant, and if the walls could talk, they would tell about the historical heyday and then the decline of the property. Also, in passing I noticed one huge, black shutter on the front of the house that seemed to need repair. We kept cruising down Highway 90 West, headed to Pickle Lane, taking a right off of 90 there. Not long afterwards, a left off scenic Pickle Lane got us traveling down Little Cat Road, which finally led to the tiny community known today as Lovett. Just beyond Lovett, there was a brown government sign with a white arrow painted on it that pointed directly to a high hill. Graham pulled off the blacktop road and parked under a huge live oak tree. Our eyes took in an expansive pasture. He snapped a photograph of the sloping hill where the Mays's plantation house once stood. I had read in a local account that Mays had been a Baptist minister; in 1841 he founded Concord Baptist Church. Looking at the site there on the beautiful, pastured hill, I couldn't help but imagine him sitting at the round table at his plantation house, as he signed the Charter of the Florida Baptist Association document. We sat there in the truck and considered walking through an open gate, so we could go and stand on the very top of the hill, seeing the view from up there and perhaps trying to think of what the view might have been from the house's vantage point. But the deer ticks have been very bad this year, we reminded each other. We were happy to simply sit and gaze up at the mansion site from afar, wondering what life was like for the people in bygone times.

After sitting for a while, enjoying the shade and slight breeze, we left, searching then for Concord Church Road. When we finally found the turn, we were soon passing by the old church. Though the historical building was not brown in color, the song "Church in the Wildwood" started playing in my head anyway, in three-part harmony like the Carter family used to sing it. Remember?

"There's a church in the valley by the wildwood,
No lovelier place in the dale,
No spot is so dear to my childhood,
As the little brown church in the dale."

The idyllic-looking country church was shaded by hardwood trees and there was also a large cemetery just behind it. On the cool Sunday morning, many kinds of trucks and cars were pulled into the parking places, and a group of men, some in collared shirts, huddled together, talking outside of the church's entrance. Two lovely wreaths crafted with lavender, yellow, white, and pink flowers adorned the entrance. We wanted to get a photograph of the church and historical sign right then, and to stroll the cemetery, but we didn't want to interfere or disrespect the worship service. Later we looped around the church, passing by it again, and Graham snapped a shot of the old building as he was moving along the dirt road.

Later, down another canopied dirt road, we came upon another cemetery. Each grave looked cared for in the small graveyard, and I also noticed the stones and slabs were substantial in size. Mama used to say to me that a person could tell a lot about a family by the graves they were buried in. She'd remind me, "Rosie, big stones mean one thing—and that's money—they would have had money enough to spare, to have a nice stone." So I wondered what sort of life these people had led as I walked around reading the names. Some of the stones memorialized the Lovetts, Arringtons, Radfords, and Densons.

I also saw a few graves of little children, and I thought of the pain a mother must endure after burying a child. After a while, I grabbed one of my history books out of the truck to check against the plantation owners' names with those etched on the gravestones. I found no match from that source. When we eventually left the cemetery, I felt a sense of terrible sadness, a longing that stayed with me the rest of the day. Funny how it sometimes takes walking through a little family cemetery to make a soul understand the brevity of life and the finality of death.

Later, at home, I checked the Internet and found the official name of the little cemetery. It is called the Radford-Denson Family Cemetery. The location was listed in Lovett.

According to the State Library and Archives of Florida site, the image taken in 1838 depicts Richard Johnston Mays. Courtesy of State Library and Archives of Florida

On Sunday morning, April 26, 2015, Graham and I and our two canine companions decided to try finding the old plantation site known as Clifton. The home was built by Richard J. Mays back during the antebellum period. Courtesy of Graham Schorb

Where the old homesite once stood was now a green, expansive pasture. Graham snapped a photograph of the sloping hill where the Mays plantation house was built, and it was then I remembered that Mays had been a Baptist minister; in 1841 he founded Concord Baptist Church. Courtesy of Graham Schorb

We sat there in the truck and considered walking through an open gate, so we could go and stand on the very top of the hill, seeing the view from up there and perhaps trying to think of what the view might have been from the house's vantage point. Courtesy of State Library and Archives of Florida

Looking at the site on the beautiful pastured hill, I couldn't help but imagine Richard Mays sitting at the round table at his plantation house, as he signed the Charter of the Florida Baptist Association document. Courtesy of Graham Schorb

Two lovely wreaths crafted with lavender, yellow, white, and pink flowers adorned the church entrance of Concord Baptist Church in Lovett. Courtesy of Graham Schorb

Later, down another canopied dirt road, we came upon a little cemetery. Each grave looked cared for, and I also noticed the stones and slabs were substantial in size. Courtesy of Graham Schorb

Creek-Seminole History in Florida

As the indigenous Native American populations began to decline, other native groups were moving into more southern regions. These people might first have entered Florida as hunters or raiders. But still hordes of others began to colonize the state in their desperate flight to avoid violent assaults by the United States military during the colonial period. Many of these migrating native groups were descendants of the earlier indigenous peoples who, in the aftershock of two hundred years of European encroachment, which had caused sweeping cultural and spiritual disruptions, had, in the 1700s, merged, synthesizing themselves into the Creek Indians. Therefore as these native cultures of Georgia and eastern Alabama were scattered by the colonizers from Europe, the remnants of those surviving bloodlines coalesced, evolving as a political force known as the Creek Confederacy. Historical accounts reveal that the first Creek settlements in Florida can be traced to the 1750s.[1]

At about that same period, the Creeks may have come into contact with a few remaining indigenous Indians surviving in remote regions. Archeological evidence suggests that those original remaining populations were then assimilated into the Creek society. During the late seventeenth and early eighteenth centuries, Englishmen in the southern colonies started using the term "Creek" to identify a variety of autonomous peoples who communicated in various languages and practiced varied cultural ways. But the natives called themselves Coosas, Cowetas, Yuchis, Alabamas, Tuskegees, and Shawnees, as well as many other names. It is from these peoples that the Creek Confederacy ultimately emerged, and from that diverse Creek ancestral culture, the Seminole Nation multiplied.[2] Dig sites show that some of the early Creek-Seminole villages in Florida were situated in the old mission sites of the Timucua and the Apalachee, especially in the vicinity of the Tallahassee at Lake Miccosukee and at Gainesville in the Paynes Prairie area.[3]

As time ticked by, ever more Creek peoples continued to flee southward during the early 1800s. It was then that the term "Seminole" had begun to be used quite commonly as a way to identify those certain Creek groups who had entered Florida. The name, however, originally came from a Spanish word, Cimarron, used by the Spanish to speak of the natives who chose to rebel against the attempt to convert them— the tribes refusing to live in any Spanish mission village site.

Even though it is easy to call all of these native peoples Seminole Indians, they, in fact, speak two different Creek languages, one Muskogee and the other Mikasuki.[4]

A Seminole warrior is dressed in traditional warrior garb. When the Seminole Nation was trying to negotiate with the United States to keep their lands, the chiefs would dress in a regal fashion. They were a proud, noble, and unrelenting group of people. Courtesy of Patrick Elliott

Two Seminole Indian boys smile and play. The photo was taken by
W. A. Fishbaugh around the 1930s. Courtesy of the State Archives
and Library of Florida

SEMINOLE INDIAN WAR BLOCKHOUSE

On this site stood a Blockhouse erected by citizens of the area to protect women, children, and old people in the threatening period of 1835-1842. It served as an informal Court House before Adoniram Vann completed the regular Court House, 1840. These facts come from W. Carlton Smith and others versed in frontier history. The Marker will remind succeeding generations of their priceless heritage.

SPONSORED BY THE SENIOR, JUNIOR AND BUSINESS WOMAN'S CLUBS OF MADISON
THE MADISON COUNTY HISTORICAL SOCIETY 1972

Four Freedoms Park features a statue of the same name, and it is also the site of the original pioneer stronghold that was built to protect women, children, and the elderly of the Madison community during the violent times of 1835 and 1842. Blockhouses were built in many surrounding communities during that Seminole Indian conflict. Courtesy of Graham Schorb

The image depicts the painting of Tuko-See-Mathla, also known as John Hicks. A swamp in Madison County is named Hickstown Swamp. There are various spellings for that swampy domain. Courtesy of the State Library and Archives of Florida

Endnotes

1. Jerald T. Milanich, *Florida Indians and the Invasion from Europe* (Gainesville: University Press of Florida, 1995).

2. J. Leitch Wright Jr., *Creeks and Seminoles: Destruction and Regeneration of the Muscogulge People* (Lincoln: University of Nebraska Press, 1986).

3. Milanich, *Florida Indians.*

4. Milanich, *Florida Indians.*

Rose Knox and Graham Schorb

Travel Notes

Conflicts between Native Americans and Early Settlers: Clifton Mansion Plantation and the Aucilla River

The plantation site at Clifton mansion in Lovett was where an incident, one that ended in bloodshed, took place in 1842. Such an episode would also be the starting point of other eventual conflicts involving native tribes and settlers. In a separate incident, a hot pursuit ensued and a struggle unfolded that would, in due course, end in tragedy near a swamp not far from the Steinhatchee River. As more new settlers began encroaching on Native Americans' former ancestral territories, conflicts were an integral part of life for both cultures.

According to a story published in a local historical work called *Madison County: From Sea to Secession*, the area writer [only a student then] tells a detailed account of one particular clash that took place between Native Americans and early settlers of Madison County. According to his account, the affair happened during the Second Seminole Indian War, when hostilities between natives and settlers were running high.

As the narrative goes, a party of local hunters had agreed to meet over at the Clifton estate. At the time, Clifton plantation was a popular area for the early settler-hunters and was known to be well supplied with plenty of game. Three of the hunters, Mr. Sessions, Mr. Shehe, and Mr. Sandrich, were the guests to arrive at the meeting site first, but they had no inkling that they were being closely watched. Not far away, there was a group of Indians hiding close by. Soon after the hunters' arrival at Clifton estate, the natives opened up on the white men using gunfire, killing all three of them. Because the natives had been run out of their homes, their families decimated, and their towns burned to the ground, they were very intent on sending an undeniably strong message to these encroachers. It is often hard for modern readers to understand that moving bands of peoples—the pioneers—were continually intruding on Native American soil, driving the Natives from ancestral lands. So after killing the three hunters, the Natives left a dire, inexorable warning to the settlers and to their families. After the men were killed, the Natives mutilated the bodies, displaying their remains in nearby trees and bushes for others to see.

The skirmish was far from over, though, because later even more violence was to ensue at that same site. When two of the other hunters finally ventured up, a Mr. Johnson and a Mr. McMullen, they were also caught up in Natives' gunfire. Johnson was hit by a shot, dying immediately. McMullen was able to take off on his horse, trying desperately to flee the scene, but his horse was soon shot down by the Natives. The scenario played out in the most dramatic fashion, for the local story goes on to chronicle that his horse, suffering with gunshot wounds, miraculously kept on running for a short way before finally collapsing. Then McMullen, injured and running for his life, was able to hide himself in a nearby swamp. Some people claimed afterwards that it was the head start provided by his dying horse that gave him the important seconds he needed to get free and away from the violence. He lived to tell about it.

It did not take long for the story to spread all around town like wildfire. Soon afterwards a group of community men armed themselves and took out to avenge their friends and the greater settler community. Some of the men who were listed in the vigilante party were William King, Farnell Drew, Joseph and John Flowers, and Joseph Watts. They eventually merged with more men from Jefferson County, led by Colonel William Bailey. Luckily for the men, one man in the gathering was known as an adept tracker, scout, and experienced outdoorsman. His name was Lewis Norton, and with his expertise, the group was able to track down the Indians to a location called Cliff Hammock. A bloody fight took place there and some of the Natives were killed. Yet, because the settlers realized they were far outnumbered at that point, they then retreated.

The Natives afterwards started moving north, up toward the Hamburg region, where a few of their avenging white pursuers had established their homesteads. Later, sometime after nightfall, the Natives attacked the home of Joe Gill. Gill's home was situated just south of where the Kinsey's store once was, on the Greenville-Quitman Highway. In the melée Mrs. Gill was killed, and the home was set ablaze. Gill was, however, fortunate enough to escape the attack, getting out of his burning home. He was then capable of finding safety by hiding in a nearby pond, and that pond was later renamed "Joe Gill

Pond" in his honor. It was likewise a geographical place, with a name now fortunately attached to it, which would keep the story of what took place there alive.

On the following day, Lewis Norton and Colonel Bailey had been successful in tracking the Natives over to the Gill place. It was there Mr. Gill joined them. In their hunt, the men noticed that a total of twenty-three Natives had attacked his home; this they surmised by counting the number of human footprints. Each Native had walked down a separate cotton row in the exodus. From that point, the settlers trailed the Natives to a place called Johannah Lake. There they discovered the Natives had stopped and made a campfire, and they saw evidence of where Natives had downed wild game. Maybe they had stopped to rest and to eat for more nourishment to build up strength. In their retreat, the Indians eventually passed over the old St. Augustine Road, and this location is not too far off from the plantation estate of Mr. Mays.

The Natives that day had journeyed close to the tiny community of Hopewell. Considering the violent mindset of the Natives that night, the Mays household and the Hopewell community were luckily spared by some random hand of fate, because the Natives did not venture into those localities. Also in the same vicinity, a fort had been built as a safe haven for settlers and as a way to try to suppress the ever-increasing Indian hostilities of the region. While at the fort, the pioneers were joined by thirty-eight "new" recruits, men who had been presently defending that particular fort. They all took chase; the pursuers' numbers at that time totaled eighty-eight men. With them, as well, on the hunt was yet another expert tracker named William Hankins. He and Norton "put their heads together" in a concentrated effort to trail the fleeing Natives.

The vigilante party kept moving along, finding ample traces of the Natives' presence, though the fleeing Indians had a two-day head start on them. Soon the pursuing party crossed the Econfina River. The trackers, Norton and Hankins, kept noticing clues that the Indians had become reckless in their movements, thinking in error that they had finally outrun the pursuing settlers. Hankins and Norton also figured the Natives would choose an already well-established trail that would lead them finally across the Fenholloway River. Indeed, the trackers were right, but when it came time to cross over the Fenholloway, ironically their own men gave them some trouble.

Here is what happened next: When the party began crossing over the river, the "fort soldiers" rebelled, refusing to go into what they thought of as "alligator infested" currents. So these men decided to retreat to the fort from where they had first come. However, the determined community men, the ones in the original party, forged diligently onward over the river, making it to a swamp located beside the Steinhatchee River. When they reached that location they were on high alert, thinking the Natives might be camped out in the scrub area just beside the swamp and the Steinhatchee River. So they scouted around the surrounding area, discovering the Natives' camp was set up in a strategic place within a pine forest, just outside a thicket of dense palmettos.

At that location, there was a creek winding between the settlers and the Natives' camp. The trackers felt that the creek would be a major obstacle to achieving a full-open charge, but there happened to be a sliver of land, a small dry ridge, where they might quickly be able to move over in groups of four. That was going to be the strategy. The plan was finally set and communicated to all. The idea was for all of the men in the party to attack the Natives together. Soon afterwards Norton, Hankins, Bailey, and a man named Rufus Dickinson crossed over the ridge and got ready to charge. But they were depending on the other men in the party to also follow the plan, crossing over the little land bridge quietly, four at a time. Plans, however, do not always go as ordered. The men, in the end, disobeyed commands, crossing all at once and making such a ruckus that one Native awoke from slumber. The pursing party knew in those vital moments that they would just have to shoot—or all would be lost. They did, and eight loads of buckshot were targeted straight at the Natives' camp.

In the skirmish Norton found himself in a perilous situation, separated completely from his party, between the Indians and his own companions. Those in the rear, strategic, position were under the impression that they had actually killed him under friendly fire. Hankins also had a close call during the violence, for a blast of buckshot had knocked his hat clear off of his head. It is no surprise that Colonel Bailey was quite angry, and told those disobedient men what he thought about their nonadherence to the specific orders in no uncertain terms. Norton had indeed lived through the episode and had been able to shoot one of the Natives during the fray.

At that point, the men spent the night camped in the same vicinity but were fearfully anxious all the night long as they expected at any second to be attacked by Seminoles. Once morning came, the men explored around the Indians' encampment, finding no people but discovering guns, shot bags, bedding, and other camp items. Soon the song of birdcall seemed to fill the air, and the men followed the sound to where they found a human foot extending out from under a cluster of palmetto leaves. Hiding there, they discovered, was a wounded Indian. Norton then attempted to get information out of the man but was unable to. Understandably Joe Gill, who had lost his home and wife to this raiding group of Natives, felt not one ounce of mercy for him and wished to kill him right off. Later though, the Native was given a trail to escape; eventually the men did catch and hang him. In the end, weary from their chase, the men decided to head back to their own homes.

Whatever came of the fleeing Native Americans? According to the written description of the ending of this saga, a few days later three Indians eventually did surrender at "No. 4" [fort] near Cedar Key. The story ended as follows: "One of them had nineteen shot holes in him, another had four, and the third was unwounded. They said that since the Cliff Hammock fight, nineteen of their number had been killed in the fighting, and one, whose arms were broken, had fallen into the Steinhatchee [River] and drowned. They had hidden the bodies of their dead by throwing them into the river to keep the white men from finding out how many had been killed. This ended the Seminole War as far as Madison County was concerned."[1]

So when travelling down lone roads in the Madison County vicinity, or near the Steinhatchee River, one might think about the tribulations that Natives and early people of the community once underwent.

A Story of Conflict near the Aucilla River: U.S. Army versus the Seminoles:

In less than fifty years of time, because of military raids by the Georgians, Andrew Jackson and his Tennesseans, and the United States Army, the Seminole Nation was finally completely driven out of north Florida; they fled in terror, moving southward, and by 1858 at the conclusion of the last Seminole Indian War, only two hundred Seminoles had survived.[2]

But until they were ultimately driven out, the Seminoles lived in the vicinity of what is today Madison County, and the following tragic incident happened around the Second Seminole Indian War, where historical accounts depict that much of the bloodshed between settlers and Natives took place near the Aucilla River Swamp. Like similar conflicts, the violence was brought on by ever more pioneer encroachment within Native Indian territories.

Rose Knox and Graham Schorb

To illustrate, one pioneer family was homesteading, living west of the Aucilla River in the winter of 1826. However, they ended up being right in the middle of a hotbed of violence, for many times, after raids by pioneers in northwest Florida, Native populations would seek safe haven in some nearby swampy place, and sometimes they were known to strike back with their own brutal violence. The Seminoles had to be quite elusive after their own retaliatory raids, and the settlers were forced to take strong action.

In a legislative decree in 1839 it was decided by those in political power that bloodhounds would be needed to successfully flush out the Natives from southeastern wilderness areas. Though such a decree seems like a desperate and cruel, although efficient, measure, the practice was not new. In fact, Cubans had already long used dogs to chase down African slaves. But even dogs could not catch the elusive Seminoles and in the end, the bloodhounds were not successful in holding a scent long enough to track down the Seminoles.

Settlers tried other measures. There were efforts to create a barrier cutting off access east of the Aucilla River in a strategic move to curtail Seminole movement. Those unsuccessful attempts were conducted by Florida area pioneers and members of the United States army. Amid all these attempts to capture them, the Seminoles kept on fervidly resisting efforts to get rid of them, because they had begun to see clearly the end of their culture as they knew it; they feared obliteration of their race and of their customs. This was also at about the same time that Osceola, the powerful Seminole leader, had begun to encourage his people to renounce any and all agreements made with the United States government, a government that wanted to remove the Seminoles completely from Florida and force them into Oklahoma. Therefore at this time Native Indian and pioneer tensions increased, and more encroaching families living on or in the vicinity of the Aucilla River became an easy target for the soon-to-be-displaced red man.[3]

To illustrate how the brutality affected one household, history recounts how a family in Madison County whose homestead was situated near the Aucilla River was once surprised by Native Americans. The family members had gathered around the table and were in the middle of eating their evening supper. During the incident, the woman of the house, Mrs. Baker, was the first victim; she was wounded and killed by gunshots. Afterwards, her husband was able to gather up his two grandchildren as he frantically tore out for the woods in hopes of finding some safety among the trees. But he and one of the children did not find a safe haven there, and in fact did not even make

96

it through the yard before they were also killed. One survivor was the other grandchild who was found the next day in the yard; the child was sleeping, nestled up beside the dead bodies.

Not long afterwards one military unit led by Lieutenant Colonel Bailey commanded several marches into the Aucilla Swamp. Some of these excursions reached as far over as the Suwannee River. As a result of increased military efforts to flush them out, the Seminoles were finally forced to leave their villages, and during these military raids, Seminole women and children were taken as prisoners. The particulars of their individual stories of terror and of their own human tragedies were not recorded, as were those in the Baker family incident. Balfour, a local writer, reminds us all that, "We are all well aware that treatment of Native Americans by the United States [government] was not a proud chapter of American history. Since they [the Native Indians] were here first, they had first title to the land, and conflicts arose largely because they were unwilling to give it up."[4]

Hankins and Norton also figured the Natives would choose an already well-established trail that would lead them finally over across the Fenholloway River. Indeed, the trackers were right, but when it came time to cross over the Fenholloway, ironically their "own" men gave them some trouble.

When we are padding on regional rivers, we always consider the stories about the place. In December 2011 Graham and Rose are introduced to the Fenholloway River by their friend, Leland Moore. Courtesy of Graham Schorb

Here is what happened next: When the party began crossing over the river, the "fort soldiers" rebelled, refusing to go into what they thought of as alligator infested currents. So these men decided to retreat back to the fort from where they had first come. However, the determined community men in the original party forged diligently onward over the river, making it to a swamp located beside the Steinhatchee River. Courtesy of Patrick Elliott

Rose Knox and Graham Schorb

Endnotes

1. Steve Knight, *Madison County: From Sea to Secession.*

2. Dana Ste. Claire, *Cracker: The Cracker Culture in Florida History* (Gainesville: University Press of Florida, 1998).

3. R. C. Balfour III, *In Search of the Aucilla* (Valdosta, GA: Colson Printing Company, 2002).

4. Balfour, *In Search.*

McGehee's Mansion and Plantation, Chuleotah: The Moseley Hall Region

"Together the McGehees and [Mr.] Hammerly planned and built a grand mansion in the Moseley Hall area near where the old Federal Road leaves the present road 360." From *The History of Madison County, Florida.*

John McGehee's name appears with the big plantation owners of Madison County. As a child, I had often heard about him from my teacher, the late Frances Sanders. She was prone to driving me and my friends around in her white station wagon, as she habitually pointed to places of interest. And while she was driving along, making sure we were all marveling at the rolling hills, with blankets of yellow, lavender, and blue wild flowers growing on the side of the road, she would weave her stories. Little did I know it back then that we were traversing, on lazy Sunday afternoons, a quite-famous fertile football-shaped domain talked about in history books of the area.

And one of "Miss" Frances's favorite subjects was the John McGehee family. So I grew up hearing snippets of his life, passed down in the storytelling tradition.[1] When I grew older and began revisiting some of those same southern subjects, I read how the elder McGehee was born in 1763 and served at the age of sixteen in the Revolutionary War. After the war he moved from Louisa County in Virginia, and while there he made his home in a place that would later be named Greenwood, South Carolina. While in South Carolina McGehee worked as a schoolteacher and later traveled to Madison County with his son, John C. McGehee.[2] Diaries of that time have described specific events and happenings surrounding the old plantation house and its owners. For example in 1833, according to the writings of Superior Court Judge Robert Raymond Reid, he was paying a visit to the older McGehee and his wife. On that day, he lauded the couple for epitomizing the best "public house" there was on that two-hundred-mile road. Reid also told a story in his journal, saying he offered half a box of snuff as a gift to Mrs.

McGehee. At that moment, she showed him a silver snuff box that had stayed in the family for about a century. On the top of that beautiful box rested a center stone. The stone was for finding spots on the sun, and Mr. McGehee claimed during their conversation that "more spots had been discovered through this stone [a stone in great demand in Carolina], than by the best telescopes."[3] Such a scene from daily life can illustrate how wealthy travelers often stopped at country homes visiting with particular families.

Before coming to Madison, his son, John C. McGehee, served as a lawyer in Cambridge, South Carolina. It was he, the younger McGehee, who would opt later to make the move down to Florida, arriving in 1831. He quickly involved himself in community affairs and became known in the region as a planter, industrialist, scientific farmer, lawyer, circuit court judge, land buyer and seller, and a Presbyterian elder. He established his plantations along the Bellamy Road, also known as the Federal Road, in Madison County.

As the McGehees became ever more wealthy, they felt it right to build a home in keeping with their high status in genteel southern society. McGehee needed an architect and he wanted only the best, so he wrote to Baltimore Technical College, requesting that they give him the name of an architect who could bring his ideas to fruition. William Archer Hammerly, a graduate of their school, had already designed one stately home for the influential family of John Brown Gordon in Savannah. Gordon later served as a Confederate general. According to local writer Beth Sims, she reveals, "Together the McGehees and Hammerly planned and built a grand mansion in the Moseley Hall area near where the old Federal Road leaves the present road 360."[4] [Hammerly was also the same man to design a home for Mr. Benjamin Wardlaw.]

Judge J. C. McGehee was also known as an enthusiastic and active supporter of states' rights and secession. After the South lost the War, he fled for a time to Mexico to avoid possible persecution from incoming Northern authorities.[5]

General Note: An historical documentary found on the YouTube channel, "Moonlight and Magnolia: A History of the Southern Plantation," features compelling photographs of many restored opulent antebellum plantation homes. The narrator nostalgically sums up the regional South, poetically referring to the societal landscape of the time, saying,

The moonlight and magnolia scented ambiance that characterized the Old South was embodied in the great plantations of that era. Plantations were the foundations of the region's agrarian economy, the pillar of the region's political thoughts, and the cornerstone of the region's societal graces. The people who lived on these estates were the contributors to this way of life that is now a vital part of America's past and proof of the nation's progress. The plantation system continues to be a hotly debated topic that entertains, enrages, bewilders, [but also] enraptures the hearts and minds that fall under the spell of its moss-shaded mystery. Regardless of a person's views of the history of the southern plantations, regardless of the crop harvest, the splendor of the big houses, the closeness of the family ties, the hard work of the slaves— regardless of how life was lived on the old plantation—this civilization no longer exists. The plantations that survive are now only monuments to a way of life that is now "Gone with the Wind."

As the McGehees became ever more wealthy, they felt it right to build a home in keeping with their high status in genteel southern society. They named it Chuleotah. Courtesy of Graham Schorb

Beth Sims, in her local historical work, *The History of Madison County, Florida*, reveals, "Together the McGehees and [Mr.] Hammerly planned and built a grand mansion in the Moseley Hall area near where the old Federal Road leaves the present road 360." The Federal Road, known also by other names such as the Old Saint Augustine Road, the Camino Real, the Old Spanish Road, or the Old Bellamy Road, ran through the extreme southeast corner of present-day Madison County and veered northwest to present-day Hopewell; then it extended to the north of Lake Sampala (but was later moved south of the lake), then southwest to Moseley Hall, then by Harmony Church, then across the Aucilla River and extended out of Madison County. Courtesy of Graham Schorb

Rose Knox and Graham Schorb

Endnotes

1. Frances Sanders, "Oral Stories of the Moseley Hall Region," Madison County, Florida, 1975.

2. Clifton Paisley, *The Red Hills of Florida 1528–1865* (Tuscaloosa: University of Alabama Press, 1989).

3. "Diary of Robert Raymond Reid, 1833, 1835," from *The Red Hills,* Paisley, p. 5-6.

4. Beth Sims, *A History of Madison County, Florida* (Madison, FL: Jimbob Printing, 1986).

5. Paisley, *Red Hills.*

Finding Chuleotah Plantation Site

"Long before I wrote stories, I listened for stories. Listening for them is something more acute than listening to them. I suppose it's an early form of participation in what goes on. Listening children know stories are there."[1]

One scenic drive is to Moseley Hall, where stories of an antebellum time come to life in memory. Those stories concern a once-opulent house, a rich planter, and a dead bride, and the same tales lurk in the burial places of those people. Sometimes Graham and I will travel the dirt-road route, down Sampala Lake Road. Other times we are not up to battling the bumps or, after a hard rain, dodging puddles. So sometimes we choose a paved road named Moseley Hall Road, though both thoroughfares will lead a traveler to the old plantation site. The place rich planters called Chuleotah was where an opulent plantation house once stood, in its architectural magnificence, up on a high hill. A dreadful story of one man's lost hope because of the sudden death of his young wife still lingers there, even though the home is long gone.

Books and articles about the Old South had given me clues regarding names of the plantations that were once located in my own backyard. It was then on a Sunday afternoon, April 19, 2015, that Graham and I and our two little Chihuahuas loaded in our 2002 Toyota truck ready to take a leisurely drive. This cloudy day was the beginning of many trips we would eventually take over numerous years to old cemeteries and to former plantation sites. We had chosen the paved road, only because it had been raining the night before.

While we were motoring down the road, I happened to be reading from one local history book, trying to find the specific hill and exactly where the elder Mr. McGehee was long ago laid to rest. As I was speaking out loud (and probably a little bit too dramatically for Graham's taste) we finally approached what we thought had to be the "right" hill. It was high and sloping indeed! When we finally got to the crest of it, I was reading the paragraph that said, "On a beautiful wind-swept hilltop here a fine marble stone, now broken to pieces, marks the grave of John McGehee." I'm not kidding you, either: the wind was actually sweeping over that gentle slope, just as this particular author had promised!

Caught in the moment, we paused to take in the view of a green rolling landscape. Later in the day, we stopped at a closed gate, parking our truck because we had spotted a small sign. The painted letters read "Chuleotah." As we enjoyed the breeze while taking in the view of a pastoral scene, watching horses and cows grazing under a big live oak tree, my imagination got the best of me. The stories I had been told in childhood came rushing back. I could see the plantation fields ripe for cotton-picking and could almost hear soulful spirituals of laboring slaves rising up to the clouds, amid a blue sky. I tried to picture the stately mansion that was once overlooking those sprawling cotton fields. This I remembered was the main plantation owned by the elder McGehee's son, John C. Then quite suddenly, I was transported back to my own past, to the summer of 1976. I was just fifteen years old. "Miss" Frances Sanders, a storytelling matriarch, had always tried reminding any soul she could get to listen to her, of the plantation days of the county's antebellum history. I could somehow hear that slow southern drawl of hers, even though Miss Frances had been dead already, by then, for going on two years. But her words still somehow managed to reach through time and space, speaking out to me there by the little sign that read, Chuleotah. Frances came to life then, saying in her voice of my long-ago memory, "If you go walking over on that hill." She'd then point directly over the landscape, so we were sure to know exactly where to go if we ever wanted to tromp around, trespassing on somebody's private property. At that moment, sitting in the truck with Graham, the idea from Eudora Welty's work started to ring true. Welty reminded me, "Long before I wrote stories, I listened for stories. Listening for them is something more acute than listening to them. I suppose it's an early form of participation in what goes on. Listening children know stories are there. When their elders sit and begin, children are just waiting and hoping for one to come out, like a mouse from its hole."[2]

So we knew the story was there when Frances continued on her narrative about the McGehees. She'd say, "And if someone was to go there, even to this very day, they could see quite a show: the breathtaking view the McGehees used to see when they'd walk around the hill just before sunset."

"What would they see?"

We'd beg Frances to tell us, hoping for a tale of some ghost that must be evermore haunting the old property, looking out for the souls of the dead in some forgotten plantation cemetery.

"They'd see the eyes of a hundred foxes," was her reply.

There would be a silence in the station wagon as we tried to imagine a scene of so many wild creatures roaming around on those beautiful hills. Then she'd plow into the crux of the story, continuing to hold us almost breathless as she recounted, and even sort of acted out, the tragedy.

She would begin: "It was in the hot, unrelenting summer of August. The year was 1858. The big house—one that had been being built for over a year—was just about ready for the married couple to move in. It was on that fateful day, Mrs. Charlotte McGehee walked through the front door of that huge mansion. She looked all around, just marveling at the beauty of it all. Still glancing about the grand, spacious main room, she said something like, 'I'm about as close to Heaven as I ever will be!'"

Frances would always pause for a long moment at that particular part in the story. Then her face would look tired, her shoulders would begin to droop. A big frown would spread across her face. She'd look so tired and worn out by then; many deep wrinkles would suddenly appear on her forehead, creating dark lines on her face. We'd all wait in anticipation, Susanne, Hank, Susie, and I, for her to move through this long minute of silence. Then she'd straighten out her body like a soldier ready for a sergeant's inspection, as an expression of determination and strength was revealed on her face, finally blurting out the words: "But when Mrs. Charlotte uttered those words, she fell straight down to the floor, and she died right then and there on the inside of that gorgeous mansion!"[3]

Frances would look down to the ground then, drooping over, and I can still see her shaking her head in sorrow like she was about to start crying. It was kind of like being at a play, and we were watching an actress express some tragic moment. And because of such dramatics, I never forgot her rendition of the story.[4]

From the road where we looked over those hills, the thought occurred to me that today there is not much left up on the hill that could even begin to speak of the grandeur of a stately home that took almost a year to build. The only passage I was able to find was a brief description I dug up from a local history book. It said that the steps and mantels had been crafted from marble. The home was adorned throughout with fine furniture; the dining area complete with silverware and china. Also near the mansion was situated a two-acre garden.[5]

Graham and I waited outside of the gate of Chuleotah for a few minutes, taking in the view. I was hopeful that the owner of the place might come along to greet us as he was about the task of feeding his livestock. Not long afterward, we pulled away from the sign that read, Chuleotah while the stories were still dancing in my head. We made our way, going further along and over to take a picture of the real estate sign that read, "For Sale" in front of the Moseley Hall Church and property. Just down the road from that church, we stopped at a cemetery. I noticed one picture of an African American male featured on a gray granite tomb. From the looks of much older graves than his, it was evident that we were walking in an old, historical place. I wondered about the stories that might rise out of these graves, if only the dead here could talk. Yet only silence and an occasional passing car could be detected. It is a certainty that most of those stories are probably dead, gone with each owner. But I paused to read and speak out loud the names I saw: names like Delaughter, Hampton, and Blue. Time had erased some of the stories for sure, and even a few of the names, because down one entire row of older graves, we noticed that the letters had been completely worn off by erosion. A quote from Ray Bradbury sums up what we saw on those bare tombs:

"I have no name. A thousand fogs have visited my family plot. A thousand rains have drenched my tombstone. The chisel marks were erased by mist and water and sun. My name has vanished with the flowers and the grass and the marble dust."[6]

Rosie's Journal: After we walked through the cemetery, trying to read the headstones, we then walked down the side of the road for a bit, noticing how the graves were positioned on both sides of the paved road, but it was all the same cemetery. It was a spring day, so I had put on my "snake boots" because I had killed a juvenile moccasin the day before. Graham also chased a big alligator-snapping turtle into the woods, shooing it away from the paved road.

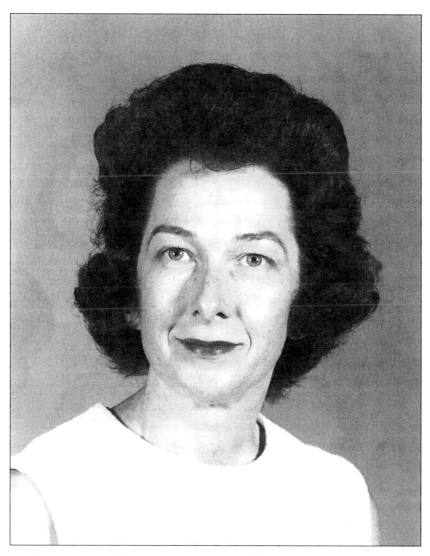

Then quite suddenly I was transported back to my own past, to the summer of 1976. I was just fifteen years old. "Miss" Frances Sanders, a storytelling matriarch, had always tried reminding any soul who would listen to her of the plantation days of the county's antebellum history. I could somehow hear that slow southern drawl of hers, even though Miss Frances had been dead already, by then, for going on two years. Courtesy of Susanne Sanders Griffin

Words from Ray Bradbury sum up what we saw on those bare tombs: "I have no name. A thousand fogs have visited my family plot. A thousand rains have drenched my tombstone. The chisel marks were erased by mist and water and sun. My name has vanished with the flowers and the grass and the marble dust." Courtesy of Graham Schorb

Artist Pat Elliott captures the majesty of a fox. As the story goes, at one plantation house in Madison County, an untold number of foxes used to gather near the home in the late afternoon, at the setting of the sun. We'd beg "Miss" Frances, our storytelling matriarch, to tell us an anecdote about the plantation, hoping for a tale of some ghost that must be evermore haunting the old property, looking over the souls of the dead, in some forgotten cemetery. "They'd see the eyes of a hundred foxes," was her reply. The artist named the piece, "Gray Fox, Gray Moss, Gray Morning." Courtesy of Patrick Elliott

Rose Knox and Graham Schorb

Endnotes

1. Eudora Welty, *One Writer's Beginnings* (Cambridge: Harvard University Press, 1984).

2. Welty, *One Writer's Beginnings.*

3. Frances Morrow Sanders, "Stories about Chuleotah Mansion in her White Station Wagon," Madison, FL, 1976.

4. Welty, *One Writer's Beginnings.*

5. Beth Sims, *A History of Madison County, Florida* (Madison, FL: Jimbob Printing, 1986).

6. Ray Bradbury, *From the Dust Returned: A Family Remembrance* (New York: William Morrow, 2001).

Oakland Cemetery: Final Resting Place of a Judge and a Secessionist

"He is not dead but sleeping." From a tombstone inscription.

On a morning in May 2015, Graham and I set out to find the Oakland Cemetery where Judge John McGehee and his wife, Charlotte, are buried. We finally found the entrance and the historical sign. The sign was in the best condition of any historical sign we had ever seen, and we wondered if it was a newly maintained one, or if an area neighbor was keeping it up. Soon we found ourselves walking through the cemetery, and as we searched out John and Charlotte's graves, we came across several small Confederate flags memorializing the Civil War dead. After seeing the grove of magnificent oak trees there, we knew why it was called Oakland Cemetery. Some of those live oaks were probably three hundred years old. While making our way up to the McGehee graves, I spied the huge cedar tree that Mr. Paisley had once described in his book on the Red Hills. McGehee's stone read:

> Judge J. C. McGhee. (His name was misspelled on the marker.) 1802-1882.

> He is not dead but sleeping. President of the Florida Secession Convention January 1861.

It was also evident that his grave was not in the same good condition as the photograph that had once appeared in Clifton Paisley's book, *The Red Hills of Florida*, published in 1989. Before taking a photograph of his wife's resting place, I had to use my writing pad to clear off the dead leaves and limbs from her raised tomb. I couldn't help but remember the story about her dying in Chuleotah mansion. What hopes and dreams of Mr. McGehee's must have been dashed at her sudden passing!

Another small stone nearby hinted of some long past tale of tragedy. The grave marker featured a black and white photograph of a little child. She was smiling and posing in her pretty dress. I paused to wonder about the story surrounding her death. A bit later, after walking around and lingering there beside the stones, we soon were back in the vehicle and driving away. As we pulled away from the graveyard, we marveled at the rolling pastures all around on both sides of the road. I tried to picture what the scene must have looked like in days gone by, in an antebellum past, when cotton crops were growing in the fields and weary voices rose on high, singing black spirituals. As we moved further from the cemetery site, I thought with regret, "There is a great deal of lost history and so many lost stories of the people buried forever in an old cemetery." But when surveying the vast, rolling landscape, I can almost hear voices rising up from the former souls living in those Red Hills. Words from the Tao echoed in my mind: "When your work is done, it will be forgotten. That is why it will last forever."

The wrought-iron sign announces the entrance into Oakland Cemetery. Courtesy of Graham Schorb

Rose Knox and Graham Schorb

The historical sign at the Oakland Cemetery gives a brief summary of McGehee's life endeavors and his ties with Madison County. Courtesy of Graham Schorb

I saw the huge cedar tree that Mr. Paisley once described in his book. McGehee's stone read: "Judge J. C. McGhee. (His name was misspelled on the marker.) 1802-1882. He is not dead but sleeping. President of the Florida Secession Convention January 1861." Courtesy of Graham Schorb

Rose Knox and Graham Schorb

Before taking a photograph of his wife's resting place, I had to use my writing pad to clear off the dead leaves and limbs from the raised tomb. I couldn't help but remember the story about her dying in Chuleotah mansion. Courtesy of Graham Schorb

Soon we found ourselves walking through the old cemetery, and as we searched out John and Charlotte's graves, we came across several little flags memorializing the Civil War dead. Courtesy of Graham Schorb

Rose Knox and Graham Schorb

As in some scene from *Gone with the Wind* or *North and South*, the old oak boughs provided a lush backdrop as well as some cool shade. Courtesy of Graham Schorb

JOHN C. MCGEHEE,
President of the Florida
Secession Convention

Image of John McGehee. Courtesy of the State Library and Archives
of Florida

Rose Knox and Graham Schorb

Travel Notes

If Walls Could Talk: History and Legends of Whitehall: Wardlaw-Smith-Goza Mansion

"An old lady came forward saying, 'my son gave his life to Virginia and this son has given his life to Florida: let me kiss him for his mother.'"
From Tracy J. Revels, *Florida's Civil War: Terrible Sacrifices*

When people take the time to explore historically significant places like pioneer cemeteries or antebellum mansions, they might pause to wonder: "What if lifeless objects could tell a story? What if walls, balconies, or etched stones were somehow capable of echoing tales from a distant past?"

If such an idea were possible, Whitehall mansion, built in 1860, might reveal tales from the antebellum era. Could one house tell about an entire region? An entire society? And in so doing, echo stories from history?

Honoré de Balzac once claimed, "The events of human life, whether public or private, are so intimately linked to architecture that most observers can reconstruct nations or individuals in all the truth of their habits from the remains of their public monuments or from their domestic relics." His words ring true to anyone who has visited the Wardlaw-Smith-Goza mansion.

Think about what has gone before. Could this house still hold the sound of desperate sighs coming from John C. Breckinridge, the Secretary of War of the Confederacy, as he sought escape from Union persecution after the South fell? There are still tales and rumors circulating in town to this day about that particular episode. Maybe if a soul were to listen closely, they might hear death cries from soldiers young and old, Yankee and Confederate, willing to die in battle. Those war dead are buried in the old cemetery just down the road, and they met death's call inside of those mansion walls. The grand mansion does indeed have a southern story to tell.

Fast-forward many decades from that Civil War and try to imagine the following scenario: Could there remain prayers from a seemingly powerless widow? Her children reminded me once how she stood resolute when she was forced to confront a siege on her home about one hundred years after those thirty-one Confederate soldiers perished from battle wounds.

Perhaps if legends remain there, then these very walls have absorbed and can reveal to a keen observer the many stories of the people who once dwelled within. The events of their lives, through the building's existence, might transcend time to reveal human experiences and people's reactions to suffering and grief, and might remind us of what Faulkner meant when he coined phrases like "grim endurance" and "tranquil desolation."

For a good listener, the dwelling makes known a history of opulence, decline, decay, and—finally, once more —revival. If walls could somehow magically talk, what information might folks learn about the paradox of the South's philosophy and of the South's devotion, passion, decimation and reconstruction? It is a fact that Whitehall has watched privation and hardship march past her doors; and inside these pine walls the tales remain.

Whitehall was the mansion's initial name, and it is a colossal two-story classical Greek Revival-style home, with twenty Greek Doric columns and manicured grounds, located in Madison County. The mansion was originally built with porches on two floors. In the 1900s columns were added, the two porches removed, and balconies were put in, under the direction of Chandler Holmes Smith. The Wardlaw-Smith-Goza home is known as the second most historically significant residence in the state, and the enormous antebellum structure is an architectural marvel, built with twelve-foot-wide interior halls, twenty-foot ceilings, African mahogany stairs, chandeliers, four iron balconies with ornamented doors, and marble hearths. The palatial dwelling is constructed of longleaf heart pine held together by wooden pegs, and the home and grounds encompass an entire city block.[1] In 1910 the original upper porch was removed, and the fluted columns were added.[2] So culturally valuable, the mansion has been included on the National Register of Historic Places and the Historic American Building Survey. In short, the home is an historic treasure, reminding us of stories from the antebellum past.[3]

The majestic home was constructed in Madison, Florida, by architect William Archer Hammerly of Baltimore, Maryland, in 1860, for

Colonel Benjamin F. Wardlaw, originally from Sea Island, Georgia.[4] Wardlaw was a prominent Madison resident, a county judge, a cotton and tobacco planter, and a Confederate officer, defending states' rights during the American Civil War.[5] Madison County during the early nineteenth century had thirty cotton plantations and numerous mansions dotting the expansive pastoral landscape. [Madison was a much larger mapped-out county back then.] Bales and bales of cotton were transported by the ton to the Gulf of Mexico via area waterways. The St. Marks and the Suwannee Rivers were two important waterways during the antebellum period. Steamships would be loaded with baled cotton, making Madison a significant location for area planters, even though the county was landlocked; and one prominent planter of that time was Colonel Benjamin F. Wardlaw.

In Madison and surrounding counties, cotton was king. The recent history of the area that is now called Madison dates back to the 1820s.[6] The frontier plantation area was known as Middle Florida.[7] However, thousands of years before this date the Paleo Indians hunted mastodon and saber-tooth cats on this land. An intact mastodon was once brought up from an area river by divers, just a few miles from the mansion's location, and it can remind us of a prehistoric past, going back at least 13,000 years.

Those ancient hunters and their later descendants, the Timucua, thrived in the area by the tens of thousands, way before the first pioneers were to come here with mule and oxen trains, cotton seeds, and slaves. And way before those pioneers arrived, Hernando de Soto crossed the Suwannee River somewhere near Charles Spring in the year 1539. His army came marching on a well-worn path; that "path" is known today as Highway 90 (in late afternoon shadows, the mansion now looms over 90's asphalt). De Soto's men would have witnessed, back in the mid-1500s, farming methods, Indian villages, and towering ceremonial mounds; these crops and structures came from a highly evolved and ritualistic Native American society living thousands of years before European occupation.

People today can still visit the Indian sites, because the former Indian Nations left remnants of their way of life in a forty-foot mound, located just a few miles west of the mansion. Yet, within three hundred years, these people had been destroyed by many methods and several generations of Europeans: they were sold into slavery, decimated by European diseases, and converted to another religion. As mentioned in previous chapters, some were forced onto western reservations by the later settlers under the dictates of the United States government's

Indian Removal Act.[8] In time the proximity of area waterways and the rich soil of the territory attracted many planters, some very prominent, into Florida, and especially northern Florida, where some were to build aristocratic homes such as Whitehall.

Since 1860 the Madison County mansion has served various purposes, including as a makeshift hospital during the Civil War. Historic oral accounts have emerged about those wounded soldiers, from both the Union and Confederate ranks. These tales portray how hopeless men were transported to the mansion by railway train after the bloody Battle of Olustee, which was fought seventy miles east of the house.[9] Approximately 10,000 infantry, cavalry, and artillery soldiers gathered on that cold February 20th morning in 1864. The Confederate rebels, determined to push the Union forces back and away from the strategic bridge at the Suwannee River, won the day, and by sunset, the Union suffered 203 killed, 152 wounded, and 506 missing. Losses to the Confederacy included 93 killed, 847 wounded, and 6 missing, for a total causality count of 946.[10]

As the story goes, by the time the men arrived via train at Whitehall, destiny was corralling them towards death. Those brought to the house had been severely wounded at Olustee. All were silenced inside Whitehall. If walls could talk, what prayers might have seeped into corridors and crept over winding steps of the Charleston staircase, as the dying struggled for one last breath. These determined men from both sides, praying for their souls to the same Christian Savior, met their Maker there. It is said that women of the town, desperate to help, tore the curtains from window frames to bandage soldiers' wounds. According to one source, survivors were transported via train to area towns; the women of each community took charge, serving in whatever ways they saw fit. In Madison Margaret Vann, along with other women, provided food and tried to offer comfort to the soldiers. Vann encountered a scene that saddened her concerning a young soldier reposing inside of a coffin, and "partially covered by flowers." A touching moment transpired then, and Vann remembers "An old lady came forward, saying 'my son gave his life to Virginia and this son has given his life to Florida: let me kiss him for his mother.'" The lady then proceeded to cover the face of the soldier with her own handkerchief. Vann recalled, "It was all so sad, so pathetically sad."[11]

The only physical evidence of that vain struggle is thirty-one markers at the town's Oak Ridge Cemetery, about a half mile from the stately home. Now nameless stones stand there as testimony to the losses of America's Civil War. Old live oak trees shade the marble headstones that are engraved with the letters, C.S.A.; the three carved initials stand for Confederate States of America.

This is one story that has perpetuated itself over time. Yet the house and land have known other owners besides Wardlaw. Some of their stories have been lost, while some still survive. Those owners were: A. Marshall Cason 1863 -67; Elizabeth T. Glover, 1867-71; and Chandler Holmes Smith and succeeding members of the Smith family, 1871-1978 (the Smith family owned the home for over a hundred years. Chandler Holmes Smith was a nephew of Oliver Wendell Holmes); and Mr. and Mrs. William M. Goza, 1978-1982. Mr. Goza is a fifth generation Floridian, and Benjamin F. Wardlaw was Mr. Goza's great-uncle. The Gozas spent a year restoring the home to its pre-Civil War condition.[12]

The couple lived in the mansion for a while but later donated it to the University of Florida Institute of Food and Agricultural Sciences. During the restoration, period furnishings were donated by Friends of the Mansion and local residents. North Florida Junior College, now known as North Florida College, acquired the historic structure and grounds through the efforts of the Florida Historic Preservation Advisory Council, with assistance from members of the Florida state legislature and supportive friends, appropriating $210,000 for the purchase of the home and grounds from the University of Florida Foundation to transfer ownership to North Florida Junior College in 1988.[13]

By 2015 the college was ready to sell the home, for there was no operating budget for the home's maintenance due to cuts in funding. As luck would have it, when the fate of the mansion was in question once again in 2015, Arthur "Art" Smith, a celebrity chef known worldwide for his culinary expertise and a native Floridian from nearby Jasper, purchased it from North Florida Community College. In my own lifetime the fate of this home has been in question. For now, however, it is in the hands of a person who values local history because he is a native of the region, and his status as a world-renowned chef will keep the mansion alive and well.

Even today, when visitors approach the home, often they are simply overwhelmed by a sense of mystery and awe. The century oak tree that predates the home is draped in thick grey Spanish moss, and if it has been raining, the limbs are blanketed with green resurrection fern. The visual effect of the home and tree seems like the estate's formal gesture, perhaps, to summon her guests to come closer and listen to the history, to hear the stories.

Other stories and legends: When the South succumbed to Northern invasion, it is believed by many that General John C. Breckenridge, who served as the Confederacy's Secretary of War, as well as former Vice President of the United States, stayed the night at the mansion on May 15, 1865 during his escape to Key West. William Carlton Smith, who lived from 1899 to 1963, was known for his extensive knowledge of local history. He worked with Dr. Mark F. Boyd on tracing the Saint Augustine Trail though Madison County and also worked in collaboration with Dr. A. J. Hanna on how Breckenridge, on his flight from Union forces, came through Madison after the fall of the South. Much later, during America's Great Depression, a local WPA office was set up in one room of the home and distributed commodities to the public.[14]

Events and Happenings: Events that drew crowds to the home in the most recent past were: the annual Old Fashioned Supper on the Lawn, Christmas at the Mansion, Art on the Lawn, and Quilt Show. Instructors and staff from the local community college also once used the site for meetings, conferences, drama productions, and Southern study tours. In recent years, Art Smith has invited the community to participate in several baking contests, where prizes have been awarded.

Additional Note: The architect of the mansion, Mr. Hammerly, remained in Madison, settling in the Hamburg area. Mr. and Mrs. Hammerly are interred in the Oak Ridge Cemetery in Madison.

In 1910 the original upper porch of the Wardlaw-Smith-Goza mansion was removed and fluted columns added. The mansion exhibits classical Greek revival architecture and was built by architect William Archer Hammerly of Baltimore, Maryland, for Colonel Benjamin F. Wardlaw in 1860. Wardlaw was also a planter, a county judge, a Confederate officer, and a member of the Charleston Convention of 1860. Courtesy of the State Library and Archives of Florida

Architectural Characteristics of Whitehall Mansion: Classical Greek Revival design constructed of regional heart pine; 9 rooms, including 4 bedrooms and 3½ baths; 6,025 square feet; two-story with columned portico on 4 sides; 1-story separate kitchen on west side; four iron balconies with double ornamented doors; exterior exhibits temple front with flat entablature, ornamental frieze, and four double ornamented doors; ground floor is T-square hallways with four 20-square-foot rooms, 16-foot-high ceilings and original wood floors; 14-foot floor-to-ceiling windows on second floor with 20-square-foot rooms; riff-cut heart pine flooring; working marble-faced fireplace; intricate handcrafted woodwork; silver-plated doorknobs; a downstairs library with original bookshelves and original light fixture; Charleston-style stairway made from African mahogany; and 20 Doric order columns. Courtesy of Graham Schorb

Originally named Whitehall, the mansion is listed on the National Register of Historic Places and the Historic American Building Survey. The home is known for its freestanding Charleston staircase. Courtesy of Rosanna Hughes, a student at North Florida Community College

The home was utilized as a makeshift hospital after the Battle of Olustee, which took place on February 20, 1864, near Lake City. Wounded soldiers, both Union and Confederate, were transported by train to Madison. Ultimately, 31 soldiers would succumb to their injuries, and they now rest for eternity in the Oak Ridge Cemetery, one of the oldest cemeteries in the state of Florida. In addition, the mansion was later used as a WPA office where commodities were distributed. Courtesy of Rosanna Hughes

When North Florida Community College owned the mansion, it was decorated in period pieces; the many fine historical items displayed throughout the home were on loan, provided by area residents. All interior photographs are courtesy of Rosanna Hughes

The mansion is pictured here with Highway 90 in the foreground.
Courtesy of Graham Schorb

Mansion bed. Courtesy of Rosanna Hughes

Inside mansion. Courtesy of Rosanna Hughes

Vase and lace. Courtesy of Rosanna Hughes

Endnotes

1. Wardlaw-Smith-Goza Conference Center Historic Florida Landmark, brochure.

2. Edwin Browning Jr., "Ellaville Stood by Confederacy," *Tallahassee Democrat*, June 25, 1970.

3. Wardlaw-Smith-Goza brochure.

4. Wardlaw-Smith-Goza informational flyer.

5. Browning, "Ellaville."

6. Browning, "Ellaville."

7. Wardlaw-Smith-Goza flyer.

8. Leslie Rose Knox and Graham Schorb, *Canoeing and Camping on the Historic Suwannee River: A Paddler's Guide* (Cocoa: Florida Historical Society Press, 2012).

9. William H. Nulty, *Confederate Florida* (Tuscaloosa: University of Alabama Press, 1990).

10. Nulty, *Confederate Florida*.

11. Tracy J. Revels, *Florida's Civil War: Terrible Sacrifices* (Macon, GA: Mercer University Press, 2016).

12. Smith family interview conducted by Rose Knox at Wardlaw-Smith-Goza Mansion, Summer 2011.

13. Smith family interview.

14. Wardlaw-Smith-Goza brochure.

Walking/Driving Tour of Antebellum Homes

"Now, just as one more-or-less consciously reads the face of every person one meets, to discover whether it is friendly or withdrawn, happy or sad, at home in the world or baffled by it, so buildings are the faces on which one can read, long after the events themselves have passed out of memory, or written record, the life of our ancestors." Lewis Mumford from *The South in Architecture*

There are many old buildings still standing in Madison County that can reveal the story of the past. The "Historic Walking Driving Tour" brochure of the town features around fifty structures, among other places of interest.[1] A few houses built around the antebellum period are still standing. Listed below are some of those structures:

Parramore-Randell House: 291 N. E. Range Avenue, c. 1839

Livingston House: 219 N. E. Livingston Street, c 1836

Nathan P. Willard, The Dream House: 146 N. W. Marion Street, c. 1849

Wardlaw-Smith-Goza: Chef Art Smith Southern Kitchen and Garden School: 121 N. W. Marion Street, c. 1860

Parramore House: 230 S. W. Meeting Avenue, c. 1865

Vann-Dickinson House: 435 S. W. Rutledge Street, c. 1850

Elijah J. and Seth H. Bunker House: 219 S. W. Bunker Street, c. 1850

245 S. W. Shelby Avenue Home: 245 S. W. Shelby Avenue, c. prior to 1850

Buildings in Downtown Madison: 100 S. W. Range Avenue to 310 Range Avenue c. 1838

Brief information about each home:

Seven generations of the Randell family have, off and on over the years, taken up residence in the Parramore-Randell house. This home was built by R. W. Parramore in 1839 and is constructed of hand-hewn boards with pegs and handmade square nails. The original placement of the home was changed in order to move it further away from the road. It was also remodeled after fire damaged the structure.

The Livingston House, built in 1836 by Madison Livingston, is said to be one of the oldest antebellum homes in the town. Oral stories surrounding the home suggest that on May 16, 1865, at the conclusion of the Civil War, the owner, Daniel G. Livingston, offered a "swift saddle mare" to John C. Breckinridge, a Confederate general, helping him escape after the South fell to Union forces. The home still has quite a few of its original features, including heart pine flooring, six wood-burning hearths, twelve-foot ceilings, woodwork, and doors.

The Nathan P. Willard Home known as "The Dream House," was built in 1849. Nathan Willard was known for establishing the second cotton mill in the state of Florida. This small cottage-like home is unique, for it mimics in architecture, structure, millwork, and layout the Prince A. Murat home located in Tallahassee.

The Smith-Wardlaw-Goza Mansion (see a detailed story in the previous chapter).

The Parramore House, constructed in 1865 at the end of the Civil War, was built by James Buchanan Parramore. After the death of his wife, he sold the house to his brother, William Laurance Parramore, and it remained in the family for over a century. The original site included servants' quarters and a greenhouse, but those are no longer standing. Constructed with wooden pegs, the home is the work of master craftsmen.

The Vann-Dickinson House was built by the Vann family in 1850. It was later owned by Governor Drew's family and later still was purchased by E. F. Dickinson and stayed in their family for half a century.

The Elijah J. and Seth H. Bunker House was built by the two brothers, Elijah and Seth, in 1850. Their family history reveals they came from France and were Huguenots. The home was built with two entry doors to accommodate the comings and goings of both brothers who lived in the house. When visitors arrived they would go to the door of the brother they wished to visit and would be invited into the central parlor. Elijah was wed to Fanny R. Mobley. In 1894 Fanny Bunker, listed then as a spinster, sold the home and property for $685 to Richard Bevan. The current owners of the home claim that supernatural stirrings have occurred while they have lived there.

The small home located at 245 S. W. Shelby Avenue was built in 1850. The structure was originally a two-room log cabin. Over the years the house has seen many changes.

Church Building: Established in 1840, the First Presbyterian Church was built in 1851. My father, Charles Samuel Knox, was a Sunday school teacher and deacon, coming from Ulster-Scot roots. He made sure all five of his children learned the catechism and attended services regularly, where seven of us filled the entire second-row pew. Tragically, the elegant, artful stained-glass-windows were sold in the 2000s and taken from the building; however, they do grace the walls of a nearby church at Honey Lake Plantation.

The Livingston House, built in 1836 by Madison Livingston, is said to be one of the oldest antebellum homes in the town. Oral stories surrounding the home suggest that on May 16, 1865, at the conclusion of the Civil War, the owner, Daniel G. Livingston, offered a "swift saddle mare" to John C. Breckenridge, a Confederate general, helping him escape after the South fell to Union forces. Courtesy of State Library and Archives of Florida

An archival image from the Madison collection depicts the Livingston home. Courtesy of State Library and Archives of Florida

Rose Knox and Graham Schorb

Endnotes

1. "Historic Walking/Driving Tour: Madison Florida," brochure.

Strolling Down Memory Lane: A Sense of Place

Winston Churchill once proclaimed that "We shape our buildings; therefore, our buildings shape us."

The experience that had an influence on my upbringing, shaping why this book was started, besides the Oak Ridge Cemetery tours, was the one about a local antebellum mansion located up the road from our family's home. Churchill's words may ring true to many of the people who grew up in the shadow of a once-opulent antebellum home. Today the address for that mansion is 103 North Washington Street. The Knox children were raised in a neighborhood called Livingston Spring Acres, situated not far from the antebellum house, and not far—as the crow flies—from the Livingston family cemetery plot. Before my Father arrived in the 1960s to build the house that would soon accommodate his growing family there amongst a pecan grove, way back before that time, the Native Americans had once lived in the vicinity, too. In childhood, I had a shoebox full of artifacts to prove it.

The Cherry Lake Highway, as locals called it, ran directly past our home. Anytime we went uptown, we would drive by a mansion built on that same road, officially known as Washington Street. The home was a subject my Mother especially liked to take up, talking about it when we would be driving past. Here is one scenario that happened often, when we would go to Pic-N-Save to purchase items for a tackle box, or swing by Seltzer's Grocery Store to get hand-cut steaks from the butcher. Sometimes we would make our way to the farm store to fetch sweet feed for Blaze and Lightning, our horses that were kept on the nearby Rock Fraleigh farm. On those excursions, Mother would pull up to the light. We always called it a "red light." It was one of only two others that had been assigned to the main drag.

Not much has changed; even today there are only three lights running through town. It was at the intersection that crossed Highway 90 that Mother would pause to tell us what she knew of the place, the mansion. She was prone to look over, gazing to the right, the shadow of the house looming over the car. It was then I would press my nose against the passenger window of the family's Plymouth station wagon while Mama's talk filled my head. She was good at concocting a story, for she'd been "dunked and baptized" in the artful craft of storytelling, all part of her coming from southern Georgia and out of that storytelling tradition. Her people knew how to weave "a sure-enough tale"; but she would tell the "mansion story" in fragments because we were paused for just a moment by the house, "stuck" there by the traffic light. Her stories seemed to come in short bursts, and when that red light would turn green, talk of the real world and things that needed to be done would resume. The old tales of the mansion were left behind right there at the stoplight; but that patchwork of story pieces always stayed with me and was fertile ground for a child's imagination. While our station wagon sat idling there, she'd throw out a few notions like: "Rosie, that house has the most beautiful winding staircase you ever saw."

I'd ask, "What does it look like, Mama?"

She'd reply, "Well, I don't rightly know because I only remember getting a glimpse of it. But I do know people who know people, who know *other* people who have actually spent time in there. One was your oldest sister. She used to visit there when she was in high school, because she was friends with the oldest Smith boy, Jim." Sue, my oldest sister, recalls in her teen years having a séance in the house with Jim and other friends, trying to conjure up old spirits of the Civil War dead. (Though I have seen Jim Smith a few times over the years, he keeps making a point that neither he nor any of his family members ever encountered any spectral happenings!)

Then Mother would add about the beauty of the Smith mansion: "They say there are even some pieces of metal inlay crafted into each stair step."

On another occasion while waiting for the light to turn green, Mother would be inclined to say, "Yes, indeed, that Mrs. Smith stood up to some powerful individuals to save it. They wanted to turn that piece of land into to a parking lot, of all things! Can you believe that? But if it had not been for Mrs. Smith, the home would have been long gone— gone for all time: and all the stories with it! Now that was a brave woman!" Mother would then sigh, taking a deep breath, as if the fight Mrs. Smith had endured somehow had exhausted even our Mother.

So in the end, any real history I absorbed came in little tidbits and pieces over the years. Hungry for more stories, I needed to have a better account than what our mother and a few others had been able to give, but it was not until I grew older, became a teacher, and continued my own storytelling, that I started searching out articles and talking to people about the history of the house. One effort included sitting down with the Smith children. They grew up in the home because Chandler Holmes Smith and succeeding members of the Smith family had owned it from 1871 until 1978.

In the 1970s the house was over one hundred years old. By then the place was in decline, and peering up at it might give any imaginative child an uneasy feeling, kind of like something out of an Alfred Hitchcock movie I had seen on television. But I was drawn to it, nevertheless—like the tongue gravitates to a sore tooth. A magnificent oak that actually predated the mansion always seemed to cast strange shadows in the yard. Gray moss and palm trees shrouded any good view from where we were always trying to see it, from the Cherry Lake Highway; funny how that same oak tree and Spanish moss still look much the same now, decades and decades later, as I drive by it these days on my way to campus. (The tree was split by a massive storm in 2016 and does not have the same majestic look it once did.)

Today when I take that same route, I am reminded of the front cover of one of William Faulkner's books, *Absalom, Absalom*; it has a photograph of a dilapidated mansion on the front cover and portrays almost that same image as our own town mansion. And long before I ever even knew of a man named Faulkner, I would stare up at the enormous house, up at the big windows, and imagine lonely faces stealing a look back at me. (I still do to this day!) The twenty stunning columns, I would later learn, were called Doric. The porch, planked with longleaf heart pine, wrapped itself all the way around the big antebellum house.

"Can't we go in and take look around?" I'd start to implore of Mother.

"Sorry, Sugar. It is not open for the touring public. I am not sure if you will ever be able to get in there."

Mama was right most days, about most things. But she was dead wrong about the mansion! Yet she did always tell me in hopeless-looking situations, "If there's a will, Rosie, there's a way."

I never gave up and my steadfastness paid off. Decades came and went. I did finally get in and have since toured the home many times. Inside there is indeed a stunning, winding staircase, just like Mother used to describe. The first time I went in at age thirty-three, I sat on the bottom step in a contemplative moment, looking at the metal inlay and running my hand over the smooth velvet feel of the African mahogany rail. Since that time I have heard historians call it by its real architectural name, "a freestanding Charleston staircase."

But back during my growing up, while at the stop light, Mother would describe what I would be able to witness firsthand, umpteen years down the road. And Mother's voice still rang out in my head!

"The ceilings are high, and the kitchen is built off of the main house on purpose, to keep the home safe in case a fire was to break out."

Our mother has been laid to rest since the summer of 1999, in that old cemetery they call Oak Ridge, the same one the Knox clan all used to tromp around in. I am sure she is looking down on me, proud as a peacock about how I finally was able to get inside the home. And I'm sure Mother would agree with what Winston Churchill once claimed, "We shape our buildings; therefore, our buildings shape us."

It was not until I was hired to teach at the local college that more stories and mysteries of the house started to surface, however. Taking up my Mama's tale, I wanted to also shape my students' views on the American South; after they had read some Faulkner, I would treat them to a field trip. For over a decade I took them to the boneyard, just like my parents did me, over to Oak Ridge Cemetery to read interesting stones and to wonder about the people, this place, and what things were like at another time. Later we would end up at the mansion, marveling at the wonder of the architecture. Over the years I have received "thank you" emails from a few students, telling me they had never in all their lives spent time simply walking around, wandering in a cemetery. In fact, one student confessed she had never before even considered it something people might do to pass the time, but assured me she was going to spend more time walking around in cemeteries!

Consequently, this sketch ties my own family connection directly to the history of the Red Hills; I find it a special place that once drew ancient people to hunt and to farm. Much later, after the indigenous peoples had all been run off, other farming communities with a few aristocratic planters migrated there with their African slaves. They came to farm some of the richest soil deposits in the entire world.

Ann Dillard, in her book *An American Childhood*, reveals what I know now when she writes, "We children lived and breathed our history . . . history so crucial to the country's story and so typical of it as well—[Yet] A child is asleep. Her private life unwinds inside her skin and skull; only as she sheds childhood, first one decade and then another, can she locate the actual, historical stream, see the setting of her dreaming private life—the nation, the city, the neighborhood, the house where the family lives—as an actual project under way, a project living people willed, and made well or failed, and are still making, herself among them. I breathed the air of history all unaware, and walked oblivious through its . . . layers."[1]

Victor Hugo can likewise remind us of an important fact. He once said, ". . . Let us, while waiting for a new monument, preserve the ancient monuments." That monument was the home; it is therefore my hope you will be as intrigued about the Red Hills as I have been. As a grandmother, staying true to the old Southern Gothic tradition, it is my goal to one day tell stories of that home and of that boneyard, reading epitaphs from interesting graves to my granddaughters, trying to preserve for them the history that can be found in antebellum houses and in old places like the Oak Ridge Cemetery.

Today when I take that Cherry Lake Highway and drive past, I am reminded of William Faulkner's book, *Absalom, Absalom.* A photograph of a haunting, dilapidated mansion on the front cover is almost that exact image as our town mansion, the way it was in the home's decline. Courtesy of the State Library and Archives of Florida

The first time I finally went in at age 33, I sat on the bottom step in a contemplative moment, looking closely at the metal inlay and running my hand over the smooth, velvet feel of the African mahogany rail. Since that time, I have heard historians call it by its real architectural name, "a freestanding Charleston staircase." Courtesy of Graham Schorb

Rose Knox and Graham Schorb

"You have to know the past to understand the present." Carl Sagan

It was not until I was hired to teach at the local college that more stories and mysteries of the house started to surface. And after I have my students do a little reading on Faulkner, I treat them to a tour. For over 17 years I have taken them to the boneyard at Oak Ridge Cemetery, just like my parents did me, to read interesting stones and to wonder about the lives of the people. Later we ended up at the mansion, marveling at the wonder of the architecture. Courtesy of Graham Schorb

The Oak Ridge Cemetery cradles the graves of many people of the area, but some of them are forever forgotten, the engravings eroded over time. To be sure, however, each stone has a silent story to tell. Courtesy of Graham Schorb

The grave of Enoch J. Vann is located in Oak Ridge Cemetery.
Courtesy of Graham Schorb

Local historians in Madison County write about how several prominent citizens were standing as sentinels at the Suwannee River Bridge during wartime. Judge Enoch Van J. Vann, President of the Confederate Senate and well known lawyer, once recalled that he and Chandler Holmes Smith, a Confederate planter who lived in a magnificent Greek revival antebellum home in the heart of the town of Madison, were standing on guard at the western section of the Suwannee Railway bridge, when a train filled with Confederate troops hurled past them as the locomotive sped toward Jacksonville in order to merge with General Joseph Finegan and his troops. The war strategy was to send fighting men to Ocean Pond in an attempt to push back the Union soldiers under General Truman A. Seymour. Vann recalls the excited soldiers were singing lively songs and shouting cheers as they passed over the Suwannee River. Courtesy of State Library and Archives of Florida

The men who were wounded at the Battle of Olustee were taken from the battlefield by train to Madison County where 31 of them surrendered to injuries. Dying to defend the Suwannee River Bridge, they are today only nameless men, hastily buried in the Oak Ridge Cemetery. Once courageous soldiers, now they repose in a regimental row, sleeping under shades of massive century oaks. Their tombstones are inscribed with only the letters, C.S.A., acronym for Confederate States of America. When I find myself standing on the embankments over at the Suwannee River, or when my shadow looms over their graves at Oak Ridge Cemetery, chills run up my spine. I pause to wonder which ones might have been singing and shouting on that railway train, in the days just before the cold February battle of 1864. Courtesy of Georgia Dietz

Victor Hugo can remind us of an important fact. He once said, ". . . Let us, while waiting for a new monument, preserve the ancient monuments."

Citizens of Madison County place small flags on Confederate and Federal tombs each April as a way to remember the fallen in the American Civil War. The photograph was taken in Oak Ridge Cemetery in April 2017. It must be understood, according to southern professor Dr. Delma Presley, that the motivation for going to war for many southerners is often still misunderstood. Presley includes an important quotation from Charles H. Smith concerning Confederate sentiments. Smith once wrote, "What a mistake to say that these men were fighting for slavery. . . . When nearly the entire voting population were Democrats . . . the slave owners . . . were generally Whigs . . . and these backwoodsmen had no love for either the negro or his master. But they fought. They fought as did their forefathers who resisted a little tax on tea, though not one in a thousand drank it." (As quoted in Presley's *The Crackers of Georgia*.) Courtesy of Graham Schorb

Rose Knox and Graham Schorb

Alex Haley explains in his fictionalized book of the Old South, *Roots*,
that elaborate funerals were often held for women who had nursed
and cared for the children of the aristocrats. The woman might have
raised many children for the family. At her death she would often
be buried in the aristocratic family plot as a way to show honor for
her nurturing spirit. That story is played out in a local cemetery.
The picture of "Mammy" originally came from Beulah Brinson in
Monticello; she married a Livingston descendent. Courtesy of The
Treasures of Madison County Museum, Madison, Florida.

Mammy was a treasured servant of the Livingston family, and she is buried in the northwest corner of the Livingston family plot in the Oakridge Cemetery in Madison. The family plot is one of the first ones, if a person is entering Oakridge Cemetery from the main entrance, off of Meeting Street. That area is surrounded by a wrought-iron fence. There is no given name, or birth or death date on her tombstone—only Mammy. At Christmastime in the year 2016, some anonymous person had placed a poinsettia on her grave as a tribute. Textual information is courtesy of Mrs. Teenie Cave and Mr. Jim Sale of the Treasures Museum. Photograph is courtesy of Graham Schorb

Endnotes

1. Annie Dillard, *An American Childhood* (New York: Harper-Perennial, 1987).

Professor Welch at Treasures Museum
Talks about Reenactments

[He calls the Civil War an] ". . . epic event" and "a horrendous tragedy. . . ." Jason Welch

Early life experiences would prove the catalyst that would ultimately influence Mr. Jason Welch. Now a history professor at North Florida College in Madison, Florida, Welch reveals that when he was growing up, his family took him to several significant Civil War battle sites, including Bentonville, North Carolina; White Oak Swamp, Virginia; Manassas, Virginia; Sharpsburg, Maryland; Gettysburg, Pennsylvania; Wilderness, Virginia; Spotsylvania, Virginia; and Appomattox, Virginia. From those pivotal experiences, and from his own curiosity in reading books about the war, he eventually became a reenactor. Today he participates in various annual events, playing the role of both a Union and a Confederate soldier, depending on the occasion.

In the spring of 2016, at the Treasures Museum in Madison, he told me that reenactors are ". . . actively trying to keep the time period of the early 1860s alive." Professor Welch also attempts to inform his students about why the American Civil War was important. He calls it an "epic event" and "a horrendous tragedy" that resulted in "over 600,000 dead Americans," this "in a free Republic." He also covers in his lectures the impact to the society. One of his major points is how women coped after the men of the community were killed or maimed; and how women also played a role before and after the war. He said, "I want students to consider the effects on people and on their relationships."

Reenactments are not just a sideline for Welch but are very connected to his family life. In fact, he met his wife at a reenactment, and even on his wedding day, all the people in the wedding party were outfitted in Civil War period attire. Welch's wife and two children have also been known to put on period clothing, sleep in tents, eat out of tin cans, and "survive" on hard tack, as they have joined him in participating in reenactments over the years. Professor Welch has been teaching history since 2001, and his excitement is quite contagious. Dozens of his students over the years have taken part in reenactments with him, such as the Battle of Olustee, the Battle of Natural Bridge, and Raid on the Suwannee. As a passionate teacher, he is passing on to them ideas about Southern history that will help them understand the complexities surrounding the American South. Since many of his students are born Southerners, he is also instilling in them an appreciation of history, as they begin to comprehend their own historical roles and learn what a sense of place can bestow.[1]

Early life experiences would prove the catalyst that would ultimately influence Mr. Jason Welch. Now a history professor at North Florida College in Madison, Florida, Welch reveals that when he was 18 years old, his family visited several significant American Civil War battle sites. From those pivotal experiences, and from his own curiosity in reading books about the war, he eventually became a reenactor. Courtesy of Jason Welch

Rose Knox and Graham Schorb

He met his wife at a reenactment, and even on his wedding day, all the people in the wedding party were outfitted in Civil War period attire. As a family man, with a wife and two children, his family members, over the years, have also been known to put on period attire, sleep in tents, eat out of tin cans, and "survive" on hard tack, as they also have joined him in participating in the re-enactments. Courtesy of Jason Welch

Endnotes

1. Jason Welch, personal interview at the Treasures Museum, Madison, Florida, Spring 2016.

Rose Knox and Graham Schorb

Travel Notes

David and the Giant: The June Smith Story

"Remove not the ancient landmark which your fathers have set."
Proverbs 22:28

"What wasn't well known about the mansion's legacy was the important part our mother played in saving it from destruction. . . . Our mother endured many challenges and obstacles. . . . We know firsthand why this house stands today. It is because of the actions of June Smith and eventually Bill and Sue Goza." Jim Smith

There have always been spiritual and mythical stories about ordinary people; those tales can sometimes remind human beings how seemingly powerless individuals can fight and, in the long run, win some of life's toughest battles, the battles over giants! Those enduring legends which fill the pages of ancient writings hold powerful morals about conflicts. Such themes are often found in epic literature from all over the world. One familiar story appears in the Christian Bible about a struggle between a boy and a giant.

Most folks are familiar with those sagas. But when people in the town of Madison today drive by an imposing house visible from Highway 90, they might not even remember the story about the courage one woman had to muster in order that a mansion—her people's mansion—could remain standing. Yes, a local matriarch once firmly stood her ground to protect her children and their legacy, and in doing so was able to save one of the most treasured historical homes in the American South.

Her given name was Junanne Baldwin Smith, but most people in Madison just called her "June." She was born June 1, 1924, and died on March 31, 1988. During her lifetime she raised four children, sometimes under quite uncertain conditions. Here is a brief chronicle of how the threads of her life are connected to a local house, Whitehall Mansion, often also called the Wardlaw-Smith-Goza Mansion. At a presentation before the Madison County Historical Society in April of 2009, her son Zet gave an ancestral timeline of the ownership of the property and details about the family's antebellum mansion. It is the home where he and his siblings were raised. Zet's goal was to show how his mother came to possess only a quarter portion of the house.

Jim Smith, the oldest of June's sons, steps aside to let Zet talk, but as an introduction he says: "Zet will now share with you how the house passed through three generations of Smiths, for over a one-hundred-year period and how the ownership of our family home came to be divided into quarters."

Zet speaks:

> Our Great-Grandfather, Chandler Holmes Smith, bought the mansion in 1871. When he dies, the mansion is bequeathed to his son, S. Alex Smith, and his wife, Birdie. When our grandparents, S. Alex and Birdie Smith, died, the home was divided among their five children: [They were:] Susan Smith Zetrouer, Elizabeth Smith Felty, Sim Smith, James W. (Bill) Smith, and Alex (Gee) H. Smith.

> When Aunt Susan died, her husband, Horace Zetrouer, conveyed his share of the house to the Smith heirs, creating one-quarter shares for each remaining descendant of S. Alex Smith. When Dad died [Gee], his portion of the house went to our Mother and us four siblings. Each of us owned one-fifth of one-fourth of the house. My siblings and I gave our shares to Mother, giving her control of one-quarter of the house.

It was that small one-quarter of the house that would ironically save it. Jim picks up the narrative during the Historical Society speech, explaining that some years after his father's passing, the Madison County Historical Society and the Madison County Historical Association, Inc., had hopes of buying the property to save it for "its historical significance and its architectural significance." Eventually, final appeal for funding to save the home was printed in the *Times-Union* on April 13, 1968, but after many efforts to raise monies, in the end, those efforts failed. That is when the real trouble for June Smith first began.

Jim speaks again, explaining the predicament and what his Mother was truly up against. He explains,

> Three years later, three-quarters of the home and property belonging to our aunts and uncles—what had been owned and lived in by our family for over 100 years—was sold to Florida First National Bank of Madison. One quarter-share remained

with June Smith, who refused to sell. At that time, the Florida First National Banks were headed by the financier of the DuPont estate, Mr. Ed Ball. It is important to understand who Ed Ball was so that we can better understand what our Mother was up against. One can't have a discussion about Florida First National Bank without bringing Ed Ball to the forefront. To say he was in charge is an enormous understatement.

Here is a brief chronicle that details some of the June Smith story as told by her children on that day of their presentation:

On March 8, 1971, 75 percent of the Smith property was purchased by the Florida First National Bank of Madison, because the ". . . direct descendants of Chandler Holmes Smith had sold their heritage for $17,000 each. . . . Overnight, our Mother had become an adversary to arguably one of the most powerful men in Florida, Ed Ball."

Because the bank now owned a huge share, many precious heirloom items in those bank-owned sections of the mansion were sold off. Some of the items included paintings by the Smith children's grandmother, hand-crafted furniture, and rare books dating from the 1700s, which were sold for 50 cents apiece. One fireplace mantel was auctioned for two dollars. The Smith children remember vividly their Mother weeping over the loss of such precious family history. Other special items that were auctioned off were chandeliers, desks, brass beds, chests, and a signed letter by George Washington. After several attempts to get June to pay for certain costs in an effort, perhaps, to financially strap her, forcing her into selling the home, the bank claimed they needed to install larger tanks for the gas station, and Mrs. Smith would be held responsible for part of the cost incurred. A letter also claiming she was now to pay rent to the bank since they currently owned a majority of the home and property, was delivered to her. At that point June promptly did what she thought was best; she moved her family of four children into the one-quarter of the house of which she held ownership.

Time crept by, but June Smith held steadfastly to her heritage, no matter what was thrown at her. By 1975 she still harbored high hopes that someone would see the historical and cultural value of the home and want to purchase it, restoring it to its former grandeur. [It should furthermore be noted that in the time between the bank ownership takeover until 1975, she, normally a friendly soul, had become suspicious of strangers wanting to see the inside of the home. At that time she suspected some sort of foul intentions by the bankers.] She waited and waited, and her miracle finally came when, in 1976, Mr. Bill Goza got word that the bank was willing to sell their 75 percent share, as it was evident to the bankers that June was holding fast to her home and to her legacy.

Jim declared, to conclude the presentation, "Our Mother's destiny was to live her life for her children and the preservation of our great grandfather's home . . . what had been owned and lived in by our family for over 100 years."

Like David defeating the giant, June stood firm, standing up to powerful forces and individuals as she remained loyal to her family and her remarkable heritage.

Additional Note: The Smith family was also quite heartened to be invited into the mansion by the Bill Gozas, once the home was fully restored. To their delight they saw paintings of their grandmother hanging upon the walls. The Gozas had been present during the auction and had purchased some of the heirloom items.

Source: April 26, 2009: Jim and Zet Smith gave a presentation before the Madison County Historical Society concerning their family's legacy in saving local history. The "June Smith" story they told was about their Mother and her bold fight against powerful entities. Transcribed segments of that meeting are included here. In 2009 her sons recounted how Mrs. Smith's efforts would eventually be enough to save the house from destruction; the rumor was that the bankers intended to tear the home down in order to install a parking lot to serve banking customers. The meeting held at the Wardlaw-Smith-Goza Conference Center chronicled some of the situations surrounding that particular event.

The Chandler Holmes Smith family, and succeeding members of the Smith family, owned Whitehall Mansion from 1871 to 1978. The house at that time was also referred to as the Smith Mansion. Courtesy of the State Library and Archives of Florida

Depicted is the 1896 portrait of S. Alex Smith in Madison, when he was around 16 years of age. He was the son of Chandler Holmes Smith and Susan Parramore Smith. Courtesy of the State Library and Archives of Florida

The photograph was taken in December 1945 on the steps at the Smith mansion. Pictured from left to right: Bottom row: Bert Felty, H. H. Felty Jr.; 2nd row: June Baldwin Smith, H. H. Felty, Elizabeth Smith Felty, Venera Minter Smith, Bill Smith; 3rd row: Alex Holmes "Gee" Smith, Grace Edhegard Smith, Susan Smith Zetrouer; Top row: Simeon Benjamin "Sim" Smith, Bertie Smith. Courtesy of the State Library and Archives of Florida

Rose Knox and Graham Schorb

Travel Notes

How the Gozas Saved a Mansion and an Interview with the Smith Children

"... It was our Dad's family house, but Mother knew from what he had told her how much the house meant to him—how much history this house meant to Madison and Madison County." From an interview with Zet Smith

The ultimate destiny of Whitehall Mansion had been in question for a while. Would the home be plowed down to make way for the parking lot for a financial institution? Would the town lose a vital piece of its Southern history and an architectural marvel full of rich stories from the past? That particular plan, coming from folks in very powerful places, was not meant to be. Thank goodness! The "saviors" of such a phenomenal home would be Mr. and Mrs. William and Sue Goza. Mr. Goza already had ties to the region for he was born in Madison, but was raised in Clearwater, where he was to practice law for forty years before retiring in 1979 from the firm Goza, Hall, and Peters.

Because he was a fifth-generation Floridian, and because his great-uncle happened to be Mr. Benjamin Wardlaw, he had direct family bonds to the area and also to the mansion. That family connection was to save the mansion from disrepair; restoration began in 1978, and by 1979, the home was ready for the Gozas to live there. They resided in the mansion until 1981 when they finally donated the $750,000 home, "Whitehall," to the University of Florida's Institute of Food and Agricultural Science."[1] Goza, an alumnus of the college, said he had made the contribution to the university because his family roots involving agriculture could be traced back five generations; his people were growing tobacco and Sea Island cotton in the region during that time.

Once, when asked about the importance of the home and its historical worth, he remarked, "After the Civil War Battle of Olustee, the house served as a hospital. Upon the fall of the Confederacy, John C. Breckinridge, Secretary of War of the Confederacy and former vice president of the United States, in his flight to avoid capture spent the night in the northeast upstairs bedroom on May 15, 1865. The room houses a plaque to commemorate this event, and the state of Florida has placed an historical marker on U.S. Highway 90 adjoining the property, noting the significance of the structure."[2]

An Interview with the Smith Children of White Hall Mansion

Introduction: Fall 2011, Rose Knox Speaks: Today we have the Smith children here, and we are honored to talk with them. They are the children of June and Gee Smith. June is the woman who stood against powerful entities and saved this architectural wonder. Here at the interview, we have Peggy, Jim, and Zet; but Alex was not able to join us. We can begin by you all recounting stories that you have of the home.

Interview Begins

Zet: We never really treated the house like it was a historical house so much. We were just children. This is the place that we lived; the place we played; it was a great place; it actually was a wonderful place to play. We had the wrap-around porch. We had the hallway to go through. On a rainy day we were set! We never had to get wet. You could even ride your bike through the house and around the porch.

Peggy: Or roller skate around the porch!

Zet: Jimmy is famous for breaking windows with rubber balls—off of these twenty-foot-tall plaster walls. You could bounce the balls; didn't even need anybody to play with. It'd come right back to you.

Jim: That sounds a little terrible the way you said it.

Zet: But it is true!

Jim: Yes, the side facing east of the house had those steps— probably eight or nine steps. It was perfect for throwing tennis balls against. If you threw the ball, sometimes it'd hit the edge of the step, and it would give you a nice pop fly; sometimes it would bounce down and give you a grounder, or sometimes it would hit the top of that step and bounce up and it'd knock out these French cut-glass segments from this side. And every time I would do it, Dad would say, "Stop!" But I obviously didn't listen to him; much later Mr. Goza had Billy Childress duplicate the pattern on the plated glass, to replace the ones that were original cut glass. But every time I would break one out, Daddy would take it from the west side of the house and replace it to put on the side facing the street. So you can go and count the number of duplicate ones, and you could probably tell me how many I knocked out!

Knox: So just from the eyes of a child, certainly, this place was a wonderland. It kind of reminds me of the scenes from C. S Lewis's *Chronicles of Narnia* where the children are playing in that antiquated home. There are places to hide and places to explore.

[Knox pauses as other thoughts come to her.]

And, you know, Robert Frost talks about the road less traveled, and Henry David Thoreau talks about marching to the beat of a different drummer, and your Mother, from what I've read and heard, stood very resolute against powerful forces. Would you care to recount some memories, just in storytelling fashion, of any stories you remember hearing in your little ears, as all of that conflict was happening?

Jim: We probably should start from the beginning. While Dad was alive, he was approached by people of the First National Bank who, at that point, were controlled by Ed Ball, the financier of Alfred DuPont estate. And they wanted to buy the house and asked if they could put a bank branch on the property. So Daddy wanted to have a clear understanding, because he was very specific in asking them, "Well, what are you going to do with the home?" And they said, "Tear it down." So he kind of gathered his siblings together, and at the time there were four; including himself, it would be five. They had a decision to make.

Zet: And that is why the bank—they purchased the property across the street—and they cleared all of the housing over on that part; that is why that bank is there today.

Knox: I see. I didn't know that there were once houses there.

Zet: The florist downtown is where the old bank used to be. And they decided to move from there to this area, and I'm sure they would need a bigger bank. They wanted this because it would be easier to tear down one building, divide one family, rather than divide several families.

Knox: So they had eyes on this very location . . .

Zet: They kept saying they wanted more parking. But they had plenty of parking.

Knox: I remember as a child, because I lived over there in the neighborhood of Livingston Spring Acres, and we would always come up this road, and I can remember stopping at the traffic light many times over my childhood and being so intrigued with the home; and then my Mother would start telling the story about your Mother and how she was resolute in standing up against these people—how they wanted to tear the house down. . . . And had it not been for your Mother standing up, there might only be a parking area.

Knox: Do you remember anything specifically about your Mother in the whole battle? What was she feeling? What was she doing?

Peggy: Well, now, me being the youngest, of course, I didn't really realize then what was going on. I think the two older brothers probably knew more than what Zet and I do.

Knox: What decades were you living here?

Jim: We moved in this house, I think, when my oldest brother Alex was born in 1947; I was born in '49.

Jim: I moved in here when I was probably one or two.

Knox: As far as when you come back here now looking through the eyes as an adult—you're talking about playing with the tennis ball, and breaking the beautiful glass, and the stories about your Mother; but back then you all were probably not understanding as a child what this house represented, an entire Southern era, a chapter in history that intrigues people from all over the world.

Zet: . . . it was our Dad's family house, but Mother knew from what he had told her how much the house meant to him— how much history this house meant to Madison and Madison County. So our Mother learned to love this house, even though it was difficult for her to raise a family here. [His idea alludes to the fact it was hard to manage electric bills and such in a huge house.]

Zet: When it gets cold in north Florida, it gets cold in this house. In fact, we only had a heater in this room and one in the back room. We did have one foyer over in the corner but very seldom did it ever really warm that room up. . . . So even though it was difficult sometimes, living in this house, because it's not a normal house, she still had great respect for what this house meant.

Knox: On this plaque right here in the June Smith room, it shows how she was saving the house in honor of your Father's legacy, also.

Zet: Right. She understood that. Unfortunately our Father's siblings did not quite understand the importance of keeping the home in the family.

Jim: We love our aunts and uncles. They were wonderful people . . .

Knox: With that situation with the bank, how did your Mother endure?

Jim: Mother became quite mistrusting of people interested in seeing the home. . . . They were mostly the Northerners coming through Florida on U.S. 90 wanting a tour of the house, which we graciously gave tours. But Mother became reluctant to let just anyone enter after the situation with the bank. But the tourists would stop, and they were intrigued with not only the home but about the moss on the tree and on the ground; we'd let them take moss home when they picked it off of the ground. [Laughter from the children.]

Peggy: We would let them have as much as they would want! [More laughter.]

Jim: Obviously we didn't like the moss. Our chores were to go out and pick up the moss.

Knox: Well, I know the Bill Gozas came in with their resources, and they were able to help your Mom save the house.

Jim: Yes, we credit Bill Goza with that . . . we appreciated what they did. They were very gracious; when the house was fully completed, they gave us a personal tour.

Knox: What year was this?

Zet: That would have been 1978.

Jim: So he was very gracious—took us through the house. He had also purchased items from the auction—this is a whole separate story.

Jim: The paintings in the house, our grandmother had painted were there again. . . .

Jim: We got to know Bill Goza really well. Zet and I decided on a project to videotape our Mother and Daddy's closest friends. We started that project because there was an article written in the newspaper here in Madison that gave credit to another individual for saving this house through a handshake with Mr. Ed Ball after meeting him over a weekend. . . . So that is when Zet and I—and quite frankly all of us—were rather upset because we knew it was just untrue. Our Mother and the Gozas saved the house! There were others of course with the Historical Society here, but not enough money was raised. Many people were interested, but Mother and Bill and Sue Goza were the ones saving this home.

Knox: Rewriting history.

Jim: We were trying to set the record straight.

Zet: We could not send a letter to the editor, because our words would never get published. And if we sent a letter to the editor to a larger newspaper in another town, that doesn't mean anything here. And at the time, both town newspapers were owned by the same person.

Jim: So we started a video project. We said, "Let's get the story out!" And it turned into a multifaceted project. . . . So we must have videotaped twenty to twenty-five couples of our Mother and Father's closest friends. One was in Jacksonville who actually was a friend of Mother and Father before they got married . . . we collected lots of stories about how Dad got his name. But I regress. [Laughter from the children.]

Jim: We first wanted to ask the Gozas questions. We met them over in Ocala. We wanted to know how much they knew about the selling of the house; the negotiations of the house; how did they get involved with it; what was mother's side; what communication did they have with her. . . . Zet, being in the production industry, he put up lights in trees, and recording mechanisms and microphones all over the place! And we thought it would take two hours, but it took about five.

Knox: Do we even know how much money was put into restoring the mansion?

Zet: I don't know if anybody knows that.

Peggy: A ton of money.

Zet: I mean there are the stories of how many times the house had to be painted because the paint would soak into the wood. They were taking and putting new bases at each of the bottoms of all the columns all the way around the house. They put on a new roof, new porch, heating and air-conditioning throughout. I just cannot fathom what the cost of just heating and air-conditioning the place might be.

Jim: Bill Goza redesigned several things. The room back here, made a bathroom, which was our kitchen. So he took the kitchen and moved it out to the original building, which is where the kitchen was in the first place.

Zet: There was no original bathroom in the house. Before, when our aunts and uncles and dad were growing up, through this door, to the exterior, they built a bathroom on the outside of the house.

Jim: With no shower.

Jim: And there were six of us, yet it never appeared to be a problem . . .

Zet: And then there was a bathroom added to the hallways upstairs. And other changes . . .

Knox: A lot of modifications done. [Knox pauses and says reluctantly] I am going to visit a subject that is supernatural in nature. Do you remember people telling stories about the house being haunted when you were growing up?

Jim: I remember when I first heard about that, I was probably in the second or third grade. I remember Mother and Father talking about Confederates that had died in the house.

Zet: And Union soldiers.

Jim: Yes, and Union soldiers.

Jim: As a little child, I thought it would be cute to play a joke. So I went to school the next day, and I told all of my friends that I had found a Confederate uniform in the house. Little did I know that they were going to go home and tell their parents! Mother got wind of it and she didn't think it was a good joke, and I got a spanking.

Peggy: Oh well, I think the only reason why I might have ever been scared in the house would be from hearing what other kids would say at school about this house. You know, I lived here and I don't know anything about what they are claiming.

Peggy: But Mama might say, "Go over and tell the boys it's suppertime." So I'd open this door and say, "Come eat dinner." And if they didn't come, I had to go over there, and if it was nighttime, because in the winter time it was dark, and unless there was a light on in the hallway, I would not go across. But being young, I guess I was a little scared.

Knox: Human beings are afraid of the dark.

Peggy: Right.

Peggy: And plus, sounds would echo because there was very little furniture in the hallway, so the echo was scary; but I never saw a ghost.

Zet: And then also Grandmother's painting was on this wall over here, and she was extremely good at painting, so that the eyes in the painting followed you wherever you went. That was part of the spookiness Jim was talking about earlier regarding her paintings.

Peggy: We would share that painting with many of our friends that would come over.

Zet: And then once you knew about the eyes following you, you couldn't avoid looking at that painting every time you came into the hallway and feel a little scared.

Jim: And there was always some sort of sound in this house.

Zet: It is made of wood; it's always creaking.

Jim: Always creaking.

Zet: And at night with this huge oak tree out front, and the trees up near the side of the house, the streetlights coming in through big windows, creating shadows . . . a kid with an imagination might see all kinds of things in the shadows that were just plain shadows. And growing up three boys in one room, these guys were notorious for pranking the younger one—me! They would sit there in the dark and invent ways to scare me. I remember we'd just watched the movie *Hush, Hush Sweet Charlotte*. And Jimmy would start singing the song very lightly under his breath—just to, uh, just to get me a little bit scared, you know? And I was six years younger, so I'm ten, he's sixteen—there is a big difference there.

Knox: So you all would not give credence to any of those supernatural stories. Although, you know, the mystery, and the age of the house, certainly lends itself to these types of spectral stories. People like hearing them and telling them.

Zet: Speaking of stories, we used to have birthday parties here, and all the kids would line up on the steps, and Jimmy might come in and tell a ghost story. You know, because it just is what kids did.

Zet: And so that kind of thing might get weird stories started.

Knox: Sure, and in a small town . . .

Jim: If there is such a thing as ghosts, which I don't really believe because I've never witnessed it, but maybe some people are just closer to ghostly encounters than others. If there is such a thing as ghosts, I'm sure they're in here, because you have a house over a hundred years old; you have numerous individuals who were living here; humans that died in the house; you had four generations of Smiths living in the house; so if there are ghosts, they're probably here. We just didn't see any of them. And if they were relatives, we would have probably been okay with it.

Knox: I know that you all had a big wedding yesterday for Peggy's Sarah.

Peggy: Yes, it was a wonderful day! Everything was set up in the yard. The wedding took place out in the garden, but of course we had the wedding party in the house all day, taking pictures, enjoying themselves.

Knox: I think that is a great legacy for your family and for Sarah, to have her wedding in the family home. I thank you all so much. I appreciate you all.[3]

Additional Conversation:

Knox: Seven years ago I told you all I had this idea for a book. The name of the book was going to be *If Walls Could Talk*. I am probably not ever going to write that book.

Update: Additional Note, April 2015: The inspiration for this work, *Mastodons, Mansions, and Antebellum Ghosts: Voices Rising up from Florida's Red Hills,* came to me in April 2015, and actually originated from the idea *If Walls Could Talk*"; the Smith family interview was the catalyst for the writing idea for this book.

[End of Recorded Material]

Transcribed by writing student, Rosanna Hughes

William Goza, past president of the Florida Historical Society and the Florida Anthropological Society, and restorer/former owner of the home, once said, "After the Civil War Battle of Olustee, the house served as a hospital. Upon the fall of the Confederacy, John C. Breckinridge, Secretary of War of the Confederacy and former vice president of the United States, in his flight to avoid capture, spent the night in the northeast upstairs bedroom on May 15, 1865." Courtesy of Rosanna Hughes

Over the years, the home fell into disrepair. The photograph shows
the mansion in 1962 and has a gloomy sort of Gothic look, which I
vividly remember as a little child. Courtesy of the State Library and
Archives of Florida

Because of the courage of one woman, Mrs. June Smith, the home was saved for posterity. Over the decades local college students have had the privilege to tour the home as part of their studies in Southern literature. Courtesy of Graham Schorb

"Mother became quite mistrusting of people interested in seeing the home. . . . They were mostly the Northerners coming through Florida on U.S. 90 wanting a tour of the house, which we graciously gave tours. But Mother became reluctant to let just anyone enter after the situation with the bank. But the tourists would stop, and they were intrigued with not only the home but about the moss on the tree and the ground; we'd let them take moss home when they picked it off of the ground. We would let them have as much as they would want!" Courtesy of Patrick Elliott

Endnotes

1. Karen Haymon Long, "Madison Mansion Given to UF," *Orlando Sentinel*, February 18, 1984.

2. Long, "Madison Mansion."

3. Jim Smith, Peggy Smith, and Zet Smith, "How Our Mother, June Smith, Saved the Home: And Other Memories," interview by Rose Knox in Wardlaw-Smith-Goza Mansion, Madison, Florida, 2011.

Rose Knox and Graham Schorb

Travel Notes

Planters Lucius Church, William Tooke, and Reddin Parramore

As has already been established, in 1850 in Madison County, two-thirds of the thirty-three large plantations were owned by pioneers out of South Carolina. Folks coming in via Georgia also dominated one particular region of the county. According to Clifton Paisley in his work, *The Red Hills of Florida 1528-1865*, ". . . in one of the principal cotton-growing regions, around, to the south of, and for six miles to the west of six-hundred-acre Cherry Lake just below the Georgia line, the planters were mostly Georgians." In fact, one of the most expansive plantations among them measured two thousand acres on Cherry Lake and was owned by Lucius Church. He was of middle age, around fifty years old then, and was originally from the northern state of New Hampshire, but before his arrival in Florida, in the 1830s he had been a Georgian merchant.

Another prominent area planter was William L. Tooke; he, too, was middle-aged. Tooke had first lived in Telfair County, Georgia, before coming to Madison, but was a native of North Carolina. It was in the 1850s that he increased his landholdings, quadrupling his land to 4,520 acres, which included what was called back then, "The Wardlaw Place." That area encompassed 2,160 acres and was located south of his farm. Though all seemed to be going well for Mr. Tooke, good fortune can prove fickle. It was on a fateful day in October of 1860 that he got into an argument with Thomas F. Drew, his plantation overseer. In that dispute, according to an old article that ran in the *Tallahassee Floridian*, Drew pulled out a knife, stabbing Tooke in the abdomen. Tooke was then knocked to the ground by Drew. After this, the overseer proceeded to get back on his horse. He rode away leaving the scene of Tooke's desperate struggle for life.

Other quite expansive plantations were situated beside Tooke's place to the west of him. For example, a Mr. Reddin W. Parramore, then fifty years old, had moved down to north Florida with the same migration that had brought Tooke to Madison. Parramore's father had originally come here from North Carolina out of Onslow County. He, like Tooke, had been raised in Georgia, in the same county, Telfair. Sadly, history has a way of slipping though our fingers, and some facts get lost through the gradual ticking of time. That was the case with some lost history of his plantation, for it was merely one folded edge of an important page in a manuscript census that kept the true account of his plantation's cotton yields and profits.

But what we do still know of his production is that he owned livestock which was worth $20,000. That amount was three times that of other planters in the immediate region. When he died in 1851, his estate was worth a literal fortune. To illustrate, he had large herds amounting to 3,692 head of cattle. At the time, the herd alone was valued at $14,768. Records of his estate further reveal his worth was $89,672.85. In addition, some of the landholdings of Parramore's estate were part of a partnership he had with Simeon Alexander Smith. Smith was Parramore's brother-in-law and he had made his way to Madison from Georgia's Thomas County. The two men made a land deal in 1842, their first, and it included the western one-third of what is today the town of Madison. Parramore also built his house there.[1]

Endnotes

1. Clifton Paisley, *The Red Hills of Florida 1528-1865* (Tuscaloosa: University of Alabama Press, 1989).

Rose Knox and Graham Schorb

Travel Notes

Way Down Upon the Suwannee River

"Way down upon the Suwannee River,
Far, far away."   Stephen Foster

As a child, I was taken to the tannic waters of a legendary river and given the opportunity to watch the slow current flow past me. In middle school Mrs. Tadlock, our social studies teacher, took our sixth-grade class to dance around the maypole at the annual Folk Festival located on the banks of the Suwannee River, in White Springs. The children on the bus sang Stephen Foster's songs all the way to the festival. After we arrived, we saw red-skinned men carving out canoes and women of that ancient race making dolls adorned with colorful clothing. As an adult I had the chance to paddle miles and miles on many sections of the river, starting at the headwaters in the Okefenokee Swamp and places nearing the Gulf of Mexico, and I've been privileged to sleep under starlit skies, setting up camp on white sand shores, as sounds of frogs, crickets, and an occasional owl provided background music.

To stand on the banks of the Suwannee River is to feel invigorated. It is easy to see why it has been called legendary. The river also has a way of reminding people of an historical past. Such an ancient waterway might harbor echoes from long ago in what is today south Georgia and north Florida. People's lives have always been intertwined with the tales that once were part of those dark currents. They are many: The voice of the Native, the Indians who once lived near the shores for thousands of years, hunting, farming, and raising families; or what about the Spanish soldier? The Catholic priest? The French pirate? The Confederate soldier? The trapper? The hunter? The slave? The pioneer? The mill hand? The entrepreneur? The tourist? There were so many people playing various roles on these shores down through time.

The river starts up in Georgia at the headwaters of the Okefenokee Swamp, and it winds a way through many counties, finally making it 242 miles to the Gulf of Mexico.

Though some of the soil around the region of the river is not as rich as the Red Hills soil in other parts of Madison County, the river was nevertheless destined to play a big role in people's lives; countless stories about the river survive today. For instance, back in the 1500s hundreds of armed soldiers marched through the Suwannee's tannic currents, led by Spanish explorer Hernando de Soto. Those same soldiers marched through other areas, finally reaching the Red Hills. On the shores of the river is also the Spanish Trail, once called the Camino Real, or the Bellamy Trail, the well-trodden path that was used by Europeans to make it to the all-important city of St. Augustine. Such a trail was a significant thoroughfare in pioneer Florida, as it connected Tallahassee to Saint Augustine. The trail was built by Indian and African slaves.

Later, in times of colonial advancement, the United States Army built forts directly on the banks of the Suwannee River to rid the area of the Seminole Indians, those various tribes that had been driven into north Florida from other states. And three wars were funded by the federal government to finally purge the Seminoles from the southeastern states. Then encroaching settlers of the early 1800s used the river for food and transportation; one busy ferry crossing was once located at what is today the Suwannee River State Park.

In the antebellum period, when cotton was king, shrill whistles from steamships announced their arrival at bustling river landings; some ships carried local passengers and wealthy tourists; others transported cotton, mail, and various supplies. One old landing is now located within the boundaries of the Suwannee River State Park, which was likewise the location of a pioneer town called Columbus. A pioneer cemetery is also nestled there in the shades of a grand old longleaf pine forest. Today, situated inside of the Suwannee River State Park boundaries, not far from the confluence of the Withlacoochee and Suwannee Rivers, is what remains of the Confederate earthworks. The earthworks were built and manned by Southern sentinels to equip the vicinity to defend the railroad bridge against Federal invasion. Fifteen thousand Florida men fought for the Southern cause in the Civil War, sometimes referred to today by Southerners as the War of Northern Aggression. The state's soldiers made up only two percent of the Confederate Army. Another Florida contribution to the Southern war effort was thousands of head of cattle, seventy-five thousand in all, keeping the Confederate Army from going hungry. The Confederacy depended heavily on the bridge to deliver the needed cattle that would sustain men, readying them for battle. Many of the cows were herded to Madison, located just across the Suwannee River from the bridge location. The bridge at the Suwannee River was only one bridge that was heavily guarded during wartime, as soldiers manned them to guard the flow of much needed supplies.[1]

Men of great prominence relocated to Madison County because of the river. One was Governor Franklin Drew who was known as a leading figure in the South, especially on the Suwannee River. He was a Northerner, born in New Hampshire, but he established himself in the South as a prosperous lumber and salt industry figure.

When the Civil War started, he held mixed loyalties. On one hand, he sided with Northern political views, but he was married to a Southern woman; this union tied him closely with Southern ways. And the Confederacy benefitted from his marital loyalties, as he helped in the Southern cause, providing them with much needed troop supplies of lumber and salt. But it was not until the last months of the war that Drew ultimately joined the Union army. However, when he later ran for governor, most Southerners were, ironically, not even aware of his past loyalties to the North. He served as governor of Florida during the challenging era of Reconstruction from 1877 until 1881.[2] The railway system in place at that location allowed Drew to board the train that had a route over to Tallahassee. Yet, much of Drew's official government business was conducted right from his mansion[3] located on the Madison County side of the Suwannee River near the confluence of the Withlacoochee and Suwannee Rivers.

At the end of the Civil War, Drew's successful lumber business situated at the Town of Columbus (once located at the site of the present day Suwannee River State Park) was now out of operation. He soon relocated to the Madison County side of the Suwannee, where he started up a new steam sawmill operation that would ultimately grow to be the largest in Florida.

The place also became a booming mill town that Drew named Ellaville. According to some local accounts, the name was derived to honor an elderly black woman who had once worked for his family. Ellaville eventually prospered, becoming a vital town with a population of over one thousand inhabitants. Residents and visitors had access to a post office, two churches, an express office, a telegraph unit, two schools, and a Masonic Lodge, but no saloons were allowed. Lumbermen and trappers were also attracted to the boomtown in their search for jobs or when they wanted to trade.

Drew built an opulent home for his family at Ellaville in 1868. It is not an antebellum mansion, as some people think. The home was then known as the Drew Mansion and was a two-story residence that had ten rooms. Inside was a beautiful staircase constructed of imported mahogany; there were also finely crafted fireplaces with elaborate facings and marble mantels. Sparkling chandeliers hung from the high plaster etched ceilings. The mansion estate was known in that time for its manicured and formal gardens.[4] Some historians claim the home was the first residence in Florida with electricity, telephone, and indoor plumbing.[5]

In 1883 Drew sold his Ellaville sawmill to Louis Bucki from New York City; Bucki then conducted business at the mill for several years, while also making the mansion his home. Other men operated the mill after Bucki; however, as yellow pine became ever more scarce, the mill was finally forced to shut down, and with the closing of the mill, the town died (officially in 1942), when the post office closed its doors.

By the 1930s the Drew Mansion was all but abandoned by its owners, according to a Madison County resident, L. A. Bailey. Bailey went to the site in 1930 while on a school field trip. His story depicts details of a very dilapidated mansion. He recollects ". . . a family of gentle negro sharecroppers lived in the downstairs area of the former governor's house. They had nailed the cellar door shut to keep the haints from coming up and had boarded off the upstairs areas of the house to keep them from coming down. . . ."

In the 1970s the Drew Mansion was completely destroyed by fire.1 Ibid. The property was later picked up by the state of Florida and today is part of the Suwannee River State Park situated on the Madison County line.

Drew Family Cemetery: Northeast of the old homesite there is a small cemetery where Drew buried his wife, several infant children, and one teenage son. Some accounts suggest that the son was drowned in the Withlacoochee River. Sometimes when I'm spending a day on the Withlacoochee, swimming at Melvin Shoals, I can't help but think of Drew's son. Some believe he lost his life somewhere on the river near those shoals.

Historical Connection to the American Civil War: At the railroad track that crosses the river from Madison County into Suwannee County, Confederate soldiers sang merrily as they rode a train that crossed over the bridge. They were on their way to Ocean Pond to push back the Federals who were marching to take the Suwannee River Bridge, and the rebels were attempting to defend that strategically located bridge. But those soldiers were to return on those same tracks— battle-weary, blood-soaked, and mortally wounded—to Madison, to a mansion that had been hurriedly turned into a makeshift hospital. One man, a prominent local citizen from Madison County, heard their songs because he was standing watch on the river bank the day when they first passed by, on what is today the Madison County side of the Suwannee River. Many of the war dead from that battle are reposed in area cemeteries in Madison, Jefferson, and Leon counties: Oak Ridge Cemetery in Madison, Roseland Cemetery in Monticello, and the Old City Cemetery in Tallahassee. The Battle of Olustee is reenacted every February near modern-day Lake City in order to commemorate what historians now call a Confederate victory.

The Suwannee River has many stories about people and their past, ranging from ancient stone tools, remnants of steam ships, resort hotel sites, and pioneer towns and cemeteries—those objects and places are a testament to their lives. After the Natives had been killed or driven out of the area, rich people flooded to those shores in droves to bubbling springs that promised healing waters. Opulent hotels were built near those cool springs, catering to their lavish lifestyles. Lively dance tunes, their entertainment, poured out of a grand piano. Might jubilant laughter from affluent tourists somehow still reverberate from once-popular resort hotels that were built for their pleasure along these very shores?

Exploring the 242-mile Suwannee River, or reading books about it, will prove a cultural and historical journey that will take folks back to a fascinating human past. A visit to the Suwannee River State Park will also be enlightening and educational.

Governor Franklin Drew built a lavish home for his family at Ellaville in 1868. The home was then known as the Drew Mansion and was a two-story residence that had ten rooms. It is sometimes mistaken for an antebellum mansion. Inside was a beautiful staircase constructed of imported mahogany; there were also finely crafted fireplaces with elaborate facings and marble mantels, and from the high plaster etched ceilings, were hanging sparking chandeliers. In its heyday, the mansion estate was also known for its manicured and formal gardens. Much later, however, the home fell into disrepair. Years of abandonment had finally taken their toll on the once-extravagant home. Cloaked in shadows of neglect, the structure existed until the 1970s, when a fire consumed the mansion, completely destroying it. Courtesy of State Library and Archives of Florida

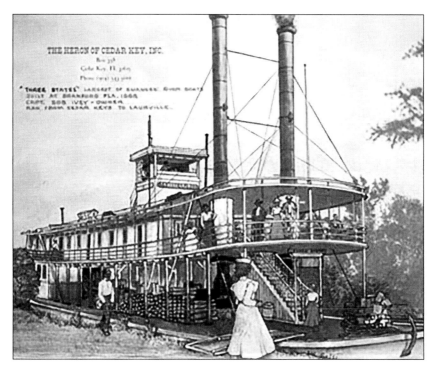

Many steamships plied the tannic currents of the Suwannee in times past. The art rendering depicts the *Three States* which was captained by Captain Ivey. Courtesy of State Library and Archives of Florida

Rose Knox and Graham Schorb

In the antebellum period, when cotton was king, shrill whistles from steamships announced their arrival at bustling river landings; some ships carried local passengers and wealthy tourists; others transported cotton, mail, and various supplies. One old landing is now located within the boundaries of the Suwannee River State Park, which was likewise the location of a pioneer town called Columbus.

A pioneer cemetery is nestled there in the shades of a grand old longleaf pine forest. Situated inside the Suwannee River State Park boundaries, not far from the confluence of the Withlacoochee and Suwannee Rivers, is what remains of the Confederate earthworks. Courtesy of Patrick Elliott

Exploring the 242-mile Suwannee River, or reading books about it, will prove a cultural and historical journey that will take folks back to a fascinating human past. Courtesy of Graham Schorb

The place also became a booming mill town that Drew named Ellaville. According to some local accounts, the name was derived to honor an elderly black woman who had once worked for his family. Ellaville eventually prospered, becoming a vital town with a population of over one thousand inhabitants. Residents and visitors had access to a post office, two churches, an express office, a telegraph unit, two schools, and a Masonic Lodge, but no saloons were allowed. Lumbermen and trappers were also attracted to the boomtown in their search for jobs or when they wanted to trade. Courtesy of Patrick Elliott

Endnotes

1. James C. Clark, *200 Quick Looks at Florida History* (Sarasota, FL: Pineapple Press, 2000).

2. Elizabeth Sims et al., *A History of Madison County, Florida* (Madison, FL: Jimbob Printing, 1986).

3. Eric Musgrove, *Reflections of Suwannee County: 150th Anniversary Edition 1858-2008* (Live Oak: North Florida Printing, 2008).

4. Clark, *Quick Looks*.

5. Musgrove, *Reflections of Suwanee County*.

Rose Knox and Graham Schorb

Travel Notes

Antebellum Ghosts of Madison: Local Lore

Wardlaw-Smith-Goza (Whitehall) Mansion and the Bunker House

"Folklorist Jan Harold Brunvand defines urban legends as 'legends that—unlike myths—are set in the recent past and involve human beings rather than ancient gods or demigods.' The most enduring legends are those reflecting the fears and the anxieties of our time."[1]

Many oral legends of now-dead people arise from these Red Hills. Or so the folktales from local people claim. One author, John Harden, once said of such histories, "Myths, legends, and folktales come from the primary literature of any people. It takes . . . time and years of loneliness to create them. It takes hunger and imagination."[2] And another writer, Joseph Campbell, once supposed that "The folktale is the primer of the picture-language of the soul."[3]

Talking to many people over the years, Graham and I have come head to head with lots of supernatural tales. Though we've personally never seen a ghoul, a ghost, or any kind of spook on our various travels, we have walked to the places where others swear something weird happened to them. Therefore, we are not proclaiming that we believe in the supernatural, but we took the time to listen to those stories. Some tales were told to us firsthand, others we only heard about, and some were taken from area books about haunted places of Middle Florida. We will, for that reason, leave it up to the reader to decide if these bizarre legends hold any credence. Here are a few stories that over the years have "found" our ears.

The first story that came my way happened many years back, as I was admiring a quilt while wandering around the Wardlaw-Smith-Goza Mansion at an event they called Down Home Days. I was standing on the threshold of the west downstairs room, just at the foot of the winding Charleston staircase, when I encountered a stranger. She was also admiring the same quilt that had been placed for display on the wall. She was a black woman of about middle age. Since I grew up in Madison but did not recognize her, I said as a way to start a conversation, "You are not from around here, are you?" She looked at me, smiling, and said in a Southern accent, "Not now. But I used to be. In fact, I used to work here in this house for Mrs. Smith."

Then even more eager to speak with her, I promptly introduced myself, telling her I was a teacher. I also asked her, since she had spent time in the home—quite a bit in her early years—if she'd ever come across any strange happenings. She told me that she could remember one story in particular, a peculiar one, but I could tell from her body language and strained expression that she was hesitant to share. I implored her again, telling her that I'd always had an interest in the house and I liked touring my students around, showing them historic places and telling them stories, and would love to hear the details of hers. Without much more prompting, here is the story she told.

First she stepped into the main foyer of the home, there by the stairs, not far from the double doors and entrance, and pointed to the room on the east downstairs wing. She said, "See that room over there?" I looked and nodded. She said that one day while she was in the home working, she heard Mrs. Smith call out to her, saying in a kind of falsetto voice, "Charlotte?" Charlotte said she moved toward the room where Mrs. Smith was sitting. Mrs. Smith wanted to know something, asking, "Charlotte, can you hear them?"

Charlotte replied, "Hear what Mrs. Smith?"

Mrs. Smith then said, "The soldiers; I can hear them marchin' down the staircase."

Charlotte said she listened for a minute to see if she might hear the rhythm of steps from marching men, but after lending a close ear she said, "No, Mrs. Smith, I can't hear a thing." It should be noted again that Confederate and Union soldiers who were transported by train from the Battle of Olustee had suffered and died from battle wounds in the mansion.

Another interesting story involved one of my former students. While I was explaining how we would soon tour the Oak Ridge Cemetery, a boneyard that cradles some of the oldest graves in Middle Florida, one student seemed very uncomfortable. I was excited, and I explained to them we would also be walking around the town square where the Slave monument and the Confederate monument are located among other historical monuments and signs. After the park tour, we would head over to the Treasures Museum, ending the outing inside of the

Smith-Wardlaw-Goza Mansion. The girl, an A student and front-row sitter, was now squirming in her seat. She raised her hand and quite politely said to me, "Ms. Knox, I will not be able to go on that tour." I assured her that I would be giving points for going, and I hoped she might change her mind. After class, she lingered until all the other students had left the classroom. She then relayed this detailed account of what happened to her father. She was sure he would not allow her to go. Here is a summary of what she said about the mansion.

She began by saying that her father was a professional photographer. He often covered weddings and had been asked to take photographs of a wedding that was going to take place at the mansion. This was before digital cameras, so he had set up a makeshift darkroom in the tiny room that is in the foyer. She told me that he would "swear that this is what happened to him as he was working under his infrared lighting." She continued, "The temperature all of a sudden dropped. It was very cold in the darkroom and just as the temperature drastically dropped, he 'felt strong hands take him by the neck' as if to try to strangle him."

At this point in the story, the student made sure that I knew her Daddy was "a big, strong man and not afraid of much." But at the moment he felt those hands gripping his neck, he "flew out of the darkroom," out into the foyer, and tore out of the huge double doors. He was so frightened by the experience that his daughter told me, "He refused to go back in. And you have to know that he had left behind 1,500 dollars' worth of camera equipment in that tiny room! Somebody else had to go back in and bring him his equipment." True to her word, she did not come on the tour. But some of her friends did. We opened up the tiny room in question, and I allowed them to peek in. I wanted her friends to tell her that they had seen it "with their own eyes." Nothing happened to us on that day, and nothing has ever happened while showing students around.

Yet another story involves going inside the mansion at night. The night was hot and muggy. A storm was approaching out of the east. In the distance, black clouds were looming and bolts of lightning lit up the night sky. Graham and I had previously set up an appointment to meet someone up at the Wardlaw-Smith-Goza mansion at about nightfall. We drove up to the wrought-iron gate at the appointed time, near where the huge live oak tree looms over the brick-lined, looping driveway. At dusk, at 8:27 p.m., we sat patiently in our little Toyota truck waiting for our escort. The light was slowly fading and darkness soon descended.

I was excited because I had never been in the house at night. On that August 31st of 2015, the mansion had just been bought from the local college by a world famous chef. I knew that my connections at the local college had always gotten me in, but I was not sure if I would ever get the chance again, and especially to roam around the rooms and up the winding staircase at night. My interest was piqued because of the strange tales that had been told over several years by the security guards responsible for looking after the place. The guards were from the local college. Some of the scenes that Captain Maurice James explained to me made me want to go in after sunset.

Just that week he had explained (after I'd asked him) that he had become fearful of checking on the place at night. The other guards had come to dread it, too. He said that the alarms that had been set in the house made him nervous. Each time the alarm went off—and that was quite frequently—he or one of his staff members had to jump in a golf cart and head up to the mansion with flashlights in hand.

On one of those occasions, he swore that he did see a light come on in the second story of the house on the east side, but he could not explain exactly why. To his knowledge, the mansion was "locked up tight" and no one was in there. He also talked about another occasion when he had entered the house after dark and was exploring around; this investigation took place after the alarm had gone off at night. He recounted that he was moving up the staircase to check out the second story of the house. He told me, "I heard creaking, like steps behind me." This took place near the top of the Charleston staircase. Maurice, a quite athletic fellow, said he was so "frightened by sounds" that he started taking three steps at a time, at record speed, to get down the stairs and out of the house!

So on the evening of August 31, Desmond, one of his staff members, arrived in the golf cart. I was glad to see Desmond, for he had been one of my former students and we'd also performed in a musical together a few years back. He smiled, giving me a hug and shaking Graham's hand, all the while expressing that he "couldn't understand my wanting to go in, especially after dark. That place is sure haunted, you know." Desmond was not kidding when he said those words, and his facial expression told us so. We stood outside of the wrought-iron gate catching up and looking at the mansion from that distance. He took out his keys, opened the gate, and led us up on the huge heart pine porch and around to the west side of the house. When we were on the porch, he informed us that "I will not be going in; I'm just going to open the door and wait outside on ya'll." I asked him then if he had experienced any happenings and why he was so resolute about not going in. He told us this story out on the porch:

> Once I came up here after dark to check on the house because the alarms went off. I came right to this very door. Before I could open the door, I saw that curtain moving around. (He then pointed at the curtain visible to us on the first story, near that downstairs west side.) I didn't want to go in after that because I thought there might be somebody at the window. But I had to check on the house. It was my duty. I went in. I looked up and down beside where I saw the curtain moving to see if there was some sort of air vent that might have made that curtain move. There was no such thing. I then walked all around each room and left as soon as I saw everything was secure. But I don't like going in there. Some strange things have happened in there.

Graham and I listened and were interested in those details. But I wanted Desmond to go in with us. I told him that I'd been in the house on many occasions with students. I always felt very safe. Also, I made it clear it would mean a lot to me for him to go with us. His presence would also provide confirmation in case we did happen to run across some weird occurrence. He didn't want to, but I was able to somehow talk him into it. We toured all around, even taking some pictures, but we saw nothing on that night. We later departed, thanking Desmond. I could tell he was relieved to get back in the golf cart and go back down the hill to the nearby campus.

Other stories have come to me over the years because people know I'm interested in the house. Here is another one I scrawled down after I heard it. On September 27, 2016, I had a book delivered to my office at the college by one of the campus security persons, Captain Maurice James. Another story had come his way, and he said it had recently been relayed to him by a reliable source, a member of our maintenance crew on campus. Captain James said, "Remember the man that just bought the mansion? Well, he had some visitors come in from Europe to spend the night. They had some candles lit. But they said they would 'never spend the night in that house again.'" He added that "you can get the rest of the story from Mr. Hackle." I immediately called Dale Hackle, the head of maintenance, and left a message telling him why I was calling. I wanted to hear the story while it was still fresh in his mind. In a few days he called me and told me that some cabinet makers had been invited to stay in the mansion by the new owner, while they were doing work. However, they ended up going to a motel room, and it was claimed by one of them that he would "never try to spend the night in there again." It seems that there were some candles lit, and an unexplained draft kept snuffing them out. I never talked to the workers myself, but this story came to me from folks I work with.

Another home in Madison that has supernatural stories surrounding it is the Elijah J. and Seth H. Bunker House. The home was built by the two brothers, Elijah and Seth, in 1850. Their family history reveals that they migrated to America from France and were Huguenots. The home was constructed with two entry doors to accommodate the comings and goings of both brothers who lived in the house. When visitors came to call they would go to the door of the brother they wished to visit and would then be invited into the central parlor. Elijah was wed to Fanny R. Mobley. In 1894 Fanny Bunker, listed then as a spinster, sold the home and property for $685 to Richard Bevan.

The current owners of the home claim that supernatural stirrings have occurred over the time that they have lived there. For example, a baby monitor was said to have picked up sounds from an unexplained source. A woman was singing lullabies, and it was surmised that she was looking after the baby at night. Other unexplained happenings have supposedly occurred in the nursery, and whenever the child's crib was left in the down position, the owners would return to find it moved to the up position.

Also, around the same time, it is said that a four-year-old child claimed to have had an encounter with and man and a woman. The couple stood beside her bed, and leaned down to give her a kiss and told her ". . . not to be afraid, that they were there to look out for her."[4] As the story goes, the child described the apparitions as a man and a woman, and after her encounter she saw a picture of the former owners and claimed she recognized the couple as the ghostly ones she had seen. The child inquired about where they were buried; she was later taken to the gravesite, allowed to spend time at their tombs, walking and talking to them near their graves. It is also claimed that other family members who had once been acquainted with the couple have heard footsteps in the house and detected the smell of pipe tobacco lingering in the air. According to an historical brochure produced by the local Chamber of Commerce, one passage states: "A child has also been sighted numerous times, standing at the foot of a bed. Its identity continues to elude the owners. They are not afraid, just curious to find out more about them."

Recently I ran across these relevant ideas from Richard Southall, when I pulled the books from the shelves at the college. In Southall's book, *Haunted Plantations of the South*, he reminds people that "There are certain conditions that need to be present in order for a location to become haunted . . . they include an emotional connection to a location, a sudden or violent death, or unfinished business.[5] In that interesting work of haunted places of the South, he often mentions the stories of numerous sites that alleged witnesses swear are true, of the sounds of shuffling or the rhythm of marching feet, a room's temperature dramatically dropping, unexplained lights coming on and off, and the lingering aroma of tobacco. In his book, he also describes how some "witnesses" can see or hear the spirit, but others standing right beside them cannot.

So these are a few Madison folk tales regarding supernatural beings that are said to be dwelling within antebellum buildings. It is up to the reader to decide if they want to believe such seemingly far-fetched stories.

Students are pictured at the Confederate Monument in the middle of Four Freedoms Park. The monument is dedicated to the Confederate soldiers. It was placed there by the efforts of the Daughters of the Confederacy and unveiled in 1905. After visiting the park, I often took students on a tour of the local mansion. Courtesy of Graham Schorb

"The temperature all of a sudden dropped. It was very cold in the darkroom and just as the temperature drastically dropped, my Dad felt strong hands take him by the neck as if to try to strangle him." Also, back in the 1960s, my oldest sister Sue Knox was friends with Jimmy Smith. She once told me that when they were teenagers, Jimmy Smith, Jeannie Brinson, and Chip Durant ". . . all played around with an Ouija board, trying our best to conjure up ghosts." This game took place in one of the upstairs bedrooms of the mansion. Jim Smith swears, however, that he has seen no ghosts in the house. Courtesy of Rosanna Hughes

Endnotes

1. Alan Brown, *Stories from the Haunted South* (Jackson: University Press of Mississippi, 2004).

2. John Harden, *Tar Heel Ghosts* (Chapel Hill: University of North Carolina Press, 1954).

3. Joseph Campbell, "Folkloristic Commentary," in *Complete Grimm's Fairy Tales* (New York: Pantheon, 1944).

4. Brown, *Stories from the Haunted South.*

5. Richard Southall, *Haunted Plantations of the South* (Woodbury, MN: Llewellyn Publications, 2015).

Origins of Southern Superstition:
Celtic Lore

"The whole of everyday life was circumscribed by the powers, good and evil, that were believed to be everywhere present, to be placated by ritual or exploited by magical processes."[1]

Ghosts and subjects surrounding folk legends of the American South are curious topics that have received attention in recent times. Haunted cemeteries and tales of strange happenings in antebellum mansions or on former plantations make up material for books and television shows, and are what make ghost tours popular. Yet it should not be too hard to believe that such ideas did not originate on the plantation; instead they all come from a belief system that has been passed down through the ages, superstition originating in Celtic history.

Anne Ross, in her book, *The Folklore of the Scottish Highlands*, illustrates that fact by writing,

> As in ancient pagan times, when the classical writers were commenting on the customs and habits of their Celtic neighbors in Europe and Britain, and the splendid repertoire of Irish and British legend and myth was receiving written form by the early Christian scribes, the life of the Scottish Highlander was . . . not only rich in lore and legend, music, and song, but completely hedged around by taboo—things to be done, things to be avoided. The whole of everyday life was circumscribed by the powers, good and evil, that were believed to be everywhere present, to be placated by ritual or exploited by magical processes. The otherworld forces, and the ghosts and monsters of hill and water were real, substantial, and infinitely menacing.[2]

In this compilation I have attempted to present a few stories of haunted places, and tell of spirits that, local legend claims, dwell in graveyards and old homeplaces of the Red Hills. If it were possible to trace back the exact origins of these varied supernatural beliefs, readers might not then be too surprised to find the Celts had a strong predilection for fantastic stories, and the tales were part of the very fabric of their everyday lives. Ross explains further, "Every place had its name and its legend—how it got its name; what famous hero or infamous savage, supernatural animal, or shaggy, semi-human sprite was associated with it were stories known at one time to all . . . these were those men of Scotland who could chant the ancient ballads, many of which contain legends common to Ireland and Scotland."[3]

These pagan chants, over time, mixed themselves with Christian doctrines. For example, the deity Brigit would be mentioned in the same prayer as the Virgin Mary. The Celts believed the prayers and chants served to ward off the evil eye and their supplications held power over evil forces. An obsession with death also permeated their lore; graveyards are the backdrop for many stories. Ross writes, "Death has always been one of the main preoccupations of the Celt; this no doubt stems ultimately from the cult of graves, ancestor worship, and the belief that the burial mound was either one of the entrances to the otherworld, or the place in which the departed continued his ghostly life, with various rites and offerings. Even the practice of placing flowers on the graves of the departed must be an almost instinctive continuation of the widespread, archaic practice of honoring and placating the dead with offerings."[4]

One illustration of such preoccupation with death concerns a boneyard and the idea of dying; a young lad is returning home from an extended journey. As he gets closer to home, he sees a long procession of people walking and carrying a casket. He recognizes many close and distant family members—and all of his friends. When he joins the processional of mourners, he grabs the coffin to help the pallbearers, which he recognizes as his dear friends. However, in that very moment when he touches the coffin, he is thrown violently down to the ground by a supernatural force! It is only then he realizes to his horror that he is the dead one. His spirit rises above the funeral march, giving him a bird's-eye view as he watches his own funeral procession.

Not only strange stories in or near cemeteries abound in Celtic lore, but Celts also believed that fairies could and would steal an unbaptized newborn child; the fairies would replace the human baby with a gaunt, skeletal infant—one who had an unrelenting appetite, and no matter how much the child ate, it never gained any weight. The superstition held that the gaunt baby must be put outside overnight, and the fairies would return to give the real baby back to its mother. Some of those children sadly died from exposure to the elements.

In addition, I grew up with a great bit of superstition that was handed down from my own Mother. We were warned never to step on the crack of a sidewalk because that meant someone who had just been recently buried would roll over in the grave; a black cat running across our path meant bad luck; walking under a ladder should be avoided at all costs to keep wicked spirits away; a sleeping baby should never be left in a room with a cat, for the cat would suck the breath and the soul from the child. A preoccupation with the idea of sudden death even manifested itself in our family's bedtime prayer. On bended knee, with hands reverently folded, the children of our family chanted: "Now I lay me down to sleep, I pray the Lord my soul to keep, if I die before I wake, I pray the Lord, my soul to take." Though we were serious about the prayer, most of what the five Knox children were told about superstition was delivered tongue-in-cheek, but it was an old oral tradition of lore that was being kept alive.

Out of Celtic lore therefore emerges an obsession with sinister and supernatural subjects. These include heroic tales and legends of birds and beasts, sacred springs, severed heads, holy trees, magic mounds, a dread of supernatural beings, roaming lonely moors or mountains, belief in hags or witches, water monsters, fairies and little people, evil dogs or goats, sinister and dangerous bulls, and a preoccupation with the past. All of these and more were passed down through the oral tradition. If anyone has ever read C. S. Lewis's *The Chronicles of Narnia* or J.R.R. Tolkien's *Lord of the Rings* or *The Hobbit*, many of these settings and supernatural happenings are part of those works, for both men took ideas from Celtic and Norse mythologies to write their compelling books of fantasy.

One online movie sums up the fear that surrounded ancient superstition: *Legends of the Isles: Fairies and Leprechauns*. In the opening scene, the narrator warns, "There's an old Irish tale that says, 'in a twilight world somewhere between heaven and hell, there lives a race of magical, mischievous beings.' Of course, we don't believe in such things anymore; but beware! The tale has a cruel twist. The less we believe, the more we have to fear."[5]

Rose Knox and Graham Schorb

Endnotes

1. Anne Ross, *Folklore of the Scottish Highlands* (New York: Barnes and Noble Books, 1976).

2. Ross, *Folklore of the Scottish Highlands.*

3. Ross, *Folklore of the Scottish Highlands.*

4. Ross, *Folklore of the Scottish Highlands.*

5. *Legends of the Isles: Fairies & Leprechauns,* YouTube video.

Jefferson County

Travel Notes

A Brief Sketch of Jefferson County

"On the very hill on which we have built must have been formerly a Spanish Town, for the traces of brick houses are discoverable everywhere." Laura Wirt Randall, 1827

Like Madison County, Jefferson County has many intriguing stories. As part of the Red Hills, its physical boundary encompasses approximately 598 square miles. The expanse is shaped in a wedge-like strip, extending about 39 miles from the Georgia line down to the Gulf of Mexico. At its northern boundary, it is approximately 25 miles wide, but begins to narrow significantly to a width of around 6 miles along the coast. The region varies vastly in its topography, with the northern two-thirds of the county having sloping hills. The soil beneath those rolling hills is known to be some of the most arable in the South, although the southern third of the county is comprised of flat woods and features sandy soil, good for the support of scrub and pine barrens.

Back in the pioneering days, it was not so easy to get into Jefferson County, as routes were not as convenient as they are today. For instance, in the early 1800s visitors might disembark from a ship in Savannah, Georgia, and take a horse or a wagon headed to Bainbridge, Georgia, moving into Tallahassee and then into Jefferson County, taking the Old Spanish Trail known also as the Old Saint Augustine Road. Still other travelers might have made their way via the Gulf of Mexico to the St. Marks River at a town called Magnolia, not too far from present-day Newport. From there a rough overland journey would get them into the area as they entered the territory from the south. But it was the rich soil of Jefferson County's sloping hills that first attracted early settlers willing to forge through harsh landscapes back in the 1800s.

One pioneer speaks of an even earlier past that hints at the sloping terrain and also the former existence of Spanish missions. Laura Wirt Randall once put it this way, shortly after arriving in 1827. "On the very hill on which we have built must have been formerly a Spanish Town, for the traces of brick houses are discoverable everywhere"[1] (as quoted in Shofner). And she was right! Archeological evidence and writings of religious scribes of the mission period reveal that one of the largest and most significant chains of Spanish mission sites once existed there, spanning the Red Hills of north Florida. As has been mentioned previously, those missions were built to convert the natives in the seventeenth century. Ayubule, as it was called, was, however, completely destroyed over 120 years before settlers like Laura Randall Wirt began to arrive.[2] Jefferson County was established in 1827, with Monticello being named the county seat in 1828. The pioneers began migrating there from South Carolina and Virginia.[3]

When the Spanish first entered the area in the 1500s they encountered the Natives known as the Apalachees, who were thriving in ordered, spiritual societies. The region of their communities was situated between two rivers, the Aucilla and Ochlockonee. Two Spanish explorers were to eventually come in contact with this highly evolved, agricultural culture. The first was Pánfilo de Narváez, who first disembarked on Florida's Gulf Coast in 1528 and then marched northward, and whose diaries speak of an Apalachee town his procession came across, called Ivitachuco, located in what is today Jefferson County. His armed and uninvited entourage was to meet with violent resistance from these native people, and those conflicts were the main reason his exploration eventually ended in disaster. History tells us that his men were forced to sail out of Apalachee Bay on makeshift rafts, trying desperately to escape the wrath of the Apalachee.

As mentioned in a previous chapter, another Spaniard later to forge through the county was Hernando de Soto, who also ended up in "the land of the Apalachee" in the year 1539. It would be over 100 years later that the Spanish finally would return to establish missions in order to attempt to convert the natives to the Catholic faith. They established numerous sites. According to Jerrell H. Shofner in his regional book,

> At one time there were 18 missions, or doctrinas, between the Aucilla River and the [mission] headquarters of the San Luis de Talimali near present-day Tallahassee. Five of those mission sites were positioned in what is today Jefferson County, and they were aligned from east to west not far from what is modern-day U.S. 27. Their names were as follows: San Lorenzo de Ybitachuco (Ivitachuco), La Concepcion de Ajubali (Ayubule), San Francisco de Oconi, San Juan de Aspalaga, and San Jose de Ocuya.

Some of the missions differed in size and population, but they were similar in their intended purposes and also in the physical layout of the site, with the church constructed at the center. Daily life rotated around regular religious services, and the natives that had given up their own spiritual practices and traded them for Christian doctrines worshipped there, being instructed in ritual and doctrine by the Spanish priests. The existing fields that had previously been used for growing food by and for the indigenous populations now were used by the mission; the natives still toiled in the field, but for now a different purpose, set in motion by Roman Catholic dictates. It would be the Indian converts who were to cultivate various crops. The crops supported not only the Spanish missions but agricultural bounty was transported to St. Augustine to help support that bustling city.[4]

One fascinating look at the mission period and the devastating impact it had on the Indian populations in North America comes from an important work, *Laboring in the Fields of the Lord: Spanish Missions and Southeastern Indians*. Jerald T. Milanich writes, "The missions of Spanish Florida are one of American history's best-kept secrets. Between 1565 and 1763, more than 150 missions . . . dotted the landscape from Florida to Chesapeake Bay."[5] In his book, Milanich tells a vivid story of those missions and the Apalachee, Guale, and Timucua Indians who lived and labored in them. He describes the mission history using old maps, archival photographs, and artistic renderings from artist Theodore Morris to show how Indian workers planted, harvested, and transported corn that helped sustain the colony. He further elaborates on how the establishment of missions was essential in meeting the goals of colonialism, adding that through the actions of conquistadors, missionaries, and entrepreneurs, the native populations were condemned to slavery and oppression, and finally their cultures were wiped out. He says, "Though long abandoned and destroyed, the missions are an important part of our country's heritage."[6]

The Spanish held possession of Florida for three centuries, except for the brief occupation of the British, and the domain between the Aucilla and the Ochlockonee had been the home of the Apalachee Natives for hundreds of years. Eventually the violent conflicts during the colonial period of the 1700s would obliterate their entire culture. Those earlier Spanish religious sites of the 1500s eventually rotted because of exposure to heat and humidity, leaving only scant evidence of their former structural existence. With the acquisition of Florida by the United States in 1821, the rich soil that had once been tended by the Natives was now open to incoming settlers, those interested in growing cotton. These newcomers, however, were to come into contact and conflict with other native people now living in the region. They were called the Seminoles.[7]

The topography of Jefferson County has always attracted humans to the region because of good soil and ample water supplies. Many beautiful watery places abound. For instance, some of the larger lakes are known as Miccosukee, Raysor, Windom, Iamonia, and Silver. About a mile to the south of the town of Wacissa runs the clear, awe-inspiring "stream" called the Wacissa River. Relics from an ancient past have been found in mounds in the Wacissa basin. One such artifact was a Pre-Columbian figurine, along with shell carvings and earthen structures that represented the religious and political influence which was wielded throughout the Southeast.

Many artifacts discovered in and around burial mounds—though they originated thousands of miles away—were indicators of the extensive communication, cultural, and trade routes that existed centuries before the arrival of the Europeans. The idol depicted here was discovered in a mound on the Wacissa River in 1936. Today the river is known by locals and outdoor enthusiasts as a bird sanctuary, and the basin supports many species of wildlife. Fed by deep underground springs, it is 150 to 200 yards wide in most sections. The currents of the Wacissa flow into the undulating, tannic Aucilla, and the Aucilla finally finds its way to the Gulf of Mexico. The Aucilla River and its tributary known as Gum Swamp flow into the eastern and northeastern sections of Jefferson County, but the outflow of the western part makes its way into Lake Miccosukee and the St. Marks River. These lakes and rivers were important to wildlife and to human beings of the region, providing sources of water and sustenance.

Fascinating stories tied to the topographical region involve "a sky river of orange" where thousands of butterflies land in the salt marsh before migrating to Mexico, and a strange tale about a volcano somewhere in the deep forest is still a mystery that has never been solved.

Communities within Jefferson County include Ashville, Aucilla, Capps, Cody, Drifton, Fanlew, Lamont (once known as Lickskillet), Lloyd, Wacissa, and Waukeenah.

The Pre-Columbian figurine, as well as shell carvings and earthen structures, represented the religious and political power exerted throughout the Southeast. Many such artifacts which were found in Florida—in and around burial mounds—originated thousands of miles away, indicators of the extensive communication, cultural, and trade routes that existed centuries before the arrival of the Europeans. The idol depicted here was discovered in a mound on the Wacissa River in 1936. Courtesy of Samuel P. Adams and the State Library and Archives of Florida

Rose Knox and Graham Schorb

The name of this mission, once located in Jefferson County, was
San Juan de Aspalaga Mission. Courtesy of the State Library and
Archives of Florida

The image depicts a painting of the mission of San Francsico de Oconee. This painting is based on data uncovered in the excavation of the Spanish mission San Francsico de Oconee. Courtesy of State Library and Archives of Florida

Endnotes

1. Jerrell H. Shofner, *History of Jefferson County* (Tallahassee, FL: Sentry Press, 1976).
2. Shofner, *History of Jefferson County.*
3. "Jefferson County: Monticello Section," pamphlet published by the Jefferson Business League, n.d.
4. Shofner, *History of Jefferson County.*
5. Jerald T. Milanich, *Laboring in the Fields of the Lord: Spanish Missions and Southeastern Indians* (Gainesville: University Press of Florida, 2006).
6. Milanich, *Laboring in the Fields.*
7. Shofner, *History of Jefferson County.*

Ancient Indians at Letchworth-Love Mounds

". . . in a time, thousands of years before the Pharaohs or the
first faint stirrings of recorded human history . . . for 12,000
years they lived and loved, dreamed and died, along the rivers
and the shores . . . of what we now know as Florida."   From
the film *Shadows and Reflections*

There once were skeptics asking questions about ancient mounds
built in eastern North America. Many people believed that these
mound builders, a "mysterious people," had nothing to do with the
Native Americans. In that period of questioning, wild speculations
emerged concerning the origins and customs of the mound builders.

Such mounds initially became a topic of discussion in the 1800s
as Celtic peoples migrated over the Appalachian Mountains, settling
in the Ohio Valley and beyond. George R. Milner writes in his book,
The Mound Builders, "Thousands of these mounds were discovered in
plains and forests—one 100 feet high—some overgrown hillocks, some
conical, others flat-topped. Speculation was rife as to the identity of
these mound builders."

Excavation of the mounds revealed that these monuments served
various purposes. Some were mortuary mounds; others were used
as the base for the chief's home; some served as "effigy" mounds
and were crafted in the form of panthers, snakes, and other sacred
creatures. Anthropologists believe that mound-building was a vital
element of the rich ceremonial life the people led. It was how Natives
remembered their ancestors, how they worshipped deities, how they
buried the dead, and how they held respect for their leaders. Over the
years, many finely crafted objects were discovered inside the mounds,
including some made of copper.[1]

Looking up at towering burial mounds is a sight to behold; much
mystery surrounds the people who built them. The Letchworth-Love

Mounds site is located in Jefferson County and encompasses what is known as the largest earth mound in the state of Florida. People today go there to hike, to picnic, and to walk up the elevated railing to get a good look at one prominent mound. At that site there still exists one significant mound, with a few smaller mounds in the immediate area. Archeological studies indicate that as many as twenty mounds may have previously been destroyed as a result of modern land use. The location has been deemed by the Florida Bureau of Archaeological Research to be a predominantly Woodland-period site.[2]

The terminology "Woodland period" came into being in the 1930s and has been used as a general classification for prehistoric sites, those cultures existing between the time of the Archaic hunter-gathers and the planting societies known as the Mississippian cultures.[3] To further illustrate how the Woodland period is described, one source reveals, "This period is . . . considered a developmental stage, a time period . . . of cultures related to earlier Archaic cultures."[4] These peoples were known for crafting stone and bone into tools, crafting pottery and leather, making bows and arrows, and for their cultivation of crops, especially corn, among other plants. The period has been dated from around 1000 B.C. to A.D. 900. During this time the development of many trends that had started during the preceding Late Archaic Period (3000-1000 B.C.) reached its height in development as it moved into what was later classified as the Mississippian Period from A.D. 800–1600. Changes in that time included social stratification, sedentariness, and elaborate ritualistic ceremonies brought on by an agrarian lifestyle.[5]

Other Lesser-Known Mounds

There is also a lesser-known mound situated off Old Lloyd Road in what is known today as Great Oaks subdivision. The burial mound was excavated in 1958-59 by the anthropology department of Florida State University. Four burials were discovered at that time, but it is believed more bodies existed there. Stone tools and pottery vessels were likewise found at the site.

For a general history of the mound builders' culture, search movies online. One interesting one is titled *Who Were the Mound Builders? The First American Civilization Built by Native Americans.* The film was produced by Ambrose Video and runs 37 minutes and 32 seconds in length. The film depicts artists' renderings based on the archaeological record.

If you are looking for a serene place to relax and reflect on the ancient past, take a drive down Highway 90, and be sure to stop at Letchworth-Love Mounds Park. We sometimes venture there to picnic and to wonder about these ancient societies.

"... in a time, thousands of years before the Pharaohs or the first faint stirrings of recorded human history ... for 12,000 years they lived and loved, dreamed and died, along the rivers and the shores ... of what we now know as Florida." From the film *Shadows and Reflections*

Looking up at ancient burial mounds is a sight to behold; much mystery surrounds the prehistoric people who built them. The Letchworth-Love Mounds site is located in Jefferson County and encompasses what is known as the largest earth mound in the state of Florida. The image depicts a mound that was built by an ancient race of people; the photograph was taken in 1932. The mound rises up about fifty feet near Miccosukee Drain and is located 18 miles northeast of Tallahassee on Highway 90. Courtesy of State Library and Archives of Florida, Photographer Herman Gunter 1885-1972

Endnotes

1. George R. Milner, *The Mound Builders: Ancient Peoples of Eastern North America* (London: Thames & Hudson, 2004).

2. Charles Harper and Daniel M. Seinfeld, "Woodland Period Settlement Patterns at Letchworth Mounds, Jefferson County, Florida," 81st Annual Meeting of the Society for American Archaeology, 2016.

3. Harper and Seinfeld, "Woodland Period Settlement Patterns."

4. Ronald J. Mason (1970), "Hopewell Middle Woodland and the Laurel Culture: A Problem of Archaeological Classification," American Anthropologist 72 (4): 802-15.

5. Thomas J. Pluckhahn, "Woodland Period: Overview," New Georgia Encyclopedia, 03 August 2015, Web, 10 February 2017.

Travel Notes

Ted Morris: Artist of Native Americans

"Back as far as I can remember, I was always drawing." From an interview with Ted Morris

It was in 2008 that Theodore Morris's *Florida's Lost Tribes* work first captivated the region's attention. I discovered the book at the local college where I teach. I had never before come across Morris's detailed work, which showed a genuine cultural history of Florida Indians. His varied depictions of early peoples were captivating. Along with the paintings in *Florida's Lost Tribes* was expert commentary from one of the most renowned Florida archeologists, Jerald T. Milanich. The compilation was an ethnographic dream come true. Any soul interested in Florida's Native American past would certainly want to read this work. Milanich and Morris fused their knowledge, wisdom, and talents to produce a true account of the first Floridians. It was about time!

For anyone out there who has not heard of Theodore Morris, he is known as the preeminent painter of Florida's indigenous peoples, and his depictions show up on the front covers of many an academic book. His portraits have also been appreciated by thousands of people visiting Florida museums and art galleries; hundreds of thousands of people have seen his online works.

But he is known for more than his Florida Indian portrayals. Morris's most recent body of work, *Florida & Caribbean Native People: Paintings by Theodore Morris,* chronicles the Caribbean Taino people. The book includes interesting commentaries from some of Florida's principal archeologists, including Brent R. Weisman and Ryan J. Wheeler among others, and it also records Morris's own specific artistic vision. As a result of such works, Morris's name is already well on its way to becoming a household word, for his paintings are displayed in many places, including private and corporate collections, and in museums throughout Florida.

The best way to know anything of Morris's artistry, though, is to experience his paintings firsthand. I will attempt to give some description in words. All of Morris's realistic oil paintings are presented in vibrant colors, and leaping off each canvas are the lives of the very people. That is not just a poetic-sounding sentence, either!

Some are beautifully haunting, while others might take a person back to their own childhood. Some speak of the love and devotion of a parent to his young child. To illustrate, a striking young woman walks alone in a lush hammock. She stares upward, her face illumined as if caught in a spiritual moment. A scrub jay has balanced itself for just a second on her finger; mist envelops the primeval forest behind her. Another painting is of a group of children about six or seven years old; one is looking contemplative, another mischievous; all have innocence written on their faces. The simple shell and bone ornaments dangling from the necks of some seem like they might have been made by the children themselves. The four of them are standing behind some coontie leaves. This plant has also been called "Indian breadroot" and was often found growing in regional hammocks, pine-oak forests, scrub areas, and beside shell mounds. Are the youngsters getting ready to play a game that children today might call chase, or hide-and-go-seek?

In yet another portrait, a young father stands confidently in his panther warrior headdress. Feathers and tattoos adorn his chiseled body. He is hugging a toddler in an embrace of fatherly love, while the little boy offers up to the viewer his toy bow. Is the young father about to go to war? Is he pondering the magnitude of the moment—of what life just might be like for small children when a father does not return from battle? Such real-to-life scenes show the true humanity of each figure.

Thus, in depicting the faces of the early native peoples, Morris somehow finds something of the ephemeral—what he needs as an artist—to capture the absolute essence and soul of his subjects. He also places particular artifacts in each painting; every one of them seems to tell a story all its own of an intriguing ethnographic past. Adding the artifacts to his canvas is what Morris likes to call his favorite part of the creation. Those pieces include various objects like projectile points, jewelry, feathers, pipes, tattoos, and ritualistic relics.

The author Marjory Stoneman Douglas describes in words what the artist has also been known to paint when she writes, "They carved and perforated bones, deer bone, and turtle bone and even human bone, perhaps the bones of a powerful enemy . . . those . . . things [they wore] on the oiled, shining copper bodies . . . those young hunters and warriors and fishermen, their black hair pinned up with pins and stuck with arrows. Their raccoon tails swished behind them. The dark eyes of girls must have watched them from the house shadows as the self-conscious young men went by . . . walking like dandies."

Morris has a way of crafting a true-to-life background of clouds at sunrise or at sunset, too. Or he paints hanging wild grapevines, or cleverly places some resurrection fern for real botanical effect. In some works, he even shows the delicate wings of a dragonfly or paints a lovely zebra longwing butterfly flitting about. With such mindful attention to detail, each person, along with all of the creatures, looks as if they might be about to emerge right out of the canvas!

As with any imaginative process, none of what Morris does comes easily. Rather, the meticulous accuracy of Ted's paintings is the result of many hours dedicated to his academic research. In that process, the artist relies on numerous sources. Some days he visits sites where the native peoples once lived or congregated. He takes photographs there, while listening intently to the sounds of nature and to what the place might "present to" him. Or he picks up ideas from Spanish diaries or other books that chronicle the lives of Natives. One of his favorite books was one written by Dr. Robin Brown called *Florida's First People.*

On a given day, Morris might travel to a university, a museum, or a conference. He gets answers or clarification from spending time with scholars. Yet probably the most fascinating of all the sources are some of the other places he visits. At actual archeological dig sites, he is able to stay in very close communication with some of the leading Florida archeologists as he watches and sketches what mysterious tales the earth is willing to give up.

It is no surprise, then, that for his painstaking portrayals, Morris's body of work has been noticed and revered, and he has private collectors from North America and from Europe. In 1997 the Florida Anthropological Society selected Morris for esteemed recognition because his works had been chosen to be synthesized into a historically revealing Public Broadcasting Service video titled, *Shadows and Reflections: The Search for Florida's Lost People.* The movie, produced by Robin C. Brown Jr. and dedicated to the memory of B. Calvin Jones, can be found online or at the Archeology Channel website.

When I finally had the honor of talking with Ted in October of 2015, I had many questions for him, because back when I was nine years old, I found arrowheads and spearheads in "just plowed up" fields not too far from the neighborhood of Livingston Spring Acres. I would scurry home from walking the rows, putting each one in a Ked's shoebox; then I would get my Mother to "carry" me over to the local college. Back then, in the 1960s, Mr. Mark Cherry, who taught an anthropology course there, willingly shared the histories he knew about my found relics, and those stories he told gave me a lifelong interest in the first peoples of the region of these Red Hills.

As did Theodore Morris with his paintings. During our conversation, Ted revealed that he always had a desire to draw. He recollected, "Back as far as I can remember, I was always drawing. I had some very good art teachers." Those early teachers helped him nurture his already burgeoning creative spirit; but the artistic Muse was there from the beginning. I later asked him how he got interested in Florida Indians in the first place, and how that all tied in with his visits to archeological dig sites. He said, "When I first started researching Florida history, I joined the Time Sifters Archaeology Society. They organized area digs, and that's where I got to know George Luer. He is a respected archeologist and a man dedicated to preserving Florida history."

Back in 1995 Morris was asked by Luer to work on a poster which would help the Florida Anthropological Society. That moment in time was a very pivotal project that would ultimately usher Ted into a new artistic realm; a threshold that would bring to the public a fantastic visual medium of real history. In due course, the marvelous, authentic stories Morris would present on canvas would be ones never before told; for these accurate cultural notions of the lives of the ancient peoples of Florida were not previously known. Sadly, much of what most people knew up until that time was a much-biased depiction that came mostly from the diaries of the Spanish in their conquest of Florida. So it was actually the conqueror's voice that ultimately told and perpetuated the biased story.

But Luer and Morris would, in time, combine their efforts as they merged the science of archeology with the vision of the artist to create a Bird Man Dancer, and such a painting would be created to represent the Apalachee tribe. But when Morris first started researching the subject, he was quite dismayed that he was not able to get many facts or accurate images about the ancient tribes. He said, "Researching Bird Man was not easy because the history of Florida's first peoples has been either distorted or misrepresented for hundreds of years." That was when his research took a turn away from the books and images which he was finding in his local library, and he started directing his attention to the men with archeological expertise. This was also back in the days before ever-present electronic communication.

At that time, Ted had to request information from several archeologists, and through handwritten letters "going back and forth" with people like George Luer, Jerald Milanich, and Jeffery Mitchem, the artist finally was ready to paint a historically accurate Bird Man Dancer based on specific finds from dig sites. Hence, his first rendering of the Bird Man Dancer was conceptualized and crafted straight from the archeological record.

Morris elaborated on that "light bulb" moment by saying, "So one day I walked past the finished poster, and I wondered what the drawing might look like in full color. Later, when I finished the first color painting, it pleased me." To this day he claims, "It is still my favorite painting because it was the bridge to a whole new life." Since that time, Morris has chosen to paint portraits instead of tribal scenes because his vision as an artist has been to introduce these ancient Floridians on a personal level. He made it clear, "I wanted to make these people human—not idealize them or romanticize them."

Another question which I posed was: "As an artist, some philosophers say that you are obligated to bring a message to the greater society; describe what Truth is preserved by your paintings." Ted replied,

These people existed thousands of years before the Europeans came. They took care of the land; they had a good life. I decided to paint them as accurately as possible so their lives could be understood—and because their lifestyles were misrepresented for so long. While I can't undo history or right the wrongs that forced these Indians into extinction, I hope through my work I can breathe new life into their existence and honor their memory to set the record straight . . . for I often meet many lifelong residents of Florida, most of them have never heard of these early native peoples; all they know of are the Seminoles.

I then asked Morris, "If your depictions could speak, what might the 'voice' of your paintings be saying?" He said, "I would hope that the Natives might be grateful that I brought the memory of their lives back—that I did something good for them to show how they lived— how they died."

As our conversation was coming to a close, one of the last questions Ted answered had to do with how he would like to be remembered. I wanted to know how he wanted his own artistic legacy to be known in the future. He said, "I'd like to be remembered as Catlin was remembered." As an historical note, George Catlin was an important artist who lived from 1796 until 1872. He traveled west during the 1830s on a quest to paint the Plains Indians. As a kind of prophet, he was convinced that westward expansion was going to be the death and the absolute end of the Indian way of life. Today Catlin's Native American paintings are recognized as an important cultural treasure, offering rare understanding into native cultures and an essential chapter in American history.

By painting true scenes of fast-disappearing native life, Catlin was able to capture the essence of their humanity, just as Morris has also created "new" life for the Florida and Caribbean Indians. The only difference was that one artist painted the Natives before they died out. Another resurrected them from an ancient past.

It is certain then that Theodore Morris's art transcends time and space, taking modern people back to a far-distant past. His telling portraits of the Florida and Caribbean peoples allow each of us to reflect on that long ago familial and spiritual existence. The emotions of love, care, reverence, courage, innocence, and sadness he depicts tell a true human story about the lives of those first Natives living in what is today Florida. So from Theodore Morris's depictions, people might just be able to reach back in time to find a lasting human connection.

Additional Note: Morris's works have appeared in many traveling exhibits all over Florida. Those locations are: Fort Walton Beach, Tallahassee, Amelia Island, Jacksonville, Gainesville, Deland, Sanford, Casselberry, Kissimmee, Tampa, Safety Harbor, St. Petersburg, Bradenton, Sarasota, Venice, Osprey, Avon Park, Sebring, Fort Pierce, Stuart, Jupiter, West Palm Beach, Delray Beach, Naples, and Marco Island.

His studio was once located on Aviles Street in Saint Augustine, but now he is living and painting in Sarasota, Florida.[1]

Morris's works can be accessed online at these websites:

losttribesflorida.com

theodoremorris.weebly.com
tainopaintings.weebly.com

Theodore Morris is known as the preeminent painter of Florida's indigenous peoples, and his depictions show up on the front cover of many academic books. His portraits have also been appreciated by thousands of people visiting Florida museums and art galleries, and hundreds of thousands of people have seen his works online. Courtesy of Theodore Morris

In depicting the faces of the early native peoples, Morris somehow finds something of the ephemeral—what he needs as an artist—to capture the absolute essence and soul of his subjects. He also places particular artifacts in each painting; each one seems to tell a story all its own of an intriguing ethnographic past. Courtesy of Theodore Morris

The writer, Marjory Stoneman Douglas, describes what the artist has also been known to paint when she writes, "They carved and perforated bones, deer bone, and turtle bone and even human bone, perhaps the bones of a powerful enemy . . . those . . . things [they wore] on the oiled, shining copper bodies . . . those young hunters and warriors and fishermen, their black hair pinned up with pins and stuck with arrows. Their raccoon tails swished behind them. The dark eyes of girls must have watched them from the house shadows as the self-conscious young men went by . . . walking like dandies." Courtesy of Theodore Morris

Endnotes

1. Theodore Morris, telephone interview and follow-up visit to his studio on
    Aviles Street in Saint Augustine, Oct. and Nov. 2015.

Rose Knox and Graham Schorb

Travel Notes

Aucilla River and a Paleolithic Past

Ten thousand years ago may seem like a long time, but lying on the bone bed of Sloth Hole and feeling all those intact remains transported my thoughts right back. . . . Being able to touch and feel those bones in their natural resting place brought the extinct animals alive for me. Tapirs, horses, llamas . . . still roam the globe, although not in Florida for at least ten millennia. Mammoths, mastodons, ground sloths . . . saber-toothed cats, dire wolves, giant tortoises, and giant beavers are gone forever; and yet, I know they have been here.[1]

That is the description one diver recounts in his underwater explorations of the dark depths of the Aucilla, for all around him on the sediment bottom of that ancient place, Dr. Bruce Means encountered evidence that human beings had indeed been there, killing and feasting. The landscape 10,000 years ago once supported more than forty-five now-extinct mammals, and the later evolution of a river was to keep that story intact, for what is today the Aucilla River was once only sinkholes with catchment basins. These age-old places once provided watering holes for many a prehistoric creature.

The Aucilla River is today known as the "River of Many Faces," and much like the Suwannee River, the topographical scenes vary, depending on the section of river. The Aucilla has also been called a "black water stream" that flows through numerous and varied topographical places, beginning somewhere in a region between Thomasville and Merrillville, Georgia. From there the main current works its way through the eastern half of Thomas County, while it also meanders through several Florida counties. The many faces of the river can be seen in open prairies of grass or in dense forests of cypress trees. Sometimes the Aucilla seems to completely disappear, finding its way underground, once in Georgia and several places in Florida. Eventually the stream ends up at Nuttall Rise where it reappears on the surface, finally on its undulating path to the Gulf of Mexico.[2]

Since the river is a hop, skip, and a jump from my home, I like to paddle it from time to time. The first time Graham and I kayaked the river together in 2005, we were able to access it from Highway 90. The black stream was running pretty fast that day, after some hard, recent rains; I got to understand in a hurry what a fallen tree can do to a kayaker. In one second, under lush shade, I found my craft headed fast for the obstacle that was sticking up just above the swift water's surface. When I tried using mere human strength to push away from the thick limb, the kayak got hung up there and I was dumped out into the dangerous currents. It was then I found out just how fast even someone paying close attention can get into trouble in strong river currents.

Yet in 2005 I only knew a bit about the river's ancient past; someone once told me that scuba divers had been known to discover animal bones and worked tools there, revealing evidence of beasts and ancient peoples. For that reason the little river, not far from my childhood home, had always held intrigue. As early as the 1920s, archeological interest surrounded the Aucilla. But it was not until 1983 that the Aucilla River Prehistory Project was launched by the Florida Museum of Natural History in Gainesville and funded by grants. The specialists in charge were Dr. S. David Webb and Dr. Jerald T. Milanich.

Dr. Webb, a paleontologist, was quite enamored with the River of Many Faces. As an expert in his field of study, he was aware of how ancient Indians were known to seek out water sources, such as indentations in limestone outcroppings and in deep springs. In these places the hunters would proceed to dismember their kill, a giant sloth perhaps, or a mastodon. Consumption of the downed beasts would come soon afterward.[3]

Dr. Webb began exploring the Aucilla in his official underwater investigations, and as a result of his explorations, many discoveries were ultimately made. What he and his crew found there in the 1980s under dark, watery depths revealed specific details about an ancient race of people and how they at one time lived near the Aucilla and within its basin. After ten years of meticulous archaeological research that required specialized diving and excavating equipment, countless clues to the plant and animal existence of the last Ice Age were brought to life. They discovered clumps of matted debris; that material turned out to actually be the digested food once eaten by an Ice Age beast, the mastodon! In that same Aucilla River exploration, one fully intact ivory tusk from the giant creature was also pulled up from dark depths. Dr. Webb commented on such an incredible find, saying:

The biggest thrill came one day in thirty feet of water with a thousand-watt light trained on our work site. Suddenly a small clink from my trowel and a brilliant orange gleam from the mud showed us a beautifully preserved tusk. A day later we had fully exposed a mastodon tusk more than seven feet long with cut marks where it had been removed from the skull . . . we [then] had evidence of the Aucilla Paleo-Indians butchering a mastodon.[4]

Regarding much earlier finds in a farm field in New York, the French scientist, Georges Curvier, after being given the chance to examine mastodon bones and teeth sent to him from an excavation that took place in 1801, was fascinated with the shape of the large teeth. Looking closely at the structure and shape of the teeth of this mysterious creature, the domelike projections made him think of a woman's breasts. He named it "mastodon" from the Greek words for breast and teeth.[5]

Yet human beings have been discovering mammoth and mastodon bones for thousands of years in places like Siberia. People have wondered, too, what these strange, massive skeletal remains really were. Lore and legend become part of humanity's way of explaining the giant bones. In fact, the ancient Greeks believed that giant men once inhabited the earth and that such immense bones were sure proof! The people of the Arctic regions told stories of mighty, evil moles that would die if they came in contact with sunlight.

Even President Thomas Jefferson had an opinion about it. Since he was a friend of a man named Charles Peale, who funded one of the first digs to exhume the mastodon from the farm field in New York, Jefferson mused that the skeleton must be some rare elephant that was still living in the deep forests of America. Around 1806 the American mastodon became the first animal to ever be proclaimed an extinct species. Before that time, people actually believed the living creatures existing on earth never changed. Therefore the discovery of mastodon bones in the early 1800s helped fuel all kinds of heated debate regarding the geological age of the earth, which also sparked many spiritual questions concerning the age of mankind.[6]

To be certain, such huge mammals were quite plentiful during the Pleistocene Age. Not only elephant-like mastodons, but armadillo-like glyptodonts roamed around in what is today North America, along with the giant ground sloth standing 6 meters tall and weighing 2,200 pounds which inhabited both North and South America. There were other huge creatures like the saber-toothed tiger; despite the name it was not a member of the tiger subfamily at all. Rather, the smilodon, as it has come to be called, had an extremely muscular and heavily built body type. In some ways the body structure resembled a bear, with powerful forelimbs used for downing prey. The beast could weigh up to 880 pounds. Skeletal remains of such Pleistocene creatures are often found in Florida springs and rivers.[7]

During the exploration of the river, it was not too surprising for the divers to also find the bones of other species of the same ancient Paleolithic past. Other kinds of bones that were pulled from the river were those of the saber-tooth cat, the camel, the jaguar, the giant sloth, and the tiny, prehistoric horse. Dr. Webb once commented, "The pond where the Paleo-Indian lived had also become the death scene of a herd of mastodons. We had uncovered evidence that the great beasts had gorged on gourds and browsed on at least a dozen kinds of trees. But later, when they went to wash it all down with a drink, many of them had been ambushed. The piece of chert (which the crew had previously discovered there) was a skinning knife, lost on the same occasion."[8]

Visitors going to the Florida Museum of Natural history in Gainesville can see the displays of many reconstructed skeletons of beasts of the Paleolithic period. A museum in Tallahassee also offers the same kind of historical record. Imagine being greeted by a magnificent beast resurrected from the Aucilla. That is what visitors to area museums will see.

The Aucilla River is also a place that has gotten international attention in recent years. The Page-Ladson site, known for those very significant underwater archaeological finds mentioned above, and which is chronicled in the *Shadows and Reflections: Florida's Lost People* film produced decades ago by the Florida Heritage Council, is still a place where archaeologists are finding ever more stories in the artifact record, telling a new story of mankind's ancient past. In fact, the site may add to the growing evidence that human beings inhabited North America much earlier than historians, paleontologists, and archeologists ever once imagined.

To illustrate, in one article entitled "Big Digs: The Year 2016 in Archeology," published online by the BBC, Dr. Louise Iles of the University of Sheffield, England, reveals the Aucilla River finds are some of the most significant archaeological discoveries of 2016. The artifacts show that tools dating back to 14,550 years ago are making experts rethink the timeline of human occupation in North America.

Another article posted on the same BBC website titled, "Crossing Continents" reveals the magnitude of the finds regarding these long-held ideas of man's presence, stating "Traditionally, hunter-gatherers are thought to have crossed the Bering land bridge into the Americas from northeast Asia no earlier than 13,000 years ago, quickly hunting local populations of mega fauna [like the giant sloth and the mastodon— Knox's addition] to extinction. . . . The Page-Ladson site pushes back that date by more than a thousand years."[9]

So if you ever find the time to venture out on the beautiful Aucilla River, a challenging, technical paddle, to try a little exploring or to do some fishing, think about the prehistoric peoples and animals that once roamed the region and how artifacts found there may help in rewriting mankind's history in North America.

The image portrays a photograph shot in 1966 of Benjamin Waller with mastodon teeth taken from the Aucilla River. Waller was a pioneer diver in Florida. He taught Lloyd Bridges how to dive and was his stand-in double for the footage of "Sea Hunt."

Regarding much earlier finds in a farm field in New York, the French scientist, Georges Curvier, after being given the chance to examine mastodon bones and teeth sent to him from an excavation that took place in 1801, was fascinated with the shape of the large teeth. Looking closely at the structure and shape of the teeth of this mysterious creature, the domelike projections made him think of a woman's breasts. He named it "mastodon" from the Greek words for "breast" and "teeth." Photograph by Don Serbousek of Ormond Beach, Courtesy of State Library and Archives of Florida

A giant ground sloth fossil was once on display at the Museum of Arts and Sciences in Daytona Beach, Florida. This impressive 13-foot tall skeleton of the Eremotherium laurilardi, or giant ground sloth, was excavated in 1975, in an important Pleistocene fossil site called the Daytona Bone Bed. Though not found in the Red Hills, ones like it have been found in the area of the Red Hills. "Mammoths, mastodons, ground sloths . . . saber-toothed cats, dire wolves, giant tortoises, and giant beavers are gone forever; and yet, I know they have been here." Divers like Dr. Bruce Means have brought up bones of these ancient species. Courtesy of State Library and Archives of Florida

Rose Knox and Graham Schorb

Endnotes

1. David S. Webb, "Aucilla River: Time Machine," in *Between Two Rivers: Stories from the Red Hills to the Gulf*," Susan Cerulean, Janisse Ray, and Laura Newton, eds. (Tallahassee, FL: Red Hills Writers Project, 2004).

2. R. C. Balfour III, *In Search of the Aucilla* (Valdosta, GA: Colson Printing, 2002).

3. Jerald T. Milanich and Theodore Morris, *Florida's Lost Tribes* (Gainesville: University Press of Florida, 2004).

4. Balfour, *In Search of the Aucilla.*

5. James Cross Giblin, *The Mystery of the Mammoth Bones* (New York: Harper-Collins, 1999).

6. Cheryl Bardoe, *Mammoths and Mastodons: Titans of the Ice Age* (New York: Abrams Books for Young Readers, in association with the Field Museum, Chicago, 2010).

7. Gavira Guerro and Peter Frances, senior eds., *Prehistoric Life: The Definitive Visual History of Life on Earth* (Great Britain: Darling Kindersley, 2009).

8. Webb, "Aucilla River: Time Machine."

9. Lazaro Aleman, *Monticello News* and *Jefferson County Journal*, ECB Publishing, January 10, 2017.

Lake Miccosukee: Oral Legend

I often wonder when I gaze across the many serene spring-fed ponds and lakes of the region, what stories the shorelines might tell if only they could talk. Like the tale recorded about the old church bell found in a Madison County lake, another body of water known as Lake Miccosukee has its own fascinating history.

Though the old tale cannot be fully confirmed because it was an oral account that has been passed down through time, it goes like this: There was a former slave named Old Daddy Parrish, and he had a son, Charles. Charles, an ex-slave, was known to spread this particular happening to many of his white friends. Supposedly, when General Andrew Jackson was warring against the natives in his efforts to remove them and send them to various reservations, the general had to journey across Lake Miccosukee, located not far from the town of Monticello.

During his travels, however, he was tricked by a carefully planned Indian strategy as he attempted a false ford the Seminoles had intentionally set up. He and his men soon found themselves bogged down, slowed by the mud. It was then the Natives attacked; Jackson was somehow capable of getting away from the danger, but not without great loss of some of his military equipment, according to the legend. Two of General Jackson's brass cannons remained bogged down in the lake.

According to one writer ". . . several of the present generation living in Monticello claim to have seen the cannon . . . when the waters of the lake stood at [an] extremely low level." To make the story even more intriguing, a big rock was allegedly also found near this same location, and on it the letters A and J were distinctly etched, perhaps by the very hand of one General Andrew Jackson himself![1]

According to local legend, when General Andrew Jackson was warring against the Natives in his efforts to remove them and send them to various reservations, the general had to journey across Lake Miccosukee, located not far from the town of Monticello. The portrait depicts Andrew Jackson, Governor of the Territories of East and West Florida. Courtesy of State Library and Archives of Florida

Endnotes

1. Mary Oakley McRory and Edith Clarke Barrows, *History of Jefferson County, Florida,* published under the auspices of the Kiwanis Club, Monticello, Florida, 1958.

Rose Knox and Graham Schorb

Travel Notes

Jefferson County: Seminole Conflicts

". . . to be limited to a portion of their own territory over which they had fished and hunted . . . was . . . unbearable and especially so to these Indians whose natures were wild and free with restrictions unknown to them."[1]

As more settlers began establishing their homesteads and plantations in the area, their presence caused extreme resentment by the Seminole Indian population. Ideas from a book titled *The History of Jefferson County, Florida* can sum up the logical reasons for the Seminole people's hatred of the incoming pioneers between 1836 and 1842, the period of the Seminole Wars in Florida. The authors of that work state, ". . . they were not satisfied with reservation life. For a people who had led a free, roving existence through the beautiful, fertile lands of Jefferson and other counties, to be limited to a portion of their own territory over which they had fished and hunted . . . was to say the least, unbearable and especially so to these Indians whose natures were wild and free with restrictions unknown to them."[2]

And much like the terror that had struck the Baker family of Madison County near the banks of the Aucilla River, the early homesteaders of Jefferson County were to realize the same sort of tragic fate. Some of the first pioneers of Jefferson County wanted to establish their homes in the area between what are presently the communities of Waukeenah and Lloyd. However, those specific locations of pioneer sites have been lost to time, because no homes were ever built there. Violent attacks by Indians were the reason no settlement was ever established, and exactly where the following episode took place is in question.

Several memorable episodes transpired, and the following stories only chronicle a few of these noteworthy conflicts. Reverend D. Purifoy's family was to become the victims of one of the first attacks by Natives on early settlers. As the story has been handed down, the Reverend was away from his home "filling an appointment" when a group of hostile Natives came upon his house. When he returned, a vision of horror greeted him. He saw his home burned and his two children dead; they had not survived the fire. Other dead bodies were scattered about the property. One local source reveals ". . . negroes were lying about the yard." His wife had somehow miraculously survived the brutal attack but she suffered from gunshot and tomahawk wounds. She only partially recovered from her physical injuries and was eventually transported back to Edgefield, South Carolina, her former home. Her name was Louise Byrd before she married the Reverend, and she was the daughter of Daniel Byrd.[3]

Other attacks have been recorded. In fact, one of the first pioneers of Jefferson County to die at the hands of the Seminoles was a plantation overseer who worked for William D. Mosely, a planter. Mr. Blackburn came across a group of Indians who were in the process of destroying a field of corn. He was angry and started to chastise them. What Mr. Blackburn did not realize was that he was actually interfering with an ancient practice traditionally conducted by the Seminoles, called the Green Corn Dance. The festival is an annual celebration of giving thanks. Upset at Mr. Blackburn's intrusion upon their sacred ceremony, they killed and scalped him.

Yet another tale recorded in the history books of Jefferson County includes the attack that transpired at a place called Turkey Scratch. It involved the John Slaughter family. Mr. Slaughter was a planter living on his plantation who had left to take care of a legal matter in Monticello. His wife and children had been left on the plantation in his absence, and while Mr. Slaughter was away, natives robbed then burned the home. His wife and children were able to escape, only because they had been aware of the approaching Indians. Fleeing the property, they made a way to a neighbor's home and were quite lucky to survive, unlike yet another attack, this time on the John Gray place. It was located in the vicinity of Elizabeth Church. All members inside the house were killed. One poetic legend follows this particular sad episode, and as the story goes, in the yard where Mr. Gray fell to his death, a rose bush sprouted, producing gorgeous red roses.[4]

That story reminded me of the southern poet, Archibald Rutledge's, words from his poem, "The Garden I Made."

". . . the red rose, the lily as white as a swan;
The garden I made will keep blossoming on,
When life with its fevers is faded and gone." Rutledge (1883-1973)

Endnotes

1. Mary Oakley McRory and Edith Clarke Barrows, *History of Jefferson County, Florida,* Published under the auspices of the Kiwanis Club, Monticello, Florida, 1958.

2. McRory and Barrows, *History of Jefferson County.*

3. McRory and Barrows, *History of Jefferson County.*

4. McRory and Barrows, *History of Jefferson County.*

Rose Knox and Graham Schorb

Travel Notes

The Legend of a Volcano

"The South's only volcano is said to have existed in north Florida from pre-historic and earliest Spanish times, down through the centuries; first Indians then whites observed a never-ceasing, towering pillar of smoke and flame billowing upwards from the dense swamps. . . . No one could approach nearer than 6 or 8 miles, the mud being too wet for walking, too thick for a boat, and the jungle-like growth impenetrable. In 1886 the mystery 'volcano' disappeared—still unexplained."[1] Such were the words of Walter Overton in his sensational description of the strange, billowing phenomenon.

Myths, legends, and rivers go hand in hand. Somewhere not far from the Red Hills, some say in Jefferson County, others claim in Wakulla County, the echo of one legend about "Florida's Lost Volcano" still reverberates over the swampy bogs of one of Florida's rivers. Many voices of the past claim the validity of the volcano's existence, starting with Indian lore.

But it was back in the 1830s that people once again began commenting on the smoke. Naysayers attributed the plume of smoke to a settlement of runaway slaves, while some doubters said the smoke billowed from campfires set by Native Americans. Still others placed the blame on moonshine whisky runners who were prone to set up their stills in the backwoods of Florida's scrub. Journalists were to also write of the strange phenomenon of a volcano in Florida, which most geologists will testify is quite geologically impossible.

In 1882 one magazine called it the "Wakulla Volcano." After that piece ran, the legend of its possible existence again spurred adventurous souls to go out into the dangerous wilds of Florida to find it. One of the first people to venture out into a snake-infested, mosquito-laden domain in search of the volcano after that particular news story ran was a reporter. It was in the 1870s that a New York *Herald Tribune* news correspondent was apparently sent out to discover the enigma behind the talk of smoke and of a volcano existing in Florida near the Red Hills region. Employing guides, the entourage ventured out where they met with many daunting obstacles like impenetrable bogs, thorns, mosquitoes, saw grass, and cottonmouth moccasins. The explanation of the legend of the volcano would not surface with that exploration, however, because the party of explorers eventually was forced to turn back. Before they could make it out to civilization, the news reporter became very sick and died.

Tales of such a dreadful happening, though, would not keep other thrill-seekers from trying their own luck. To further illustrate the interest in the alleged volcano's existence, in 1891 J. H. Staley and C. L. Norton went to find it, but they had to turn back, with Norton later saying that he came very close to death while out there. Not to be deterred, however, Staley's determination drove him on as he tried again that same year, taking with him two more men. But the bogs— some have called it the Wacissa Swamp—and wilderness would defeat him once again.

Later still, in the 1920s, James Kirkland, a forester, and A. L. Porter, a Wakulla County judge, said that they discovered a gigantic crater while out hunting for deer in an area in Jefferson County called Gum Swamp, not far from the Pinhook River. According to a letter he submitted in September 1956 to the *Tallahassee Democrat*, Porter claimed he had climbed up a rocky slope and found a crater. He described the crater as "the size of a dishpan." And the bottom seemed too dark and too deep to comprehend. But neither Porter nor Kirkland ever made it back to that spot for, according to Porter, the place had grown over with thick vegetation and was filled with wiregrass and jack pines, making it too difficult to get back in.

The undiscovered mystery was to continue to hold intrigue for yet two more men who were following previously recorded directions documented by a Chicago reporter. Apparently, this newspaperman had come very close to finding the source of the smoke but exhaustion had set in, so he had forced himself to turn back. In 1932 these two men, one named Fred Wimpee, a Jacksonville businessman, and a Mr. William Wyatt, a Tallahassee office-supply businessman, went out there. Before their trip, they talked about the volcano with two interested professors from Florida State University and also communicated with the state librarian. In 1964 Wyatt said of those contacts, ". . . if they had known the danger we faced, they would not have encouraged us to go."

Wyatt recounted that they forged onward, first in a Model T. Ford. They had packed a few sandwiches and their supplies included a flashlight, a hand-ax, and a machete. They eventually left the vehicle and started making a way on foot, until they came across an old, abandoned sawmill. The mill was situated about thirty miles southeast of Tallahassee. After a difficult trek toward the swamp, chopping their way through thick scrub, they later reported encountering a strange phenomenon. They claimed to have seen humongous rocks, some as massive as a house. Wyatt said of the huge boulders that they were so large that the sight ". . . appeared to be a stone wall." Wyatt also claimed the huge rock piles appeared to have been "blown out" of the ground. To this day, the mystery of the billowing smoke and of the very existence of a volcano is still unsolved.[2]

Rose Knox and Graham Schorb

Endnotes

1. Kathleen Lanfenberg, "The Quest for Florida's Lost Volcano," in *Between Two Rivers: Stories from the Red Hills to the Gulf,* Susan Cerulean, Janisse Ray, and Laura Newton, eds. (Tallahassee, FL: Red Hills Writers Project, 2004).

2. Laufenberg, "Quest for Florida's Volcano."

A "Peculiar Institution": Antebellum Life of the Red Hills

"The early settlers brought with them the economic and social ideas and institutions to which they were accustomed in the older states. Most of them came from areas where plantation agriculture supported by legal racial slavery was the dominant economic pursuit. [In the "new world"] slavery was about 150 years old by the time these settlers began arriving in Florida, and its legal basis and the ideological assumptions which supported it were well-established."[1]

Cotton was king. That is surely a fact. The plantation way of life dominated the goings-on of the region, as census records of the 1840s, 1850s, and 1860s show that sixty percent of all Florida slaves lived in the five-county area of Middle Florida known as the Red Hills. Those counties previously mentioned are, again, Madison, Jefferson, Gadsden, Leon, and Jackson. It should be noted that Hamilton County has commonly been included as part of the Middle Florida, "black belt" region because it lies west of the Suwannee River, but Hamilton's plantation society did not equal that of the other five counties. Early on, planters who owned more than five hundred acres were relatively few in number, but they dominated the slaveholder class. For instance, they comprised just 13.8 percent of the population by the year 1830; but about thirty years later their numbers had burgeoned to 21 percent, with 397 planters owning more than twenty slaves. Later still, at the start of the Civil War, the great majority of Middle Florida's plantation owners recorded having between twenty and forty-nine slaves. At the dawn of the war, those "smaller" planters made up 73 percent of the planter class.[2]

Since a good number of South Carolina planters came to Middle Florida with their African slaves, it is important to have an historical perspective, some brief history, on how the African ultimately made it to Charleston. In his book, *Slaves in the Family,* Edward Ball writes,

Africans came steadily into port. The black traffic was controlled from England. In 1672, the London-based Royal African Company secured from King Charles II a monopoly on the black slave trade into British colonies. The company sent most of its ships to a long stretch of the West African coast between the mouth of the Gambia River and the eastern edge of the Gulf of Guinea. From depots, so called slave factories, the ships brought their cargo to Barbados, Jamaica, the Bahamas, and other Caribbean islands. Until the end of the 1600s nearly all of the blacks the Carolina whites enslaved were brought from Barbados."[3]

Louis B. Wright also gives insight into the history of South Carolina and slavery when he writes, ". . . growth of a plantation economy based on the cultivation of rice in the Low Country had created an increasing demand for laborers, and South Carolina quickly became the largest mainland importer of African slaves."[4] Yet the institution of slavery was not of English origin. Such a kidnap-and-sale system with restrictions on personal movement, which was perpetuated against foreign people for the purpose of forced labor, was very, very old. Edward Ball further illustrates, "By the time the Carolina colony was founded . . . slavery was already thousands of years old." The institution of slavery had flourished among many societies and affected numerous peoples. Some were Jews, Greeks, Romans, black Africans, and ancient Germans, and slavery had existed also throughout the Holy Roman Empire, especially around the Mediterranean. Even the word "slave" comes from "slav." The Slavs were victims of European slavery for a long time.[5]

In the Red Hills during the antebellum period, the incoming people of African heritage were held against their will as slaves; they were not allowed to leave the plantation unless they carried with them written permission from either their owner or the plantation overseer. However, such a code was not always strictly enforced.

A great deal has been recorded about how the enslaved population ended up in Middle Florida and about the inhumane slave auctions at New Orleans, and of those slave traders who transported Africans from that location and brought them into the north Florida region with intent to sell them there. Though some blacks did indeed come from New Orleans auctions, the greater majority of them arrived in Middle Florida from the same places from which the pioneers had come. Black slaves consequently made up the majority of Jefferson County's population by 1860; they had been brought from other plantations to the Red Hills from many states, including Virginia, Maryland, Georgia, and North and South Carolina.

One good example of the record of settlers bringing in their slaves to the region comes from the Waukeenah area. Both John and Robert Gamble from Virginia emigrated in wagons to Middle Florida with their original slave forces. Finally entering the state of Florida, the Gambles' slave population began razing forests, clearing the land for future agriculture, and constructing cabins. Jerrell H. Shofner, in his research of the records from the Superior Court of Jefferson County, reveals that tremendous thought went into keeping slave families intact in the buying and the selling process.[6]

There was much to be accomplished in order to begin and to maintain a plantation. The African people are only now being credited with the arduous labor and fine craftsmanship which they contributed in their enslaved situation. The system of their toil was stratified. How labor on each plantation was divided differed depending on the personal operational methods of the master and the size of the plantation. However, there were some practices that were commonly observed on most plantations in Jefferson County.

For instance, it was a common idea that it took thirty workers or more to produce a profitable crop. Of course, the more affluent planters always used a bigger work force; but with at least thirty slaves, an overseer was seen as a necessity. One individual was also hired by the master to serve in the role of a "driver." He was in charge of the field hands, who were often separated into groups or "gangs." These field slaves in such groupings would be sent out to conduct a specific labor assignment. How people were chosen for particular tasks depended on the physical capabilities of each individual.

To illustrate, there was the group of slaves called the "hoe gang." They were made up of women, children old enough to work, and older men–those not physically strong enough to perform heavy, laborious tasks. They were responsible for hoeing the ground for planting–until agricultural equipment was eventually invented. They likewise tended the fields, extracting weeds from the rows where the cash crop plants were growing. Other slaves were selected to clean the Sea Island cotton and often they were part of the same hoe gangs. Some planters later used mechanized roller gins to do the job of cleaning the cotton.[7]

Another gang went by the name of the "strong force," and it was comprised of young, strong males who were responsible for tilling the rich soil. This strong force also razed forests, readying the acreage for eventual planting. They cut trees to be used specifically for materials to build homes. Roads, fences, and blockhouses likewise had to be made and then maintained by them. During the Seminole conflicts, for example, it has been documented that Colonel Achille Murat utilized about a hundred slaves to construct various blockhouses. Some slaves were even trusted to serve as sentinels, guarding such safe havens for the protection of the settlers, and these slaves were provided with loaded weapons.

As for what the laborers ate, slaves in Jefferson County were provided sweet potatoes, corn, and pork. A few masters allowed slaves to plant personal gardens, which also produced food. Robert Gamble was known for this practice, and his hoe gang tended those slave gardens along with their other regular labors. Besides cotton and some sugarcane, large and small planters alike often grew turnip or mustard greens, okra, sweet potatoes, and squash, among a variety of other crops. Attention was given to farmyard animals, according to Margrett Nickerson, a former slave. She once said, "Dere wuz . . . cotton, co'n, tate fields to be tended . . . and cowhides to be tanned, thread to be spinned."[8]

In times of surplus, milk and butter were provided to field hand slaves, but this practice was very rare. Children, however, were allowed to drink milk. Cows were a part of almost every plantation in the area— the animals looked after by a female slave. Fish out of area waterways was moreover an important provision for the slave of Jefferson County.

On many of the larger operations lived various kinds of skilled laborers, and they were worth more than common field hands. Any working plantation had need for skilled labor, so such slave labor provided the tasks of doing bricklaying, carpentry, and blacksmithing, among other skills. Such a trained person was worth $1,500 or more, compared to a field hand who went for an average price of $500. Other semi-skilled slaves knew how to run screw-press operations, or they had special knowledge of the workings of a saw or grist mill process. Some of the more expert workers might be summoned to other plantations, their skills hired out by the slaves' owner.

In clothing each slave there were several methods used, because clothing was a costly item and was provided by the plantation owner. Sometimes the clothes were manufactured on the plantation, and something called "rough cloth" was used for slave clothing. A few plantations were set up for the making of shoes. William J. Bailey of

Lyndhurst had a tannery, and animal hides were made into leather there.[9]

In Monticello the Bailey Cotton Mill, known as the Jefferson Manufacturing Company, produced much-needed cloth for the area. The Bailey mill served to meet demands for cloth on other antebellum plantations, but when the Civil War broke out, the mill was used to produce much-in-demand cloth for the Confederacy. Production was accomplished in the following manner: "The mill, driven by a wood-burning thirty-five horsepower steam engine, was designed to manufacture both yard and cloth. Equipped with fifteen hundred spindles and fifty looms, the Bailey Mill could manufacture 400,000 pounds of cotton into 600,000 yards of Osnaburg [a kind of fabric] and 100,000 yards of yarn annually."[10]

Another planter, John Finlayson, owned looms where cloth was made. The work to create all of these items was performed by slaves. And at Casa Bianca there were looms and a shoe cobbler. The pregnant slaves who were "lying in" were put to the task of making clothing, as were some house servants and "retired" elderly women.[11] In nearby Madison County there was a shoe factory located ten miles west of the town of Madison. With the labor of twenty-six slaves, eleven thousand pairs of shoes were produced each year. Those shoes were sold within the state, and the high-quality leather products produced there also provided necessities for other area plantations.[12]

According to John E. Johns, in his work *Florida During the Civil War*, "While the plantation slavery regime supplied the paramount influence in all aspects of life in antebellum Florida, the overwhelming majority of the white population of the state did not own a single slave; of 77,747 whites only 5,152 were slave owners.[13]

It is also interesting to note that some planters of the region were trying their hand at other crops, such as sugarcane. Those agricultural experiments required the hard labor of many slaves, and according to Larry Eugene Rivers in his work, *Slaves in Florida*, brought on ". . . the harshest slave-labor conditions." These instances of trying to cultivate sugarcane took place in Madison, Jefferson, and Leon Counties. For example, William Bailey, William B. Nuttall, and John and Robert Gamble were known for harvesting big cane crops, but because of the climate, frost often destroyed these crops; consequently, after the mid-1830s sugarcane never emerged as a vital cash crop. As for the planting time for cotton, the season began about March or April. The slaves would plant the seeds and cover them over by hand using a harrow.

Later, in May throughout August, slaves tended the young plants using shallow plows or sweeps. From August until January the cotton was picked, ginned, processed and transported to market.

A slave's day started early. In Jefferson County, on the Kidder Meade Moore plantation, a bugler and wagoner stood outside his cabin at sunrise, waking the slaves with the sound of his horn. On another plantation, Achille Murat made sure his slaves were already in the fields most days at daybreak. One plantation owner once recorded "Slave workdays began before dawn. The sound of a bell, a horn, or conch summoned the slaves to the fields." They would take breakfast and lunch with them, but supper was had in their slave cabins.[14]

Generally speaking, tending to the big tracts of land on an antebellum plantation therefore required work from men and women alike. The assumption that men performed the most laborious tasks, which included razing trees, digging out ditches, and tilling the soil, was not always the case; rather, some slaveholders treated female slaves like they treated the men when it came to the division of labor. According to Deborah Gray in her work, *Arn't I a Woman?*, female slaves on the plantation ". . . often treated black women like men." In many cases ". . . there is no question that slave women worked as hard as their male counterparts."

Such a scenario played itself out in Middle Florida. Not only did women perform the heavy tasks like plowing, digging ditches, and cutting down trees, but they were also responsible for other duties, like sowing the cotton seed and corn and working as hoe gang hands, as previously mentioned. They, too, were known to drive the horses, pulling harrows to bury the seeds. To further illustrate how labor was sometimes established, records kept by local plantations of the region sometimes named their female slaves. Those documents reveal that females in Jefferson County at El Destino plantation had several divisions of labor; for instance, Kate labored on the plow gang, while Harriet, Penny, Betsy, Mary, and Maria worked the hoe gang. On William Wirt's estate, women were responsible for hoeing weeds and keeping grass from smothering the young cotton plants, while the men and boys on that plantation tilled the soil.

As for the children, they started work at an early age. Documentation from that period notes that young children were in charge of tending to livestock, running errands, picking up firewood, and knocking down dead cotton stalks. One record at Wirtland shows "Caroline, a little negro" waited on tables, and she also worked as a chambermaid.

Many compelling narratives were once compiled of the life of slaves. One good source is the book, *My Folks Don't Want Me to Talk about Slavery: Twenty-One Oral Histories of Former North Carolina Slaves*, edited by Belinda Hurmence. She writes of her book,

> In the midst of the Great Depression, Federal Writers' Project assigned field workers to interview ex-slaves who could be located. More than 2,000 former slaves contributed their personal accounts and opinions, and their oral histories were deposited in the Library of Congress . . . These first person accounts . . . paint an authentic and remarkably eloquent picture of what slavery meant to countless black Americans. The narratives illuminate views that former slaves held about daily life on the plantation, about good 'marsters' and bad, about the Civil War, and about Reconstruction. Most importantly, they speak poignantly of human bondage in the 'land of the free.'"[15]

Larry Eugene Rivers, in his work *Slavery in Florida: Territorial Days to Emancipation*, also presents a much more definitive history of the daily life of slaves, including a detailed look at the slave experience in Middle Florida. Rivers examines, in his in-depth study of the antebellum past, the dynamics of the family unit, how spiritual beliefs played a part in the lives of the enslaved, and the resistance of slaves, as well as the social interactions with the planter society and with the Indian races.[16] Anyone interested in a specific look at plantation life in the Red Hills should read Rivers's comprehensive historical chronicle, which includes some compelling archival photographs of the period.

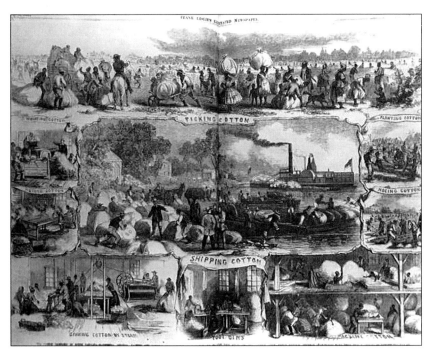

There was much to be accomplished in order to begin and to maintain a plantation. The African people are only now being credited with the arduous labor and fine craftsmanship which they contributed in their enslaved situation. They were instrumenntal in the creation and maintenance of the plantation , including planting and harvesting of cotton. The Red Hills of Florida's agricultural financial accounts chronicle the first introduction of a different kind of cotton. "Sea Island [variety cotton] had begun by the 1840s to take over the pinelands of inland southeastern Georgia as well as some counties in northeastern Florida." It was prolific, growing east of the 242-mile Suwanee River. Sea Island cotton burgeoned into the crop of choice because of the price that plantation owners could fetch for it at market. That price was twice the profit for that of the "Upland Short Staple" cotton variety. Courtesy of the State Library and Archives of Florida

Ellen Thopson was an enslaved person in Jefferson County, Florida. The photograph was taken sometime in the 1880s. Thompson worked for the Margaret Murry May family. Courtesy of the State Library and Archives of Florida

Rose Knox and Graham Schorb

Endnotes

1. Jerrell H. Shofner, *History of Jefferson County* (Tallahassee, FL: Sentry Press, 1976).

2. Larry Eugene Rivers, *Slavery in Florida: Territorial Days to Emancipation* (Gainesville: University Press of Florida, 2000).

3. Edward Ball, *Slaves in the Family* (New York: Ballantine Books, 1998).

4. Louis B. Wright, *South Carolina: A History* (New York: W.W. Norton, 1976).

5. Ball, *Slaves in the Family.*

6. Shofner, *History of Jefferson County.*

7. Shofner, *History of Jefferson County.*

8. Rivers, *Slavery in Florida.*

9. Rivers, *Slavery in Florida.*

10. John E. Johns, *Florida During the Civil War* (Gainesville: University of Florida Press, 1963).

11. Shofner, *History of Jefferson County.*

12. Ball, *Slaves in the Family.*

13. Ball, *Slaves in the Family.*

14. Rivers, *Slavery in Florida.*

15. Belinda Hurmence, ed., *My Folks Don't Want Me to Talk About Slavery: Twenty-One Oral Histories of Former North Carolina Slaves* (Winston-Salem, NC: John F. Blair, 1984).

16. Rivers, *Slavery in Florida.*

Landed Gentry: How the Elite Lived

Many of the big plantation owners of Jefferson County were involved in politics and law, and they lived lives much like the European aristocrats. In fact, their families were known to travel to Europe, and when they were not traveling abroad, they spent time in Tallahassee and in Washington, D.C., in order to tend to the political matters of the day. Some of them left the management and responsibility of the plantation to overseers.

When at home in their mansions, like European aristocrats they took part in entertaining activities. Some of the popular pastimes of this elite class were recorded, passed down first in the oral tradition; some of the stories [according to local authors' accounts] of their lives also survived in depictions in paintings, showing memorable scenes of the Old South in romanticized reminiscences of times gone by.

One form of entertainment was the grand ball. The extravagant event would bring people together in a festive atmosphere, and women and men would sport their most formal attire for such an important social occasion. At the ball, they danced in a refined fashion. Imagine, if you can, how these members of the Southern landed gentry once glided across polished heart pine or marble floors to the music, the ladies dressed in their flowing, elegant gowns and the men in their handsome fitted suits. The waltzing they did was courtly as they enjoyed musical tunes like the "Auf Wiedersehen" and the "Blue Danube." When they were not waltzing, they delighted in other dances like the polka, galop, schottische, and varsovienne.

These Southern aristocrats also took part in a modified version of the masquerade balls of the wealthy Europeans of the past. They disguised themselves, not with elaborate masks, but by covering their faces with pillowcases and waltzing the night away with various unknown partners. At the striking of the clock at midnight, the participants would abruptly identify themselves. These revelations often brought laughter at the realization of the pairing of certain individuals. Shades of European entertainment that extended back to the Middle Ages likewise manifested themselves in contests held by the men. One such amusement, a game of skill and athleticism, was called the "Fantastic Tournament." It resembled a medieval jousting or tilting contest.

At these elaborate social affairs, a young woman, "The Queen of Love," would be selected by the winner, a young man dressed in "black or fanciful" tights. He would mount his horse and with a wooden lance attempt, at full gallop, to drive through, using the tip of his lance to target rings that had been set up and were dangling from posts. Such tournaments were held on Jefferson Street in Monticello.

Great feasts of delectable dishes would be served after such thrilling contests. Try to picture the festival atmosphere of a jovial community of nobles gathering, with tables loaded down with many kinds of foods: platters piled high with fried chicken or with roasts and turkeys. The presentation of the food was indeed a grand affair, too. To illustrate, roasted pigs were sometimes displayed upon china platters, a red apple filling the mouth of the beast. That tradition extends all the way back to the early Middle Ages. Desserts, too, were presented with the most inventive, fine touches. The icing on huge layer cakes, for example, revealed details of the artist's touch in decorative magnolia blossoms, scrolls, leaves, and other intricate, feathery renderings.[1]

Large-scale Planters of Jefferson County

William Bailey (The Cedars)

William J. Bailey (Lyndhurst)

Zachariah Bailey

Ellen A. Beatty (Casa Bianca)

Emmala A. Bellamy

David Barrow

James S. Bond

Daniel Bird (two places, including Nakoasa; other spellings say Nacoosa)

Edward C. Cabell (Dulce Domum)

William G. Clark

Caroline G. Cole (Rosewood)

John Doggett

John Finlayson (Glendower)

Octavius H. Gadsden

Robert H. Gamble (Welaunee)

William Gorman
Benjamin Johnson
John Johnson
Mary Johnson
G. Nobel Jones (El Destino)
Richard Lang (Mount Pleasant)
Hampton S. Linton
John G. Mathers
Catharine Murat (Lipona)
William D. Moseley (Edwards Place and Sutherland)
William S. Murphy
Martin Palmer
Thomas Randall (Aucilla Place and Belmont)
John M. Raysor
James Scott
Smith Simpkins
Thomas Townsend
Martha P. and Dorothy Triplett (Lebanon)
James R. Tucker (Wareland)
William H. Ware (Wareland)
Elizabeth Wirt (Wirtland)[2]

"Architecture is the printing-press of all ages, and gives a history of the state of the society in which it was erected." Lady Morgan (Sydney Owenson)

Many of the big plantation owners of Jefferson County were involved in politics and law, and they lived lives much like the European aristocrats. Courtesy of the State Library and Archives of Florida

Casa Bianca Plantation: In 1827 Colonel Joseph M. White acquired
land located three miles southeast of Monticello. He was a very
influential individual, born in 1781 in Kentucky. On the Florida
land, he built a big antebellum home. Colonel White was wed to
Ellen Adair who was the daughter of General Adair, also from
Kentucky. The name of their place was Casa Bianca. Courtesy of
State Library and Archives of Florida

She was nicknamed "Florida" White by Washington, D.C., society, where her husband served for 12 years as a delegate to Congress for the Territory of Florida (1825-1837). Text and image courtesy of State Library and Archives of Florida

"Now, just as one more-or-less consciously reads the face of every person one meets, to discover whether it is friendly or withdrawn, happy or sad, at home in the world or baffled by it, so buildings are the faces on which one can read, long after the events themselves have passed out of memory, or written record, the life of our ancestors." Lewis Mumford from *The South in Architecture*.

In the ten years before the Civil War would economically devastate the Southern states, some planters owned huge plantations. Those places with names like El Destino and Chemonie were located east of Tallahassee and existing in Jefferson, County. They encompassed about 10,000 acres. Those two plantations were owned by absentee owner George Noble Jones who made Savannah, Georgia his home. The "El Destino" plantation was purchased June 4, 1828 by the Nuttall Family. Text and photo courtesy of State Library and Archives of Florida

The El Destino plantation, near Tallahassee, was purchased June 4, 1828, by the Nuttall family for $2,350.00. The plantation contained some 480 acres and was primarily a cotton-growing operation. El Destino was located in western Jefferson County at what is now Waukeenah. It extended into Leon County by six miles, just three miles south of the W. G. Ponder Plantation. Text and image courtesy of State Library and Archives of Florida

The photograph depicts a scene on the Bellamy Plantation. Courtesy
of State Library and Archives of Florida

Rose Knox and Graham Schorb

Endnotes

1. Mary Oakley McRory and Edith Clarke Barrows, *History of Jefferson County, Florida*, published under the auspices of the Kiwanis Club, Monticello, Florida, 1958.

2. Clifton Paisley, *The Red Hills of Florida 1528-1865* (Tuscaloosa: University of Alabama Press, 1989).

Life on Lipona: Plantation of a Prince

"He loved the voices of the plantation, the plaintive 'moos' of the hungry cows waiting to be milked, the cackling of the fowls . . . . . ."[1]

There were many big and small plantations on those sprawling acres and sloping fields in the Red Hills. Each plantation has a compelling story of its own, from the difficult, laborious life the slave was destined to live, to the life of the owner, his wife and children, and the owner's overseer. Many of the details of local history concerning those people's lives have sadly been lost forever to the annals of time. But some stories do remain.

One interesting narrative of such a time involves a prince. His name was Charles Louis Napoleon Achille Murat, and he was the oldest son of Napoleon Bonaparte's sister, Caroline. Caroline's husband was king of Naples. After being driven from Italy and France as an exile, Murat would find himself living a new life in the fertile hills of north Florida, after some persuasion by Lafayette who had established a land grant in the region.[2]

Murat immigrated to America in 1821, six years following his uncle's defeat at Waterloo. He first spent some time in New Jersey and later in St. Augustine before moving to the Red Hills in 1825. His plantation named Lipona was twenty miles east of Tallahassee and located on the Aucilla River. It encompassed over one thousand acres with more than a hundred slaves.[3]

Stories reveal that this man of European nobility, after his relocation enjoyed life in the countryside. The prince had two homes built. One was for living and entertaining, and the other was for his diversions, which were his experimentations with dyeing and his interest in cooking.[4] Murat was widely known as quite a colorful character among the elite class. Because he loved experimenting with cooking, he was known to come up with many unorthodox concoctions. For example, Bertram Groene, in his book *Ante-Bellum Tallahassee,* explains, "His menu ran the gamut from fried toadstools, a rattlesnake and baked owl

Rose Knox and Graham Schorb

with the head on, to cows' ears stew. Try as he would, though, he could never conquer the masterful art of cooking a turkey buzzard."⁵ Not only did he participate in these pastimes of entertaining and cooking, but he was also an avid reader, a writer, (his books were widely read in Europe), and a lawyer, and he served as a judge in Jefferson County.

As a lover of the Red Hills, he was known to be standing at the threshold of his front door where, as far as his eye could see, was acre after acre of fertile land, a gift bestowed on him from a land grant. One local account says of such a scene, in a much romanticized tone of the aristocratic South, "He loved the voices of the plantation, the plaintive 'moos' of the hungry cows waiting to be milked, the cackling of the fowls . . . while from the corn and cotton fields came the sweet, musical voices of the negro slaves, singing or calling to each other at their work." Historical accounts of the period show, too, that Madame Murat, his wife, was considered a welcoming hostess, and the Murat home drew men and women of high standing and importance to her doors. The prince was known to entertain guests at his home with his humor and his tales of journeys abroad.⁶

Though he had a love for the Red Hills, his heart was still in Europe. In 1830 Murat made plans to go back to Europe to try to claim the throne of the Kingdom of Naples. Thomas Brown, an aristocratic planter, held a grand ball at the Planters Hotel before Murat's departure back to Europe. But years would pass, and Murat would find himself returning to north Florida, "poorer but wiser."⁷ On his return in the spring of 1839, he discovered that his Lipona plantation was in foreclosure to the Union Bank. It was then that Prince Murat and his wife, the princess, moved to Econchatti, a smaller plantation, where he died in 1847. Seven years would pass and his wife would relocate to a five-hundred-acre plantation on Jackson Bluff Road, two miles west of the old city of Tallahassee. The name of that plantation was Bellevue. It was said that she then spent time in both places, dividing her days between Econchatti and Bellevue. She died long after the Civil War.⁸

As one additional historical note of the prince's life, during the conflicts with the Seminole Nation, Prince Murat commanded troops that patrolled the frontier settlements. He is buried in the St. John's Episcopal churchyard in Tallahassee. His wife, who died in 1867, reposes beside her husband there.⁹

The image depicts an etching of Bellevue, home of Princess Murat, built in 1830 in Tallahassee. The princess, known as Princess Catherine Dangerfield Willis Gray Murat, was George Washington's great-grandniece. Seven years after the death of her husband, she relocated to a 500-acre plantation named Bellevue on Jackson Bluff Road, two miles west of the old city of Tallahassee. Here is an interesting note about this cottage-like home: The Nathan P. Willard Home, known as "The Dream House" that was built in 1849 in Madison, Florida, mimics in architecture, structure, and millwork, the floor plans of the Bellevue home, which is located in Tallahassee. Nathan Willard was known for establishing the second cotton mill in the state of Florida. Text and image courtesy of State Library and Archive of Florida. Note: Some sources spell the princess's name "Catharine."

Prince Murat is buried in the St. John's Episcopal churchyard in Tallahassee. His wife, who died in 1867, lies beside her husband. When Graham and I visited the graveyard, we stood over their tombs and wondered about their lives in Europe and in Florida. Courtesy of Graham Schorb

Endnotes

1. Mary Oakley McRory and Edith Clarke Barrows, *History of Jefferson County, Florida,* published under the auspices of the Kiwanis Club, Monticello, Florida, 1958.

2. Bertram H. Groene, *Ante-Bellum Tallahassee,* Florida Heritage Foundation, Tallahassee, 1981.

3. Groene, *Ante-Bellum Tallahassee.*

4. McRory and Barrows, *History of Jefferson County.*

5. Groene, *Ante-Bellum Tallahassee.*

6. McRory and Barrows, *History of Jefferson County.*

7. Groene, *Ante-Bellum Tallahassee.*

8. Groene, *Ante-Bellum Tallahassee.*

9. McRory and Barrows, *History of Jefferson County.*

Rose Knox and Graham Schorb

Travel Notes

Music and the African Tradition:
Slave Songs

"My Lawd, I've had many crosses an' trials here below;
My Lawd, I hope to meet you,
In de manshans above."[1]

Songs have always had a way of inspiring human beings, and music seems to connect people with past events. The music sometimes alludes to human struggle, as in an old hymn.

As with the music of many ancient societies, the main purpose of African music was to retell the central historical accounts of human beings. Bands of singers from a Sudanese tribe, for example, would recite family and natural history; they did so with the accompaniment of musical instruments. These men and women from various African regions were considered professionals in their crafts, as magicians, storytellers, gossipmongers, poets, mimes, and musicians. They served as ancient troubadours, carrying on and preserving important historical and communal records of places, people, and times.[2] Louis B. Wright also reminds us that, "The African brought with them a body of interesting folklore, animal tales, superstitions, folk medicines, song rhythms and dances."[3] Some of the professional musicians served as "living encyclopedias" of the oral tradition that told of what people in a culture most valued or feared.[4]

Dancing and musical instruments such as ancient drums and wind instruments also accompanied the performers.[5] According to one scholar, "Africans danced for joy, and they danced for grief; they danced for love and they danced for hate; they danced to bring prosperity, and they danced to avert calamity; they danced for religion, and they danced to pass the time."[6]

Once Africans were brought to America, their love of singing survived but changed with the environment. The slaves of north Florida had long been Christianized; therefore, the verses and choruses that could often be heard rising up from slave quarters or from the fields reflected that Christian belief system and their plantation environment. One good example of such a song was:

Good Lawd, in de manshans above,

Good Lawd, in de manshans above,

My Lawd, I hope to meet my Jesus

My Lawd, in de manshans above,

If you get to Heaban before I do

Lawd, tell my Jesus I'm a-comin' too

To de manshans above

Lawd, tell my Jesus I'm a-comin' too

To de manshans above

My Lawd, I've had many crosses an' trials here below;

My Lawd, I hope to meet you,

In de manshans above.[7]

Through the words in their songs, they also developed a unique, clever vocabulary and a means of expression all their own. So by adding into their harmonies various concepts, images, and metaphors they had borrowed from their ancient African past, they, in time, created a special language that was unfamiliar to the greater planter society. Miles Fisher explains such language when he says, "By developing this symbolism as a universal language among themselves, they were able to harbor and express thoughts that were not understandable to others. Their masters never realized this; therefore the Africans were able to keep for themselves a small degree of intellectual freedom."[8] Such songs, sometimes in the form of spirituals—often called "black spirituals"—were a vital component in the life of a slave. Not only did the songs help pass along the hours while people labored in the fields, but the very songs carried with them remnants of the old, oral tradition.

One excellent example of how the spoken tradition helped in preserving the ways of a people comes from author Alex Haley, the writer of *Roots: The Saga of an American Family*. Haley was capable of piecing together his own family history, starting with his family's oral tradition. When he was a child in Henning, Tennessee, his grandmother often told him stories about his family. Such a storytelling tradition had stretched back to her grandparents, and to their grandparents, finally passing through many generations back to a man she spoke of as "The African." Her specific memory of the geography of the setting of the happenings was what would ultimately help Haley trace his ancestry all the way back to his regional roots. After twelve years of determined research, and half a million miles of travel that took him to three continents, Haley finally found his roots. His grandmother had always spoken of exactly where "The African" once lived. It was across the ocean near a place she knew as "Kamby Bolongo." With that one clue, and his eventual feat of years of genealogical research, Haley ended up in Juffure, the same village in Gambia, West Africa, where "The African," his early ancestor, was captured in 1767. Kunta Kinte was sixteen years old at his abduction, and it was the Lord Ligonier ship that took him to Maryland where he was then sold to a Virginia planter.

But Haley's book reveals something more than just one author's individual quest. One 1976 commentary illustrates, "But Haley has done more than recapture the history of his own family. As the first black American writer to trace his origins back to their roots, he has told the story of 25,000,000 Americans of African descent. He has rediscovered for an entire people a rich cultural heritage that slavery took away from them, along with their names and their identities."[9] In one scene in his book, Haley adds the sounds of the enslaved at early dawn, singing. The words go like this: "In de mawnin' gwine to rise up, Tell my Jesus, Hidy! Hidy!"[10]

Maya Angelou, the renowned American poet, told Bill Moyers that when she returned to the South, to Stamps, Arkansas, a place she had grown to love and to dread, a place she confesses she "was greatly hurt" and "vastly loved"—she said of the black spiritual music of her youth, "The best way for me to get out of Stamps was through the music and the poetry. . . there was a promise, always in the black spirituals that things were going to get better—by-and-by—you understand [and] not in any recognizable date [she laughs]—but by-and-by things were going to get better. . . . And then there was this incredible poetry, which I do not know why I knew at the time that it was great poetry. But . . . there's a line in a spiritual that always made me weep when I was about eight and the line is [she sings to Bill Moyers]:

'Green trees are bendin'
Ole sinner stands a-tremblin''

She added, ". . . listening to it, somehow I seemed to transcend the pit."[11]

"My Lawd, I've had many crosses an' trials here below;

My Lawd, I hope to meet you,

In de manshans above." From an old Black spiritual

Charity Stewart might have sung such a song as an enslaved person. She was born in 1844. During the Civil War she was hidden in the swamps of Jefferson County to make soap for the soldiers. After freedom, she returned to her former owner's home where she stayed until they died. For many years she lived alone in an old log house in Jefferson County. She was 93 when this photo was taken in 1937. Some text and photograph courtesy of the State Library and Archives of Florida

This is a portrait of Mauma Mollie who served as a nurse and cook. Mauma, a Partridge family slave, was brought to South Carolina on a slave ship from Africa. She came to Jefferson County with John and Eliza Partridge in the 1830s and was Frances Weston Partridge's nurse. Frances later married Charles Thomas Carroll. "We buried either in 57 or 58 our faithful old 'Mauma' Mollie—her who had nursed nearly all of the children of the family; been a friend as well as faithful servant to my Mother; in whose cabin we had often eaten the homely meal of fried bacon & ash cake and where we always had welcome and sympathy and whom we loved as a second mother. Black of skin but pure of heart, she doubtless stands among the faithful on the right of the King." Photo taken 1855 (from Diary of Henry Edward Partridge, written in 1873). Exact text and image courtesy of State Library and Archives of Florida

George Carson worked in Jefferson County, Florida. A former slave who came to Florida in 1875, he holds his former owner's Bible in which his birth is recorded. Text and image courtesy of State Library and Archives of Florida

Endnotes

1. Miles Mark Fisher, *Negro Slave Songs in the United States* (New York: Citadel Press, 1963).

2. Fisher, *Negro Slave Songs.*

3. Louis B. Wright, *South Carolina: A History* (New York: W. W. Norton, 1976).

4. Fisher, *Negro Slave Songs.*

5. Fisher, *Negro Slave Songs.*

6. Catherine Miller Balm, *Fun and Festival from Africa,* pamphlet, New York, 1939.

7. Fisher, *Negro Slave Songs.*

8. Fisher, *Negro Slave Songs.*

9. Alex Haley, *Roots: The Saga of an American Family* (New York: Doubleday, 1976).

10. Haley, *Roots.*

11. "Creativity with Bill Moyers: Maya Angelou," Films Media Group, 1982.

Rose Knox and Graham Schorb

Travel Notes

Rose Knox D

Plantations of Jefferson County.
A Brief Sketch

There were many large and small plantations established in Jefferson County as Florida was opened up as a territory. Below is a brief sketch of some of those operations. The local history book written by McRory and Barrows was the helpful source that provided the information below. Their book offers many more specifics of the people and situations concerning plantation life. Their stories also show the interrelationships of planters and how those people were connected by the planter-society to other affluent families in surrounding counties of the Red Hills. If the information below differs from other material in this work regarding ownership of a certain plantation, that is because the land was passed down to a family member or was later sold to another individual.

Welawanee–John G. Gamble of Virginia received a land grant; he called his place Welawanee. Welawanee Plantation was renamed much later, after Ted Turner bought the property in the 1980s. He named it Avalon, and the plantation he owns encompasses 31,000 acres.

The Gadsden Place–In 1827 General James Gadsden, a South Carolinian, established the Gadsden Place with the aid of a government grant.

El Destino–William Nuttall started El Destino, located near Tallahassee. It was purchased June 4, 1828, by the Nuttall family for $2,350. The El Destino plantation contained some 480 acres and was primarily a cotton-growing operation. It was located in western Jefferson County, at what is now Waukeenah, and extended into Leon County by six miles, just three miles south of the W. G. Ponder Plantation, according to the State Library and Archives of Florida.

Lipona–Prince Achille Murat developed Lipona.

305

r. Pinkney Bellinger, a South Carolinian, had a plantation, but no name was provided by the source, a local history book.

Pinetucky–Kidder Meade Moore, from Virginia, named his plantation Pinetucky.

Belmont–Judge Randall owned Belmont.

Clermont–George Whitfield owned Clermont.

Jack Bellamy–He was the owner of several thousand acres situated eight miles east of Monticello. When Jack Bellamy died his home and land went to his youngest son, William. William was married to Emmala Simkins.

Richard Call Parkhill was a plantation owner.

Junius Turnbull–His plantation joined Richard Turnbull's on one side and Captain R. C. Parkhill's on the other.

Wareland–Many acres of land near Lamont were acquired by Colonel Thompson Ware in 1837. He came from South Carolina; born in 1786, he first settled in Georgia. In 1836 he made his way to Florida and named his plantation Wareland.

Croom–Beside the village of Lamont was the Croom plantation, owned by Church Croom. He was a neighbor of the Wares.

The Cedars–William Bailey married Elizabeth Mary Bellamy, daughter of Jack Bellamy. They owned thousands of acres of fertile farmland and virgin forests. They named their plantation The Cedars.

Panola–John Bailey, though he died and never lived there, had a place named Panola, a magnificent estate that was known as the "talk of the countryside."

Glendower–John Finlayson owned Glendower plantation. It was located on the road to Ashville, fifteen miles from Monticello. John's father was Daniel Finlayson from Scotland. At his death, John left his great wealth to his children. Glendower was given to his oldest son, John, who was married to Elizabeth Hines.

Lyndhurst–Lyndhurst plantation was owned by William J. Bailey. It was located near Ashville, fifteen miles from

Monticello. He built an opulent antebellum home on the property.

Thomas S. Johnson, a planter from Virginia, brought his wife and children, slaves, cattle, and possessions and cleared and farmed land between Waukeenah and Lloyd.

John Cuthbert arrived in Florida in 1829, bringing with him his family and his slaves. It is said that he came from "cultured, refined" aristocratic roots. He purchased many acres of land from A. B. Shehee. The acreage was one mile northeast of Silver Lake.

Wilkins Cook Smith, a South Carolinian, arrived in Florida in 1840. Wilkins purchased a two-thousand-acre plantation from A. B. Shehee. It was located on the Ashville Road across from Silver Lake.

Casa Bianca–In 1827 Colonel Joseph M. White acquired land located three miles southeast of Monticello. He was a very influential man, born in 1781 in Kentucky. On the Florida land he built a fine antebellum home. Colonel White was wed to Ellen Adair, who was the daughter of General Adair, also from Kentucky. The name of their place was Casa Bianca.

Forest Farms–One of the first pioneers to the area, Needham Bryan, settled in Jefferson County in 1824. He established a mill dam, and the area was called Barne's Mill Creek. He also plowed and cultivated crops, and his slaves helped in salt-making to aid the government. His plantation was called Forest Farms.

Jumper Run and Dulce Domum–The acres that made up the Jumper Run plantation were given by the United States to Abram J. Cabell, signed off to him by Andrew Jackson. The Cabells named their estate Dulce Domum, which means "Sweet Home." Eventually the place came to be called Jumper Run and was once the central location of Chief Jumper, who was acting as a subchief under Seminole leader, Tiger Tail.

Bunker Hill and Nacoosa–In 1832 Daniel Bird from South Carolina brought his family, slaves, and possessions to Jefferson County, finally settling at a place called Bunker Hill. It was situated on a knoll northwest of Monticello, and was sold to Bird by Needham Bryan. He also later purchased Nacoosa from the widow of Jessie Simkins.

Treelawn–Pickens Brooks Bird bought land from Needham Bryan. The plantation was called Treelawn. Note: The three Bird plantations, Bunker Hill, Nacoosa, and Treelawn, were quite productive before the Civil War, and even a few years after the war. The many changes that came with the fall of the South affected production. A book called *The Orchard Princess*, written by Ralph Barbour, further details a setting that resembles Nacoosa.

Edgewood–Acreage located one mile northwest of Monticello was first owned by Gordon Clarke, who relocated to Florida from South Carolina. That land ultimately passed to a Mr. Charles M. Pugsley from Buffalo, New York. The name of that place was Edgewood.

Colonel Richard Parrish arrived in Jefferson County in 1819, coming from Wilmington, North Carolina. He was 49 years old by that time. He was granted government lands in Leon and Jefferson Counties. That domain bordered Lake Miccosukee, where he owned a plantation.

Dr. James Theodore Turnbull, born in Abbeville, South Carolina in 1811, settled on a plantation located three miles south of Monticello. He married one of the Parrish descendants, and they had a plantation that was called Sunrise. It was eventually purchased by Alex Ritter.

Dilworth–The area situated between Lloyd and Monticello was cultivated by slaves of Paul Ulmer, and adjoining the Ulmer property was William Dilworth's plantation.

Some plantations and plantation owners south of Monticello were named as follows: James Kilpatrick, John Cooksey, Alvin May, Samuel Neeley, and James D. Morris Devere.

Some plantations and plantation owners north of Monticello were: Asa Anderson, Rutheford Shuman, Robert Davis Johnson, and Benjamin Linton.[1]

Jack Bellamy was the owner of several thousand acres situated eight miles east of Monticello. When Jack Bellamy died his home and land went to his youngest son, William. William was married to Emmala Simkins. The image depicts a scene in 1891. Courtesy of State Library and Archives of Florida

The Cedars Plantation: William Bailey married Elizabeth Mary Bellamy, daughter of Jack Bellamy. They owned thousands of acres of fertile farmland with virgin forests. They named their plantation, The Cedars. "This palatial plantation home is located east of Monticello on the old plantation, The Cedars. The Cedars was owned by pioneering families Bailey, Bellamy, and Eppes. The Eppes are direct descendants of Thomas Jefferson, for whom our county is named." Eventually the plantation passed to other owners, and the land was used as a game preserve. Image and text courtesy of State Library and Archives of Florida

William J. Bailey served as captain of a company of Florida Mounted volunteers in the Seminole War and won distinction for his bravery. He was the owner of Lyndhurst Plantation. Bailey also was known as one of Jefferson County's wealthiest planters, and during the Civil War the textile mill located on his plantation provided material to make Confederate uniforms. Text and image courtesy of State Library and Archives of Florida

The Lyndhurst Plantation was located 15 miles north of Monticello; it was built in 1850 by Colonel William J. Bailey. Photograph taken by Benjamin L. Kerce, courtesy of State Library and Archives of Florida

Plantation homes were often furnished with the finest of furniture, and the Lyndhurst Plantation was no exception. Courtesy of State Library and Archives of Florida

Rose Knox and Graham Schorb

Endnotes

1. Mary Oakley McRory and Edith Clarke Barrows, *History of Jefferson County, Florida,* published under the auspices of the Kiwanis Club, Monticello, Florida, 1958.

American Civil War: The Aftermath

"... the level of enthusiasm by some was lukewarm at best."[1]

Poets and philosophers have had a lot to say about war. Even when soldiers are not convinced of why they are fighting, they are forced to combat an encroaching enemy in order to save their loved ones and their homes—and all they believe in and hold dear. Walt Whitman would lament the tragedy of the aftermath by saying "the dead, the dead, our dead"; and the loss of the war would ultimately haunt the collective memory of Americans, even into the modern day. Whitman creates a vivid picture as he laments. "The DEAD in this war—there they lie, strewing the fields and woods and valleys and battle-fields of the South . . . [a] bloody promenade of Wilderness . . . the dead, the dead —our dead–South or North, ours all . . . our young men once so handsome and so joyous, taken from us . . ."

And Unionist Richard Keith Call from nearby Leon County cautioned against war's unsuspected lure as celebrations were breaking out in many places in the Red Hills, coming with the talk of secession. Following the signing of the Ordinance of Secession, ex-Governor Call warned, "You have opened the gates of Hell, from which shall flow the curses of the damned which shall sink you to perdition."[2] Still, in many places in the region, an atmosphere of jubilation ensued, with the ringing of church bells, gun salutes, parades, bonfires, and celebratory toasts.

No prophet was among them to predict for sure that war would endure for four long, hard years, and many of those boys and men then laughing, eager for a taste of battle, would get their wish but never live to see the end of it. It was true that many of the citizens of Middle Florida, including Jefferson County residents, supported the South's decision to secede. But not all were embracing war. According to Derylene Counts, a local writer, "... the level of enthusiasm by some was lukewarm at best." That is because many people were not rich aristocratic planters with hundreds of slaves, but poor dirt farmers who owned no slaves—or they may have been pioneering people from places up north. With all wars, though, there were deserters. Counts continues, ". . . many felt little loyalty to or desire to fight for the Confederacy. A number of individuals disappeared into remote areas of swamps and forests."[3]

Then there were others who had connections to the big plantation owners and wanted to fight for the cause. James Patton Anderson was one of those men, and he would be put in charge of commanding one of the first companies from Jefferson County. His background was as a lawyer, and he had also served as a lieutenant colonel during the Mexican War. Later he was given a promotion to the rank of major general, and was ultimately given command of all Florida soldiers until the war's end. Some of those deserters would wish they had never met the man. Because some of them became outlaws, doing whatever it took to survive. Nearby Taylor County became a safe haven for deserters and conscripted men. In search of food and supplies, these desperate men would often raid area Jefferson County plantations, taking slaves in the process. Because of such acts, the people of Monticello were frightened and called on General Anderson and his troops to give them aid. Anderson's men responded to the plea and hunted and captured some deserters, while also burning their homes or camps. The deserters, along with their families, were marched over to Tallahassee where they were confined by stockade. Eventually the families were given up to a Union blockading vessel waiting at St. Marks. Anderson was later criticized for his drastic actions directed at the deserters' family members. Ironically, the Union Army would rally some of those very men to their cause, and they would come to serve the United States Second Cavalry, battling against the Confederates at Natural Bridge.

During the war, the impact on society was far-reaching. Men, women, children, rich, poor, white, black, old, and young would feel the sting of war as many became innocently intertwined in the events of wartime. There are books that contain compilations of diaries of women of that time attesting to hardship and the new roles they had to take on as each man left home. Among the poor white Crackers and smaller farmers, the boys, elderly, and disabled men were forced (out of pure necessity to keep from starving) to perform the work that had mostly been done by the able-bodied men. Generally speaking, during the war the slaves remained on area plantations. The reasons for their choosing to stay have been discussed in much detail in critical essays and in books. There were, however, some slave revolts and abandonments in areas where leagues of Union soldiers may have set up camp.[4] And more duties were heaped upon women, who were then responsible for providing for the family and—if they were women of plantation owners—for the slaves. Serving oftentimes as overseers of the slaves, women stepped into authority roles. As food shortages became a reality, as a result of Federal blockades interrupting the trade supply, more women were forced to do hard labor in an effort to keep the household or the estate intact. Counts illustrates, "They plowed, performed blacksmithing, drove wagons, tended sick cattle, butchered hogs, and harvested crops." Those women who had known physical labor prior to the war were more prone to endure such tasks. But those ladies who had formerly depended on store-bought commodities suffered the most.

As for the role of plantation slaves, the situation varied. For example, plantation slaves were given no choice about supporting the Confederacy. They worked for the Southern cause, a work force that built forts, rail tracks, and roads, while some slaves even followed their masters into war as servants. Yet many slaves stayed in Jefferson County to labor on the plantation. Some, though, did escape, becoming refugees and searching out places that were occupied by Federal troops. Others became soldiers for the Union cause. Counts explains further, "How they reacted was determined both by their temperament and how they had been previously treated."[5]

Another interesting aspect of the war was the production of salt as a critical commodity because it preserved food and was used for tanning hides. In fact, there were salt works operations in several of the marshy, coastal areas, including Taylor, Wakulla, and Jefferson Counties, although Jefferson County's salt works were more difficult to get to. Not only did Jefferson County contribute salt for the Southern cause, but Monticello was also the center of production for Florida during the war.[6] Though an entire chapter could be devoted to the production of salt, it should be noted that the largest industry emerging in wartime during the Civil War was the production of salt by boiling salt water from coastal regions. Without salt, people and the Confederate army would have been unable to preserve food, which would eventually have led to mass starvation of civilians and soldiers. Salt production was quite significant for survival.[7] And although there was never any real battle fought in Jefferson County there is a story about a confrontation at the mouth of the Aucilla River where Confederates surprised, killed, and captured some Union troops.

In summation of the war's toll, when the South finally fell at war's end, many of the former residents had perished or had left for other more promising opportunities elsewhere. Some had been the men and boys who had gone off to fight. One local historical narrative says of such a decline in the adult population of the region, ". . . her sons, having fallen in large numbers on the many bloody fields on which their loyalty to the lost cause was displayed." And as for the large tracts of land that had been in operation before the Civil War, the same author states, "Large plantations lacked the masters that formerly reaped the riches from their slave-worked acres. The boys went to the cities. The slaves, now free, drifted in the wreckage of reconstruction. . . ."[8]

Dr. Tracy J. Revels, in her work, *Florida's Civil War: Terrible Sacrifices*, further chronicles Florida's plight. "Ignored and abandoned by the Confederate government, Florida struggled to craft its own defenses and provide provisions for the army, to which it had contributed a disproportionate number of residents. . . . For this willingness to meet the needs of the Confederacy, to yield to calls for more men, money, and supplies, Florida received no great accolades or special recognition. Florida was lost even to the 'Lost Cause.'"[9]

By the early 1900s those sprawling antebellum plantations had been cut up, bought by various entities. The land would produce tobacco, pecans, cotton, watermelons, sweet and Satsuma oranges, grapefruit, and other kinds of orchards. Some of that land would go to later sustain herds of cows, and horses, and likewise be a place for pig farming. Sportsmen, too, started to congregate to the region to try their luck at fishing in local rivers, lakes, and ponds. Hunters were interested in the wild game of turkey, bobwhite quail, black bear, white-tailed deer, snipe, squirrels, coon, and opossum.[10]

There are indeed many more fascinating stories surrounding Jefferson County, the Civil War, and Reconstruction. They can be found in the work *Familiar Faces and Quiet Places* by Derylene Counts. The author includes numerous archival photographs and art renderings in her work on the history of Jefferson County.

Unionist Richard Keith Call, from nearby Leon County, cautioned against war's lure, as celebrations were breaking out in many places in the Red Hills. He warned, "You have opened the gates of Hell, from which shall flow the curses of the damned which shall sink you to perdition." Courtesy State Library and Archives of Florida

Endnotes

1. Derylene Delp Counts, *Familiar Faces and Quiet Places: A Pictorial and Narrative History of Jefferson County, Florida* (Virginia Beach, VA: Donning Publishing, 2005).

2. Counts, *Familiar Faces.*

3. Counts, *Familiar Faces.*

4. Louis B. Wright, *South Carolina: A History* (New York: W. W. Norton, 1976).

5. Counts, *Familiar Faces.*

6. Counts, *Familiar Faces.*

7. John E. Johns, *Florida During the Civil War* (Gainesville: University of Florida Press, 1963).

8. Counts, *Familiar Faces.*

9. Tracy J. Revels, *Florida's Civil War: Terrible Sacrifices* (Macon, GA: Mercer University Press, 2016).

10. "Jefferson County: Monticello Section," pamphlet published by the Jefferson Business League, n.d.

Monarchs: Sky River of Orange

There is a coastal landscape which in times past supported thousands of Native Americans, as they lived off of the rich bounty of the sea. It is likewise the selfsame landscape that once challenged Spanish conquistadors after they had marched through the Red Hills region in their search for gold.

In the period of the American Civil War, the coastal area was vital to life, as it was the place to mine salt. Salt preserved food and kept soldiers and civilians from starving. The marshy place also attracts a natural wonder of sorts and is the story of the remarkable journey of the monarch butterfly, amid a scene that transpired for thousands of years. What might the ancient peoples have thought of such a phenomenon when peering upwards as they stood witness to the "sky river of orange" appearing in the firmament, as hordes of butterflies took a miraculous transcontinental odyssey?

It is one of the most profound mysteries in the natural world—the migration each year of millions of monarch butterflies. From as far north as Canada, they make their way to Mexico. But before their flight to points further south, they make an all-important stop in Florida. I have had the chance to see them there in the lowland coastal regions, not far from the Red Hills of my home. A similar version of the following story was once featured in *Florida Wildlife* magazine and is a memoir about how students and I were to end up tagging monarchs on the coast with scientists, not far from the Red Hills region. The narrative also tells about a species that is threatened in modern times by interference of today's society. Here is how the day started on the morning we tagged hundreds of butterflies.

It is 3:30 on a frosty Saturday morning in early November, and I am scheduled to hitch a ride for the brief journey to the coast. Meeting a college scientist, Barry Barnhart, at our agreed destination, we soon find ourselves leaving the Red Hills and heading southwest over to Saint Marks coastal area where we are to join up with another scientist from our college, and several of her students.

Rose Knox and Graham Schorb

When we get there at 5:15 a.m. under a blanket of darkness, each of us is armed with a headlamp flashlight that we wear on our foreheads. A cold front has come through during the night, and the temperature now is in the mid-thirties. Soon after our arrival, we meet David Cook, a wildlife biologist with the Florida Fish and Wildlife Conservation Commission in Tallahassee. He makes sure we know what to expect, saying, "Since it is still dark, the monarchs are resting among the foliage. Our time is limited; we must catch them while they are asleep. We will use our flashlights to locate them. Sometimes they will alight alone, but oftentimes they are found in clusters. Gently pick them from the perch, and place them in the mesh cages. We will tag them later."[1]

There is a sharp chill in the air and I fill my lungs, as I breathe the scent of salty air. Moving as a group, at first, onto a finger of land surrounded on three sides by water, we approach the saltbushes. The vegetation provides the monarch with food and safety. Soon we disperse, scattering like leaves in a blast. Each of us begins to spy monarchs lighted on the spiny branches. I hear exclamations of delight pierce the morning silence as students and volunteers come in contact with their first "prize." I, too, am awed at how the orange and black, delicate insect sleeps, and as I touch the fragile wings for the first time, the moment seems like a prayer.

At first I am a tad reluctant to pluck the butterfly from the branch, so I stand still for a few seconds admiring the delicate wonder. After the first few, I get the hang of it, which brings confidence. Without any communication whatsoever, total strangers start to work in unison. Ruth, an older woman with a northern accent, comes up behind me after she notices I am in the midst of a significant cluster. She presents the round mesh cage, arms extended, with the anticipation of a child. Ruth and I begin to move like synchronized dancers, from bush to bush. But soon we change roles: I take a step back to let her experience the chance to pluck an orange-winged "miracle" from its place.

I call the monarchs a miracle because what they do is indeed miraculous! Until that day, I did not realize that it takes three generations of them to travel from Canada, through North America, and then on to Mexico. Just imagine 100 million or more brilliantly orange monarchs that start their migration, in what some more poetic descriptions reveal as a "sky river of orange. Can't you just see it—a line of fluttering, undulating orange"—a ribbon to the heavens? Traveling fifty to sixty miles a day, (and some have been known to soar on fronts for as many as a thousand miles in a day) they journey, determined to make it to their final destination.[2] I stopped to wonder then what

322

the ancient peoples might have thought of such a scene. When the butterflies finally reach Mexico, the locals have a celebration in their honor. There people believe that the monarchs are sacred, housing the spirits of the dead within them. The holiday is called el Dia de los Muertos or Day of the Dead. Sadly, though, like many species on the planet, thousands of butterflies do not make it. Much of the reason is man's encroachment and the use of pesticides; but most importantly I think it is humanity's inability to understand the monarch's sacred place in our modern world.

Before long, our group is migrating, too. We move away from the finger of land, across the tar parking lot, and out past the lighthouse. Now we are on the beach in the newness of early morning light. The sun is a huge orange ball on the horizon. Suddenly I hear the sound of many voices, a cacophony of chatter rising forth. Then I begin to see small children run towards us coming down from the sandy path, the towering alabaster lighthouse behind them. They are ten- and eleven-year-olds from a private school. Their diesel engine bus hums as they rush in excitement with their own mesh nets to the salt marsh bushes along the beach. Thirty to forty of them dash here and there as they see the butterflies, which are becoming active now. Watching the sheer wonder of children—their fascination at the mystery of the monarch—is an experience all its own. As a teacher, I am glad to know someone is instilling the love and the idea of the mystery of nature by using this event to illustrate the monarch's importance, for only if we can care for the monarch's safety, their numbers, and their lives, can we perpetuate their existence.

As the morning ticks by, walking along the white sand beach and marveling at the blue sky set above the sparking Gulf of Mexico, I start to see a few small orange, fluttering dots high above. These are monarchs that we missed. I take a minute to ingrain the sight for future memory: the bright orange dot set against the sky is a pure mixture—the alchemy of God! But I must get back to work, because there is still so much more to do—no time for delay, no time for reflection.

The sun is now fully ablaze in the midmorning hour, and all of the volunteers gather on the porch of the visitor's center at the refuge. There we are instructed on how to handle, identify the sex, and tag each butterfly appropriately. Mesh bags hold hundreds of insects. Bonnie, the club sponsor, holds one of the mesh bags as I slip my hand in. I am privileged to feel the vibrancy of wings brush all parts of my hand and fingers. Catching one, I bring it up to my eyes for closer inspection. David Cook shows me how to discern its sex, saying "If it has a smooth, round abdomen, it is a female; but if the abdomen has two extensions, it is a male."[3] Liz, one of our volunteer students, brings over two sets of tags–a 5 by 6 sheet of wax paper that holds small round blue and orange stickers. We begin the careful process of tagging and recording each butterfly. I hold the monarch in my right hand and use tweezers to lift a sticker from the wax sheet. As I place it on the right back wing, another person steps into our circle. She is dressed in the uniform of a park employee. She records the number and the sex of each butterfly. Over the next several hours, we manage to tag over fifteen hundred of them using this method.

Later we all move from the porch to a high platform overlooking the salt marsh. The sun warms us as we work up on the high deck. Hours pass. People start, little by little, to leave. The children, one by one, step back on their touring bus as one chaperone informs us they are now headed for the butterfly museum in Gainesville, which will punctuate their Saint Marks experience. The Florida Museum of Natural History offers visitors exhibits of photographs and collected specimens featuring butterfly and moth species there. Another attraction is the butterfly rainforest.[4] Other volunteers climb down from the platform, leaving only those from our college. Finally the last butterfly is taken from the mesh bag, tagged and released. David thanks us, but we linger for a few minutes more saying our goodbyes. It is a few days before we know exactly how many we have tagged. It turns out we caught 1,564 and tagged 1,513.

Leaving the 68,000-acre refuge, I stare out of the window at the vast landscape that is the salt marsh, while pondering the idea that we have just taken part in an extraordinary experience. Some would venture to say it was a spiritual encounter. The rangers say that 250,000 visitors a year come here, some from across the globe. Many travel to the refuge to marvel and to take part in such a fleeting happening.[5] I think of the hundreds of monarchs we just tagged, and I wonder about their survival. I envision them forming high above the earth, making a spectacular orange river on their way to Mexico. I even picture the joyful faces of those waiting to celebrate their coming. In Mexico they are considered sacred to the people there. As they finally arrive at their warm destination, the miracle begins again. But only a few of the thousands tagged at the Saint Marks Wilderness Refuge in a season will ever make their final journey. It is then that I think on the migration of the butterfly. Though fragile and quite delicate, it is hardy enough to sustain itself for thousands of miles.

Millions follow the same path annually in a spectacular sky river of orange. Despite storms, extreme distances, and man's encroachment and pollution, three generations endure. Their innate tenacity, their regeneration, their beauty are all part of the mystical, magical, and spiritual nature of what makes them revered by those in Mexico. That is truly the miracle of the monarch! Perhaps if more human beings took a moment away from cell phones, television sets, computers, and the many distractions of this modern, technological culture, we too might consider the magnificence and the sacredness of the butterfly. Imagine our changed selves if we all could know, understand, then celebrate the monarch!

Each time I visit the coast, I think of Pánfilo de Narváez's men as they trudged westward, leaving the sloping Red Hills, laboring their way through what is called today the St. Marks National Wildlife Refuge—that southern domain, some of which includes Jefferson County. His men made a way through bogs, swamps, and tributaries not too far from where we were tagging butterflies that day. Not only was the landscape to challenge them on their trek, a journey spurred on by the thought of gold and riches, but they were swarmed by mosquitoes, and attacked by area Indians who drove them out of what is today's Jefferson County. The Spanish conquistadors continued moving westward, but the ill-fated expedition would end with only four men surviving. When my eyes sweep over the marshy areas of the refuge today, I always wonder what hopeless thoughts those Spanish may have been having.[6]

Note about tagging: To contact the Saint Marks Wildlife Refuge and participate in tagging monarchs:

Phone: (850) 925 6121

Email: saintmarks@fws.gov

Website: www.fws.gov/saintmarks/

The monarchs come south and have peak migrations at Saint Marks between mid-October and mid-November. Each visitor will need a flashlight; a headlamp flashlight is recommended for hands-free collecting. Wear shoes that can get wet, and do not wear bug repellent. Dress for warmth.

To visit the butterfly exhibits in Gainesville, contact:

Rose Knox and Graham Schorb

Florida Museum of Natural History
University of Florida Cultural Plaza
SW 34th Street and Hull Road
PO Box 112710
Gainesville, FL 32611-2710
(352) 846-2000
www.flmnh.ufl.edu/butterflies/

North Florida Community College faculty and students participate
in tagging monarch butterflies at the Saint Marks Wildlife Refuge
in Saint Marks, Florida, in early November, when thousands light
to rest and nourish themselves before their long journey to Mexico.
Courtesy of Bonnie Littlefield

I've had the chance to see them and to tag them in coastal regions not far from the Red Hills and I've wondered what the Native Americans of this region might have thought about, when they looked up to see such an annual marvel as the "sky river of orange." Courtesy of Bonnie Littlefield

Endnotes

1. David Cook, personal interview, St. Marks Wildlife Refuge, November 3, 2008.

2. Claudia Hunter Johnson, "The Monarchs of Eden," in *Between Two Rivers: Stories from the Red Hills to the Gulf*, Susan Cerulean, Janisse Ray, and Laura Newton, eds. (Tallahassee, FL: Heart of the Earth and the Red Hills Writers Project, 2004).

3. Cook, interview.

4. Florida Museum of Natural History, Gainesville, Florida, www.flmnh.ufl.edu/butterflies/

5. Saint Marks Wildlife Refuge, www.fws.gov/saintmarks/

6. Derylene Delp Counts, *Familiar Faces and Quiet Places: A Pictorial and Narrative History of Jefferson County, Florida* (Virginia Beach, VA: Donning Publishing, 2005).

Rose Knox and Graham Schorb

Travel Notes

Haunted Jefferson County

"The stories of the slaves, planters, and soldiers often converge on the plantation. Slaves spent years working on the plantations with very little recognition for their hard work. Planters spent a great deal of time and money making certain that their plantations were successful. During the Civil War, Union and Confederate soldiers often took over the mansions and used them as a field hospital to tend to and sometimes bury their comrades. For all people involved, the plantation was a very emotionally charged location."[1]

In the Red Hills, enemy soldiers did not take over mansions, but the battle-wounded boys and men were brought to area homes of the affluent. Those soldiers are buried in the local cemetery at Roseland. As I began researching strange stories of Monticello's past, reading about weird tales and talking to folks, I tried remembering back to when I was a child, and the games my playmates enjoyed; those verbal games involved the passing on of a particular story. One I sometimes played was whispering into a classmate's ear part of a short narrative, only to find out after the account had been told to each child in the room—by the time the ideas finally got to the last child—oh, how the story had changed!

It was not hard, then, to recall memories of that same childhood game when I was reading books, running across articles, and hearing strange tales about the subject of haunted Monticello. The stories I found in those books and articles were sometimes discredited by lifelong, local residents. Or the native Monticello citizen would claim that the story I had told them about (even ones now being told on local ghost tours in town), had been greatly embellished. Please keep these ideas in mind when reading the following folktales. For who really knows the exact details of the original tales? Nonetheless, the storyteller in me felt compelled to pass on what I had come across. Here they are: Those chilling stories of ghostly happenings, in a place that has come to be known by some as "haunted Monticello."

Betty Davis, in her book, *Haunted Monticello, Florida*, touches on the same idea of how certain stories are continuously perpetuated, when she writes,

> As the years passed, one constant through all of the tragedies, turmoil and triumphs were tales of ghostly happenings; mysterious lights in cemeteries; doors opening and closing by unseen hands; ghostly faces appearing out of windows from long-abandoned houses; the sounds of ghostly footsteps; one street on which—be it the cold of January or the heat of August —the temperature is always cooler than on any other street; music emitting from empty buildings; and the residual sounds of a long ago party. These tales have been handed down for generations from great-grandparents to grandparents to parents and, finally to their children, and all are a part of the local legends and folklore.[2]

Several places in Jefferson County have also been chronicled on television shows and in various regional books because of their alleged hauntings. For example, Jefferson County High School, built in the 1850s, is known as the first brick schoolhouse in Florida. During its restoration, workers said that they could hear the sounds of children's laughter. Yet another place of strange, supposed spectral happenings is located on North Jefferson Street and is the Wirick-Simmins House built in the early 1800s. It is known as one of the oldest houses in Monticello. One writer and psychic, who likes to hunt for ghosts and to promote the haunted South to attract paying tourists, claims ". . . guests have photographed apparitions of a woman in pink looking out of the upstairs window and another woman sitting on the porch."[3]

The Palmer House is another haunted place and is one of the most talked-about areas in the town of Monticello. In fact, it is touted as "the most haunted house in the South's most haunted small town." The home was originally owned by Dr. John Palmer. Some of the purported happenings there include unexplained footsteps and voices. Bloodstains have also been claimed to appear above the hearth. The hearth area has been painted over numerous times, but the mysterious bloodstains still seem to reappear.[4]

Here is how that legend of the Palmer house goes: Built in the mid-1800s, the home stayed in the family for generations. Dr. John Dabney Palmer, a fifth-generation physician and a gifted scientist, inherited the house and, it seems, the ghoulish stories that today go with it. Tales of strange happenings and ghostly visitations are therefore part of the local lore that surround the doctor, his assistant, and the Palmer home and property; and the story is connected to the local town cemetery. People have reported unexplained sounds such as knocking, thumping, and even screaming; visitors have been known to feel the sensation of someone touching them; other folks claim they have had actual sightings of spirits or have experienced inexplicable occurrences like draperies getting moved when no person is around.[5]

It was not uncommon during that time period for a physician to also serve as an undertaker. The narrative that keeps perpetuating itself goes like so: Dr. Palmer had both his doctor's office and a mortuary set up on his property. The mortuary was located on the second story of the house, and a separate outbuilding was situated in the corner of his front yard. But many claimed that Dr. Palmer tended to his business in a strange way when handling the body and extracting the blood. He had an assistant working for him, a black man who went by the name of "Poltergeist," and the name had been given the man because it was rumored that he could cast no shadow! Poltergeist was known for riding a buckboard hauled by mules and was in charge of digging graves for Dr. Palmer. When someone died, Dr. Palmer would drain the blood from the person and save it in a container. He would then hand the container to Poltergeist who was instructed by the doctor to go back to the cemetery and to empty the blood in the freshly dug grave. Not long afterward, the body would be buried. Many subsequent owners of the home claim to have had trouble trying to remove what looked to them like a recurring bloodstain. One source even went on to say, "The wall has been scrubbed, painted . . . and wallpapered, but no matter how many coats of paint were applied, the stain returned."[6]

Some folks swear that when the moon is full, people who might happen by the old Palmer property are prone to see some spirit image of a gentleman. He has often been seen carrying a doctor's bag, dressed in his frock coat, and may be sporting a top hat. This ghostly apparition is famous for traipsing across his yard, coming from the outbuilding that served as his office as he makes his way back over to the Palmer home.[7]

Odd tales have consequently surfaced about how once, when an argument ensued between the doctor and his assistant when Palmer was handing over a blood-filled vessel to Poltergeist, the angry worker flung the container of blood. Some of it hit the doctor and also splashed on the wall and on the body of the dead person in the mortuary.

Not only are certain buildings purportedly visited by apparitions, but Jefferson County's Roseland Cemetery has peculiar stories concerning ghostly encounters as well. The cemetery is located on Madison Street, three blocks east of Jefferson Street. It was established in 1827 and many early prominent citizens are interred there, including the Denham and Clarke families. Many graves tell a silent story about the art of stone masonry at that time. For example, there are towering obelisks, Gothic-style coffin-shaped tombs, and gravestones that exhibit an Egyptian-influenced design; such types of art were often created by Freemasons of the period and their handiwork is apparent in many cemeteries in the region of the Red Hills.[8] Also resting for eternity are the Civil War soldiers brought to the town after they were wounded at the Battle of Olustee, and there, too, are many infant graves. Because several epidemics swept through the area in the 1800s, disease claimed the lives of many area residents, including quite a few very young children. Michelle Davidson, in her work *Florida's Haunted Hospitality*, tells a chilling tale that, for those true believers in ghosts, might make a person shiver with fright! She writes,

> Roseland Cemetery is the most haunted cemetery that I have been to. . . . I visited on a harvest moon with my electromagnetic field (EMF) reader and digital camera. On the north end of the cemetery, near the fence, I received high EMF readings. I sensed a spirit presence that continued to follow me throughout the cemetery. I caught an astounding amount of orbs in motion over gravestones. What I didn't expect was that a particular spirit would take interest in me. This spirit decided to follow me back to the bed-and-breakfast I was staying in, eventually following me home. [Also] what I learned from investigating cemeteries and other haunted locations is that you have to constantly protect yourself at all times. I learned the hard way when I let my guard down at this cemetery. From now on, I will protect myself with a vision of white light. I carry sage with me and burn it in my car after I leave a haunted location.[9]

Ghostly stories about many of the former residents of Jefferson County therefore surround the cemetery at Roseland. Some of the tales revolve around a jilted bride, a jealous wife, a gossipmonger, epidemic and fire victims (many small children), Union and Confederate soldiers, (buried side by side), an insane physician, a weeping widow, and people who were supposedly buried alive in Roseland quite by accident. All of their restless souls are said to manifest in several ways, such as crying, ghostly appearances, unexplained lights, moved objects, and recurring whirlwinds over particular tombs.

The day Graham and I visited the cemetery in January of 2017, we walked through the oldest section as we stopped to see tiny Confederate flags placed over a few graves; we noticed many brick tombs, placed sort of harum-scarum. According to one source, those graves were epidemic victims buried quite hurriedly. We also took in the sight of several artistic stones which were created in Gothic style and coffin-type tombs; we marveled at the variety of other designs that were a curious sight to behold, such as obelisks. On that day we heard no cries; saw no whirlwinds or lights or ghostly apparitions. It was a good thing, too. We had no sage to burn!

Another weird story involves a folktale from someone I know. Jhan, a local citizen and former schoolteacher from Jefferson County, relayed a story about the local opera house in Monticello. She told me on January 26, 2017, that back sometime around the 1990s, she and four other adults were chaperoning a high school prom. A lattice "wall" and an area of fake grass had been set up in the lobby of the Monticello Opera House, intended to make the scene look like an outdoor park. The teenagers were beginning to mill about. Many of the young men were dressed in white tuxedos. As the four chaperones were sitting at the table greeting people, they happened to notice a "person's" feet and white pant legs "standing" behind the lattice.

Because there was an exit door behind the lattice, they began to wonder if perhaps the prom goers might be sneaking other, unauthorized people into the event. So Jhan and another person proceeded to investigate; each of them walked around the two separate sides of each end of the lattice. They stood there staring at each other, once they reached the back of it, in utter disbelief because no one was there! Jhan then asked the other chaperone if he had seen anyone walking away from the area, back towards the exit. He confessed that he had not seen a soul. To this very day, none of them can explain exactly what they may have seen, but they do not rule out a supernatural visitation, a ghostly apparition perhaps, dressed in white pants![10]

One more tale, out of many more that are not covered here, is about an old tree. However, I will place a disclaimer on this story, for local folk have said to me that the details of the legend are incorrect. Such is the anomaly of folktales, but for the sake of regional lore, I am choosing to add the following account. As my mother would have warned, "Take it with a grain of salt!"

"The Old Hanging Tree" is a huge tree that is said to be more than 250 years old and grows just beside the historic courthouse in the center of town. Like many early American pioneering towns, hanging as a way to render fast justice happened just outside of a town's courthouse, and hanging as a form of execution was a standard practice before the year 1923. Some of the last hangings in Monticello took place on January 13, 1911; the men to be executed on that day were Sam Newkirk and Joseph Curry. They had been found guilty by a jury of their peers of murdering a local citizen, Jim Horton. Thursday was the chosen day for hanging people, and on the day of a scheduled execution, the shops and area businesses would close down at noontime as folks of the town would gather around the tree. Families with packed picnic lunches would wait to watch the execution. Even today, the sidewalks "roll up" on Thursdays as a way to hold to the remembrance of those hanging-days, when quick justice was meted out near the courthouse. The old oak also goes by the name of the "Meeting Oak" and is the place where Civil War soldiers gathered to get their military orders. Family members and other loved ones of those men and boys were known to assemble near the tree to extend their last farewells before each soldier headed off to war.

As for ghostly hauntings, a few people claim that they have captured weird images that later appear on photographs. There are tales of night travelers who, negotiating the sharp turn around the courthouse, have ended up wrecking their vehicles near the tree. Some of those drivers have asserted they lost control of the automobile because they saw the spectral image of a Confederate soldier with weapon in hand. Could those be outlandish claims? Or might the local journals of the time have encouraged ideas of the place—how some spiritual, historical energy may be lingering—a history of how loved ones said those last goodbyes to the men and boys who were later to die in war. Might some of those spirits still be trying to make a way back home?

During its restoration, workers said that they could hear the sounds of children's laughter. Courtesy of Graham Schorb

The Palmer House is another supposedly haunted place and is one of the most talked about places in the town of Monticello. The home has been called "the most haunted house in the South's most haunted small town." Courtesy of Graham Schorb

Some folks swear that when the moon is full, people who might happen by the old Palmer property are prone to see a spirit image of a gentleman. He is often seen carrying a doctor's bag, dressed in his frock coat; he may be sporting a top hat, for this ghostly apparition is famous for traipsing across his yard, coming from the outbuilding that served as his office as he makes his way back over to the Palmer home. Courtesy of Graham Schorb

Because of several epidemics that swept through the area in the 1800s, disease claimed the lives of many area residents, including quite a few children. Courtesy of Graham Schorb

One writer and ghost tracker claims, "Roseland Cemetery is the most haunted cemetery that I have been to. . . . I visited on a harvest moon with my electromagnetic field (EMF) reader and digital camera. On the north end of the cemetery, near the fence, I received high EMF readings. I sensed a spirit presence that continued to follow me throughout the cemetery." Courtesy of Graham Schorb

Located on North Jefferson Street is the Wirick-Simmons House built in the 1830s. It is known as one of the oldest houses in Monticello. Courtesy of Graham Schorb

One writer and psychic, who likes to hunt for ghosts and to promote the haunted South for visiting tourists, claims about the Wirick home ". . . guests have photographed apparitions of a woman in pink looking out of the upstairs window and another woman sitting on the porch." Courtesy of Graham Schorb

Thursday was the chosen day for hanging people, and on the day of a scheduled execution, the shops and area businesses would close down at noontime as folks of the town would gather around the tree. Families with packed picnic lunches would wait to watch the execution. Even today, the sidewalks "roll up" on Thursdays as a way to hold to the remembrance of those hanging days, when quick justice was meted out near the courthouse. Courtesy of Graham Schorb

The iconic Monticello Opera House, located near the courthouse in the center of town, is said to have its share of hauntings, like sounds emanating from a piano, moved objects, and ghostly visitations like the ones a few chaperones say they encountered on one particular prom night. Courtesy of Graham Schorb

Endnotes

1. Richard Southall, *Haunted Plantations of the South* (Woodbury, MN: Llewellyn Publications, 2015).

2. Betty Davis, Big Bend Ghost Trackers, *Haunted Monticello, Florida (Haunted Florida)* (Charleston, SC: History Press, 2011).

3. Michelle Davidson, *Florida's Haunted Hospitality* (Atglen, PA: Schiffer Publishing, 2013).

4. Davidson, *Florida's Haunted Hospitality*.

5. Davis, *Haunted Monticello*.

6. Davis, *Haunted Monticello*.

7. Davis, *Haunted Monticello*.

8. Davis, *Haunted Monticello*.

9. Davidson, *Florida's Haunted Hospitality*.

10. Jhan Reichert, conversation about Haunted Monticello: North Florida Community College Library, Madison, March 2017.

Leon County

Rose Knox and Graham Schorb

Travel Notes

Apalachee Natives

The ancients told many stories that involved mythical happenings. Sadly, most of the Apalachee legends were lost during the destruction of their culture. Some ideas remain, however, from other native voices. Here is one from the Eastern Band of the Cherokee, and it speaks of the importance of the land in relation to the people. Writer Susan Anderson reveals, "Many native people tell of a creation time when they emerged from the belly of the Mother earth at a place they know as the center, the heart of their land, the heart of their people."

Many ancient races believed in this same concept because they were an agricultural and a hunting people; the land was therefore the sustainer of the entire community.

In the Red Hills the Apalachee Confederation, like their neighbors the Timucua, grew crops and hunted game for survival.[1] They were also superb farmers, and their crops were pumpkins, maize, beans, and many kinds of fruit; they often enhanced their food crop by trapping turkey, deer, bear, and bison, making snares to catch the smaller game. Other foods in their diet were shellfish and fish they were able to catch from rivers, creeks, ponds, and lakes.[2] Often described as a "peaceful nation," they were the first of the Florida indigenous peoples to suffer almost complete decimation.[3] But the perception of their domain was misunderstood. According to two expert scholars on this confederation of peoples, "The Apalachee chiefdom may have been perceived as bigger and more important than it was because of its trade network and possible alliances with other important mound centers. . . . These centers extended north through Georgia into Alabama and westward into the Mississippi Valley and Oklahoma. . . .[4] Because of that misperception, European mapmakers gave the Apalachee's name to the Appalachian Mountains."[5]

As for their decimation, some written Spanish accounts from the early 1600s chronicle that disease had already destroyed much of the Native population. Only 107 Apalachee towns had been able to survive by that time; another account reveals there were only 8,000 Apalachee still alive by 1650. These Native people, like the Timucua, were eventually converted to Christianity; however, many resisted conversion for they longed to keep true to their own traditional spiritual ways which they had practiced for thousands of years. The destruction took many forms, but finally took its toll on the indigenous populations.

During the European encroachment, the Apalachee were also sold by the thousands as slaves to work on plantations of the Carolinas and in the Caribbean. Historical accounts give horrifying descriptions of how Native Americans living at the Apalachee mission site in what is today Tallahassee were set afire and burned alive. Other rebellious ones were flayed alive as punishment. But they, like the Timucuan peoples, had been a religious and self-sufficient society before the intrusion of the Spaniards.[6]

To sum it up, the indigenous people of what would eventually be named La Florida by the Spanish, would suffer from interaction with Europeans and also those peoples brought over later from Africa. The Africans became plantation slaves. By the middle of the seventeenth century, disease and enslavement had almost entirely decimated the coastal, indigenous populations. Native American groups in the interior fared slightly better, though in the long run, they too would experience the dire impact of ecological and environmental change brought about by the arrival of the Europeans and, later, the Africans. The Europeans relied heavily on African slave labor following the annihilation of Florida's indigenous Indians. After just 350 years of the European invasion, through disease, war, starvation, and forced exile, only 250,000 Natives still remained as of 1850.[7]

Other Suggested Reading: Miles Harvey, *Painter in a Savage Land* (New York: Random House, 2008).

The image of natives toiling in vast fields appeared in the artwork created by the artist de Bry. He named the piece "Grand Voyages: How They Till the Soil and Plan." De Bry published Le Moyne's watercolors in order to try to bring in support for European colonization. By depicting the Indians as primitive, yet also as a hardworking people, de Bry's hope was to calm any fears people had about exploring in the New World. In so doing, he wanted to encourage the spread of European civilization among the indigenous populations.

The following textual information chronicles the translation from De Bry. Plate XXI.

Mode of Tilling and Planting: "The Indians cultivate the earth with diligence. They have learnt to make hoes with fish bones and to fit them with wooden handles. With these they can dig the soil quite easily as it is not heavy. Once the earth has been well broken up and leveled, the women sow beans or millet or maize. To do this they are helped by people who precede them with a stick, and make holes in the soil where the grain or bean or millet is thrown. The sowing completed, they leave the field alone. It is, in fact, then their winter season which is quite cold in this region and which lasts three months, from 24 December to 15 March. Being always naked, the Indians then seek shelter in the forests. The winter over, they return to their houses, anticipating the ripening of the crops.

The harvest gathered, they store the corn for the year's uses, and do not trade with any of it except perhaps for some exchange of household articles." Text and Image Courtesy of the State Library and Archives of Florida

Rose Knox and Graham Schorb

Endnotes

1. Theodore Morris, *Florida's Lost Tribes* (Gainesville: University Press of Florida, 2004).

2. William R. Ervin, *Let Us Alone*, W and S Ervin Publishing, 1983.

3. James W. Covington, *The Seminoles of Florida* (Gainesville: University Press of Florida, 1993).

4. John H. Hann and Bonnie G. McEwan, *The Apalachee Indians and Mission San Luis, A Florida Heritage Publication* (Gainesville: University Press of Florida, 1998).

5. Hann and McEwan, *Apalachee Indians.*

6. Morris, *Florida's Lost Tribes.*

7. Covington, *Seminoles of Florida.*

Panfilo de Narvaez Marches through the
Land of the Apalachee

The Apalachee Indians had situated their chief villages among the lake regions of Tallahassee and around the St. Marks River and basin. Known as a fierce, courageous tribe, they occupied areas as far away as Pensacola. To the east of Apalachee country, however, ran the winding Aucilla River, where the Timucuan Indians lived and dominated.[1]

Though the Apalachee peoples had lived and farmed the fertile fields of the Red Hills for centuries without European intrusion, in 1528 they were to encounter the first of several Spanish invasions that would prove disastrous to their way of life. It was in that particular year that Pánfilo de Narváez, with his hundreds of men and forty-two horses, set out, venturing inland from the Tampa Bay area. He was going forth on his second attempt to find wealth and fame, for it had been in the spring, eight years prior, that Narváez had been taken prisoner by Cortez.

Narváez had tried unsuccessfully to take from Cortez the chance to exploit Mexico and he had lost his army and all that he had in trying to do so. But Charles V had granted him a second go at "glory," giving him the title of *adelantado*. The word means that he was granted special permission to go forth and find "new lands" to further the wealth, power, and domains for the crown.

In one diary entry by Cabeza de Vaca, he revealed why Narváez's army originally decided to head northward toward the land of the Apalachee. The entry read, "Having by signes asked the Indians whence these things came, they motioned to us that very far from here was a province called Apalachen where [there] was much gold and . . . an abundance of everything that we all cared for."[2]

The Apalachee peoples of these Red Hills, whom those other Natives had directed the Spanish toward, came from Muskogee lineage—but they were linguistically more closely related to the Choctaw than to the f3f335afa44a

Creeks. The name "A'palachi" translates from the Choctaw language and means "people on the other side."[3] These Spanish soldiers, with a lust for gold and fame, would eventually trudge into the domain of the Apalachee, but it would take many months of hard marching and hacking a way through La Florida's wilderness. Finally on December 27, named St. John's Day, a weary, footsore army showed up. These men were exhausted from long months of enduring the weight of burdensome armor, but they pressed on as they held the hope of gold in mind.

Cabeza, one survivor of this doomed quest, penned his first impressions, giving a descriptive visual of what the village, the lakes, forest, and wildlife looked like back then. He wrote, "The town consisted of forty small houses low and of thatch. . . . Throughout are immense trees and open woods. . . . There were many lakes great and small, and much larger than those we found before coming here. In this province are many maize fields; and the houses are scattered. There are deer of three kinds. . . . It has fine pastures of herds . . . geese in great number, royal ducks, night herons, and partridges."[4]

Some of his accounts were not so pleasant. In fact, cross-referencing de Soto's records, among the four accounts of de Soto's march, the record kept by Garcilaso de Vega is the most voluminous of all. Yet there seem to be some discrepancies when comparing those of Cabeza de Vaca's accounts. Garcilaso himself wrote about the varying depictions his sources supplied, and compared them to the description of the Land of Apalachee that was portrayed by Cabeza de Vaca. One modern translated entry of Cabeza de Vaca reveals, ". . . we made three expeditions through the land," which was "very poor in people and very bad for moving about because of the bad trails and woods and ponds it had."

Ewen and Hann express also that perhaps some of the descriptions may have come from the bad experiences that Narváez's army faced, when they write, "It could be that the Narváez expedition's hardships in Apalachee–failure to find the expected gold, the mauling that his men took, illness, and the beginning of long years of trauma in which most of the expedition perished–made Cabeza de Vaca remember Apalachee far more negatively than he otherwise would have." He also recorded the great destruction of forests, the many fallen trees; that entry suggests that a huge storm with wind of hurricane proportions had passed through right before Narváez and his army got to Apalachee.[5] For twenty-five days, which might have seemed like an eternity to his men, Narváez and his entourage wandered around in the vicinity of the sloping hills of Apalachee; by the end of July, they still had not found any signs of gold; plus they had been defending themselves from the violent attacks by the now-dispossessed Indians. Discouraged by these factors, they left Tallahassee, marching southward to Aute (known today as St. Marks). Little did they know that their hopes of fame and riches would soon be terribly dashed, because each mile they made led them ever closer to doom. They were trying to find Mexico via sea voyage by then, but a storm ended up swamping their crude, makeshift crafts, and most of the people on the expedition perished.[6]

Eleven years would go by before the Spanish would try their luck again at finding gold in these Red Hills of Apalachee.

For 25 days, which might have seemed like an eternity to his men, Narváez and his entourage wandered around in the vicinity of the sloping hills of Apalachee. By the end of July, they still had not found any signs of gold; plus they had been defending themselves from the violent attacks by the now-dispossessed Indians. Courtesy of State Library and Archives of Florida

HERE LANDED
PANFILO DE NARVAEZ
APRIL 15, 1528
FROM THE SITE OF THIS ANCIENT INDIAN
VILLAGE WAS LAUNCHED THE FIRST
EXPLORATION BY WHITE MAN OF THE
NORTH AMERICAN CONTINENT

The historical site and the surrounding recreational park are maintained and protected by the City of St. Petersburg. The area is situated near the eastern shore of Boca Ciega Bay, at Park Street North and Elbow Lane (17th Avenue) in the city. Courtesy of Graham Schorb

Rose Knox and Graham Schorb

Endnotes

1. Bertram H. Groene, *Ante-bellum Tallahassee* (Tallahassee: Florida Heritage Foundation, 1981).

2. Groene, *Ante-bellum Tallahassee*.

3. Groene, *Ante-bellum Tallahassee*.

4. Groene, *Ante-bellum Tallahassee*.

5. Charles R. Ewen and John H. Hann, *Hernando De Soto among the Apalachee: The Archaeology of the First Winter Encampment* (Gainesville: University Press of Florida, 1998).

6. Ewen and Hann, *Hernando De Soto*.

Hernando de Soto: A Quest for Gold

"They were the people through whose lands and bodies Hernando de Soto hacked a path from 1539 to 1542 in his search for wealth equal to what he had seen in Peru." Alfred Crosby[1]

Many depictions have been painted of the conquistador de Soto, and he has been called names ranging from a dashing knight to an untrustworthy, brutal fortune-seeker, and an exploiter in his lust for gold. No matter how he has been described, his presence in the Red Hills certainly made an impact on the people once living in the region. As has been chronicled previously in this work, it was early in October of 1539 that he finally arrived with his entourage of six hundred men, two hundred horses, his war dogs, and his swine. The pigs were brought along as a precautionary measure to use as a food supply, since earlier explorers had been forced to eat their own horses in times of desperation; the swine were first introduced to the New World during de Soto's quest. His expedition began from a pivotal staging point in Havana, Cuba, where he had been named governor. On May 18, 1539, he set sail, finally finding the shore off the west coast of La Florida a week afterwards. Why he chose to land in that coastal area, and to explore domains where other explorers had failed, is unclear. Perhaps he thought the resistance the Natives had shown in the past might be proof that they were cautiously guarding wealth, like gold, which he wanted to take. Or perhaps it was his ego at work, hoping to exploit the area where other renowned explorers had been unsuccessful. Some of those men were Juan Ponce de Leon (1521) and Pánfilo de Narváez (1528). Yet those leaders had perished during their quest for gold and glory. Because of those previous, ruinous explorations, de Soto made sure to put together one of the largest, most well-equipped, and most experienced group of soldiers to sail forth into the lands of the New World. Leaving from Cuba was also a strategic choice; departing from that location lessened the voyage time. His hope was that a shorter voyage might preserve the health and vitality of the horses, which were thought to be a crucial factor in the success of his exploration.

Rose Knox and Graham Schorb

As de Soto marched through La Florida, he chose to take an aggressive stance against the Natives, because Leon and Narváez had met with great hostilities from the Indians. In fact, Ponce de Leon had been hit with an arrow just after he landed, and he ultimately died from that wound. To illustrate the brutality the Natives suffered at de Soto's command, according to authors Ewen and Hann, ". . . often [de Soto's methods] took the form of holding a chief hostage or mutilating him as a warning to let the Spaniards pass unharmed."² Not surprisingly, such a fierce ploy to make the natives bend to his will, subservient to his passage, actually made them consistently more aggressive; therefore, de Soto's army was plagued with many ambushes and raids as they trudged forth through the Red Hills. When the Spaniards reached the lands of the Apalachee, de Soto's army also met with violent resistance from them, but de Soto's men were eventually able to take over the main village that was called Anhaica Apalachee. The village was large enough to house de Soto's soldiers, and the supply of maize they had stolen in their takeover of the Natives kept them well supplied with food.

Their winter encampment lasted almost five months, and proved anything but restful. Because the Natives resented the forced intrusion of their villages, and the raid on their stored supplies, they besieged the Spaniards at every turn. Records from the diaries of that expedition show that the Apalachee killed many in de Soto's entourage, while they also burned the village twice. In 1540, when the Spaniards decided to leave, they reported hauling stolen maize on the backs of their horses, while they used labor of captured men who had been forced, according to the diaries, to endure the winter with the Spanish invaders, while "naked" and in "chains."

The area of the winter encampment was later tested by the archeologist, B. Calvin Jones. Jones once stated about how he was randomly testing the site, actually in search of an old mission. ". . . the more I observed the Martin property [the ridge top] the more I sensed the realization that Spanish and Indians had shared their lives there."

Previous to Jones's discovery, the trek that de Soto and his entourage made, and the place he set up his first winter encampment, had been the subject of debate by many an archaeologist, cartographer, and historian. In the book, *Hernando de Soto among the Apalachee: The Archaeology of the First Winter Encampment*, the authors proclaim, about a vital and unexpected discovery of such great importance,

The odds against the discovery were enormous. If Calvin Jones hadn't believed that the Tama mission was located on the ridge east of the state capitol building, and if he hadn't taken note of the development activities before any serious construction began, and if he hadn't been bold enough to ask for permission to put in test pits, and if the developer hadn't been enlightened enough to grant that permission, then it is likely that the location of de Soto's winter encampment would still be lost to us today.[3]

Some of the test pits were conducted north to south between the Governor Martin Mansion and East Lafayette Street and continued in a curve around to the eastern side of the home. An east-to-west transect was also set up, and it ran along East Lafayette Street west of the drive. Among many other artifacts which were discovered, were coins, a crossbow, wrought-iron nails, seed beads, glass beads, and fragments of chain mail.[4]

Additional Note: Regarding the Cody Scarp area, according to a regional historian, the path of the march is described as such, "With cold weather approaching, de Soto was anxious to set up winter camp. Pushing on northwest, his probable trail took him through the Cody [Scarp] area, past Chaires Crossing, and into what is now Tallahassee."[5]

The legacy left by Spanish conquistadors like Narváez and de Soto was the spreading of contagious diseases like measles and smallpox. For over 150 years these infectious illnesses would continue to devastate the Native American communities, contributing greatly to the destruction of a once-powerful and self-sufficient race of people.[6]

The frantic war scene of George Gibbs's portrayal reveals the fervor
and the terror of conflicts involving Natives and conquistadors.
His painting, though not a Florida scene, depicts nevertheless the
collision of two varying cultures and belief systems. The battle
depicted here took place in what is today the state of Alabama.
Courtesy of Grace E. King, Macmillan Publishers, George Gibbs,
and the State Library and Archives of Florida

The scene shows state archaeologist, B. Calvin Jones, as he was excavating Hernando de Soto's 1539 winter encampment in Tallahassee, Florida. Jones received permission to explore the location prior to some construction, and during his work there, he uncovered coins, pottery, chain mail, beads, and pig bones that identified the encampment site. At the time of the excavation, this location was the only verified site for the entire de Soto expedition. Later the dig site was named a state park after the state purchased the area in 1988. Courtesy of Mike Ewen and the State Library and Archives of Florida; the photograph was taken in April of 1987.

Rose Knox and Graham Schorb

Endnotes

1. Charles R. Ewen and John H. Hann, *Hernando de Soto Among the Apalachee: The Archaeology of the First Winter Encampment* (Gainesville: University Press of Florida, 1998).

2. Ewen and Hann, *Hernando de Soto*.

3. Ewen and Hann, *Hernando de Soto*.

4. Ewen and Hann, *Hernando de Soto*.

5. Derylene Delp Counts, *Familiar Faces and Quiet Places: A Pictorial and Narrative History of Jefferson County, Florida* (Virginia Beach, VA: Donning Publishing, 2005).

6. Counts, *Familiar Faces*.

Apalachee: Mission of San Luis

In time, such Spanish invasions would change the lives of the Native Americans in significant ways, and colonizing occurred in numerous places. Well before the establishment of the first stable English colony in the United States, in Jamestown, Virginia, around the year 1620, Jesuit—and later, Franciscan—missionaries began establishing religious missions in territories that are now the states of Florida, Georgia, and South Carolina.[1] The period from 1568 through 1684 was the era of Catholic missions throughout present-day Georgia and Florida. During the conversion time, methods of worship, marriage, ceremonies, games, and manner of dress of the Natives were changed, or completely eradicated, in order that the Indians would begin to conform to Catholic traditions and doctrines. Any rebellious Indians attempting to resist the sweeping changes in their long-held cultural practices were mistreated, and many times even killed, by Spanish soldiers to serve as an example of what might happen to others if they attempted to defy conversion.[2] According to anthropologist, John E. Worth, the Mission at San Luis depicts the life and times of that period.[3] The ultimate objective of the mission period was to evangelize the native people, whom the Spanish referred to in their diaries as "pagans" and "infidels." The friars' main mission was to convert natives into the faith by baptizing them, teaching them the Catechism, and familiarizing them with particular rituals to go along with religious sacraments.[4]

In time, attacks on Spanish settlements and missions by the British and the Creeks significantly reduced agricultural and herding activities in La Florida. In 1704 Carolina settlers and their Creek Indian allies invaded Mission San Luis. Such a blow against the Spanish mission system displaced Apalachees living west of the Suwannee River. Apalachee refugees then fled, migrating to St. Augustine or west towards Louisiana, and some became captives of the Creeks and the British. The British enslaved hundreds of Apalachee Indians who were used as labor on sugar-producing islands in the Caribbean. Creek Indians also participated in the process of enslavement, though they likely adopted some of the Apalachee tribe members into their own ranks. Because of those persistent slave raids and warfare in the late seventeenth and early eighteenth centuries, such conflict and decimation created a population vacuum in northern and central Florida. After the destruction of the mission system, Spanish settlers, their slaves, and the few Apalachee Indians remaining in Florida retreated to within a short distance of St. Augustine and Pensacola until the 1760s. Later still, Native American immigrants from the north gradually moved into the now-abandoned lands. By the 1750s Seminole towns had replaced previous settlements west of St. Augustine.

Researching a Spanish Mission Site: When Graham and I toured the Spanish mission site in Tallahassee, we analyzed the portrayals there by two artists, John Lo Castro and Edward Jonas. The artists had been commissioned to bring the Spanish mission period back to life, creating historical scenes on murals and canvases which are positioned throughout the former mission site known as San Luis.

Several paintings were quite thought-provoking. To illustrate, Edward Jonas, using specific archeological notes, reconstructed the mission church very accurately on his canvas—even before the now-standing reconstructed building was ever erected. Since no image was available to us, I will paint a verbal picture of what we saw. [The museum owned the rights to the painting and would not give permission for us to use it, though the artist was open to our including his art.] In one of his elaborate paintings, Edward Jonas brings the time period to life, as he portrays the natives lining up to walk inside the mission church. One Indian mother holds her baby as she prepares to cross the threshold of the church. She will soon have her child baptized into the Catholic faith. In addition the symbol of a cross is visible in the background. In the foreground, Natives stand watching the procession of other Indians still awaiting baptism. The church bell used for beckoning people from distant areas is also visible. Jonas wrote to me once about his work. He said of his mission canvas:

> . . . the slope of the church in the painting is set to only a 30 degree slope! I began the painting before the reconstruction of any of the historic buildings was begun so there was no church, council house, or friary to paint 'from life.' In fact, I was only provided the dig plan that showed the positions of the post holes for any of these buildings, which meant that much of what I painted was speculative even though I did have the council (sic) of the leading authorities in colonial architecture."[5]

Yet another painting which was particularly engrossing there at San Luis was of a mission priest directing the placement of a wooden cross. Under the heavy beams, bearing its incredible weight, were three strong, muscled Natives laboring together. They were working to place the wooden symbol upright under the specific directions given by the friar. The priest stands in the foreground pointing and giving instructions to the natives.

Each painting might portray significant metaphors. For example, the depiction of a threshold of the church reveals how the Native Americans were being brought into a new world, and a new way of living. In time, walking through that entranceway would alter their existence, because conversion meant they were not only giving up their own deities, but were walking away from their cultural past. As in most colonial periods of history, they were given little choice in the matter.

The other image illustrates natives holding up a heavy load, the cross, and that image is yet another symbol that reveals the new challenges of converting an eternal soul to the faith. The painting symbolizes the sweeping consequences of how the indigenous cultures would soon face annihilation of their own belief systems, a heavy burden to bear for their entire culture, as the Spanish priests systematically altered and/or eliminated all of their ancient Indian customs.[6]

The council house at San Luis, it is believed, was one of the largest Native American gatherings provided space for many activities, both spiritual and recreational. They included rituals, preparations for war, and dances. The structures also provided the place where Apalachee rulers met each day to discuss community affairs. Courtesy of Graham Schorb

On the evening before the ball game, certain rituals had to be conducted inside of the council house. An elevated bench was reserved for the chief. New fires were lit between the chief's and the players' benches; those new fires were to be used only for lighting the chief's tobacco pipe. In order to be ritually purified, the chief also fasted, and he spent the night smoking tobacco and drinking cassina, the black drink. It was a dark brew loaded with caffeine. The consumption of the black drink would bring on nausea. Courtesy of Graham Schorb

Over the last two decades much research has been conducted concerning the missions of Spanish Florida. An expert on the subject is Bonnie McEwan and she states in her article titled "The Spiritual Conquest of La Florida," "Religious architecture and mortuary data are more closely related than one initially might think since most mission cemeteries in Florida have been located beneath church floors." Such is the case at Mission Luis. The San Luis Mission in Tallahassee, Florida, attempts to recreate the history of the mission period. Since all residents of San Luis were Christians or had been converted to Christianity, many of them were buried in the church's cemetery. Prominent people of the community were laid to rest closest to the church's altar. Courtesy of Graham Schorb

Rose stands at the gate of the reconstructed Spanish Fort at San Luis. From the 1650s when San Luis was initially founded, its military garrison was a blockhouse. However, a full-scale fortification was not built until the 1690s when the danger of British invasion became imminent. Later, persistent attacks on Spanish settlements and missions by the British and the Creeks significantly reduced herding and agricultural activities in La Florida. In 1704 Carolina settlers and their Creek Indian allies destroyed Mission San Luis. Such a decisive blow against the Spanish mission system displaced Apalachees living west of the Suwannee River. Courtesy of Graham Schorb

The San Luis site reconstructs the living quarters of some of the Europeans during the mission period. Courtesy of Graham Schorb

Europeans of higher status slept in a bed that looked like the one pictured here. Courtesy of Graham Schorb

Rose Knox and Graham Schorb

Endnotes

1. Georgia Historical Society, "Spanish Missions: Early Encounters between the Christian and the "'Noble Savage,'" brochure.
2. Georgia Historical Society, "Spanish Missions."
3. Edward Jonas, email communication, "Mission at San Luis Art and Excavation," April 2012.
4. Georgia Historical Society, "Spanish Missions."
5. Jones, "Mission" email.
6. Georgia Historical Society, "Spanish Missions."

A Trip to Ancient Temple Mounds:
Leon County

"In a certain way, I feel the land has a memory of its own. The memory of the suffering can still be felt in the Southeastern United States. You can go into the sites where Indian villages (and even we might say cities once were) and you can see the ruins, you can see the mounds where people were buried–and you don't see the people; and you know immediately there was a great and tragic story there. I think the story still lives, even if it is not in the history books; it is still there, in the land itself." Anthropologist Jack Weatherford[1]

Graham and I, with River, our little dog, awoke bright and early on December 31, 2018, and headed west. We were to meet our friend, Pat Elliott, at an intriguing archaeological site. Pat is a regional artist who has spent a lifetime studying and painting southern subjects for museums and environmental projects in the Southeast; he wanted to stroll around the ancient site with us.

Visiting the temple mounds and plaza was an exciting prospect! Relics found at that location have offered clues about a birdman dancer–the symbol that held significance for the people of this once-structured society. We met Pat in the parking lot and headed for a short walk to the picnic area, a pavilion that displayed thought-provoking, artistic renderings and photographic history. There were mounds visible in several locations as we moseyed along the sidewalk. We learned that the site, now called the Lake Jackson Mounds and Archaeological State Park, located at 3600 Indian Mounds Road in Tallahassee, was once a significant socio-religious complex. Situated directly on the shores of a large lake today called Lake Jackson, archaeologists refer to the area as the "Southern Cult" or the "Southeastern Ceremonial Complex," which was thriving around A.D. 1200. The site, however, dates back to 1000 A.D., extending to around 1450 A.D., which is known as the Fort Walton period. The location was most likely the religious and political center for the Native Americans during the timespan of A.D. 1200 to A.D. 1500.

Within the complex are seven earthen temple mounds, rising high over the landscape.[2] Spanish diaries and the temple mounds themselves can tell an important story of life and death, according to scholars. In the very stratified society of the Apalachee, Confederation chiefs and other high leaders were given special treatment. Such privileges were many, including the control over storehouses of food; receiving exemption from hard labor; entitlement to goods or riches obtained from raiding enemies; and exemption from disciplines such as beatings. The chiefs furthermore held power to keep all panther and bear skins that had been hunted on domains that were under their jurisdiction. Leaders even received royal treatment after death, and in prehistoric times a high chief, members of his family, and perhaps even his servants were ceremonially interred within the platform mounds, buried with relics and clothing that signified the status of the person.

To contrast with the burial chiefs, common individuals were most often buried outside of their homes, interred in pits.[3] Gazing across the lone field today, it might be hard to envision a busy village, but try to imagine thatched huts dotting the landscape; the laughter of children as they are darting about, or swimming and splashing, immersed in the gurgling creek; women cooking, making clay bowls, or preparing maize; fishermen coming in from the lake in dugout canoes, carrying a bounty of otter, bass, or alligator; fires burning, the delicious aroma of venison, fish, or geese wafting in the air; muscular, young men readying themselves for a fierce, athletic ballgame; or traders negotiating the value of various items. The village was indeed a hustle bustle place in antiquity.

Archaeological digs have certainly given modern-day people clues about these Indians. As aforementioned, skeletons of high-ranking citizens were buried there, lending credence to the political and religious significance of the place. Along with human remains, in some of the mortuary mounds, burial objects tell a story, too. Found inside the mounds were impressive copper breastplates, with the image of a birdman carved into them. Other items included bracelets, anklets, beaded necklaces, and cloaks. According to one state source, "These exotic artifacts indicate pre-historic Indian ceremonial centers in the southeastern United States such as Etowah in Georgia, Moundville in Alabama, and Duck River in Tennessee."[4]

From the oak-shaded picnic pavilion at the Lake Jackson locale, we began to approach the largest mound, making our way across the footbridge and crossing over the creek. The mound rises thirty-six feet above the plaza and is a striking sight! There is a wooden staircase leading to the top, where a detailed art rendering depicts what the hectic village complex might have once looked like. Looking across the expanse of the field, and over toward the large lake, we all tried to imagine how life was lived back then. Pat looked skyward and spotted an eagle. What an appropriate sighting over the very place where two birdman copper plates were once interred, along with some high-ranking individual of the society!

Graham and I have also visited the Etowah site in Georgia, where a large stone bird-effigy was laid out by the ancient peoples. Rock Eagle effigy mound is 102 feet long from head to tail and it has a 120-foot wingspan. The large stone bird measures eight feet vertically, from the ground to the top of the bird's chest. The head of the great bird faces east, the direction of the rising sun. The bird is constructed entirely of white quartzite rocks of various sizes. Many of the rocks were too large for one individual to carry by hand; archaeologists believe they were dragged to the site using deerskins. Archaeologists and anthropologists are convinced that these people of the Southeast were well connected with one another.

Those folks interested in hiking on a trail can walk the wooded loop in the park called Butler Mill Trail where interpretive signs remind visitors of Florida's Territorial Period and early statehood from 1825 until 1860. At that time the land was owned by Colonel Robert Butler, a wealthy plantation owner. Remnants of an 1800s grist mill are still visible.[5] Wildlife abounds, so be on the lookout for birds of many kinds, including eagles, hawks, osprey, cardinals, and hummingbirds, among other kinds of birds. Deer, squirrels, and turtles live also in the surrounding area.

Oral Legend: Hawkman and Turtleman

Emma Johnson, of Black Creek heritage, recited the following story. Her narrative of a Birdman and Turtleman has been passed down for generations, and comes from the Paleolithic oral tradition.

J. R. Daniels from Jacksonville, Florida, recorded her story during the 1940s and 1950s when he entered her home and asked her to explain the meaning behind the drawings he saw of copper breastplates that she had displayed. Theodore Morris, the painter of the lost tribes of Florida, read the poem at a seminar titled "Art and Archaeology." I requested the story from Morris, and I typed it below in the exact same manner that Morris sent it to me.

Emma Johnson began telling J. R. Daniels the following tale, which was written down in the phonetics of her special speech patterns:

Duh Hawkman kom wid federed robe

foe to ber ma chile away

He fly now to dem heben's high

in duh stahrs he gonna stay

Dat Turdle man, he dived duh mud

he spraid et out in a day

He taught us pilgrims how to swim

under the Father's Eye they say

He brokes his back wid a wicked word

crak dat shell wid dem ebil ways

But duh Hawkman kom wid duh federed robe

foe to ber ma chile away

Done took ma boy from dis Turdle land

done put 'em in duh Father's Eye

Can't call dat chile by name no moe

can't call him down from duh sky

But Breather got 'em in his hand

gonna git us all by and by

Gonna take us off dis Turdle land

Hawkman takes us when we die

Opa hoots on dem dark ole nights

dat burd is got a lonesome cry

He calls for the Hawkman in dat robe

foe to bring us to duh sky. Leetsha!

Other Version: Translated

The Hawkman came with feathered robe
to bear my child away
He's flown now to the heaven's high
in the stars he's going to stay
The Turtle man, he dived for the mud
he spread it out in a day
He taught us pilgrims how to swim
under the Father's Eye, they say
He broke his back with a wicked word
cracked the shell with those evil ways
But the Hawkman came with the feathered robe
to bear my child away
Took my boy from this Turdle land
and put him in the Father's Eye
I can't call that child by name anymore
can't call him down from the sky
The Master of Breath has him in his hand
he'll take us all by and by
He'll take us off this Turtle-land
Hawkman takes us when we die
Owl hoots in the dark dark night
that bird has a lonesome cry
He calls for the Hawkman in the feathered robe
to take us to the sky! Legar'!

Rose Knox and Graham Schorb

From the oak-shaded picnic pavilion, we began to approach the largest mound, making our way across the footbridge and crossing over the creek. The mound rises 36 feet above the plaza and is a striking sight! There is a wooden staircase leading to the top, where a detailed art rendering depicts what the hectic village complex might have once looked like on any given day. Looking across the expanse of the field and over toward the large lake, we all tried to imagine how life was lived back then. Pat looked skyward and spotted an eagle. What an appropriate sighting over the very place where two birdman copper plates were once interred, along with some high ranking individual of the society! Courtesy of Graham Schorb

We met Patrick Elliott, our friend and Tallahassee artist, in the parking lot and soon headed for a short walk to the picnic area, a pavilion that displayed thought-provoking artistic renderings and photographic history. There were mounds visible in several locations as we moseyed along the sidewalk. We learned that the site, now called the Lake Jackson Mounds and Archaeological State Park, was once a significant socio-religious complex. The Apalachee Confederation was a highly organized political, social, and religious system. This particular site is situated directly on the shores of a large lake, today called Lake Jackson. On top of the mound, and behind us as we posed, was an open field. Gazing across the lone field today, it might be hard to envision a busy village, but try to imagine thatched huts dotting the landscape; the laughter of children as they are darting about, or swimming and splashing, immersed in the gurgling creek; women cooking, making clay bowls, or preparing maize; fishermen coming in from the lake in dug-out canoes, carrying a bounty of otter, bass, or alligator; fires burning, the delicious aroma of venison, fish, or geese wafting in the air; muscular young men readying themselves for a fierce, athletic ballgame; or traders negotiating the value of various items. The village was indeed a hustle bustle place in antiquity! Courtesy of Graham Schorb

Rose Knox and Graham Schorb

Morris depicts the reverence the natives had for birds. The Hawk Man, a story about a bird deity, illustrates such reverence. Courtesy of Theodore Morris

Endnotes

1. DeSoto & the Mississippi Valley/1539 (500 Nations: The Story of Native Americans), published by PANGA, Youtube video, November 7, 2017.

2. Florida State Parks, Florida Department of Environmental Protection, "Lake Jackson Mounds Archaeological State Park," October 2015.

3. John H. Hann and Bonnie G. McEwan, *The Apalachee Indians and Mission San Luis, A Florida Heritage Publication* (Gainesville: University Press of Florida, 1998).

4. Florida State Parks, "Lake Jackson Mounds."

5. Florida State Parks, "Lake Jackson Mounds."

Rose Knox and Graham Schorb

Travel Notes

Cascades: Crystal Fountain Gushing

[The place] ". . . might be taken for a land of Fairies . . . a crystal fountain, gushing . . . sound of a beautiful cascade . . . the water is plenty and good . . ."[1]

When my child, Jessica, was toddling around, I often showed her special wonders of the natural world. We were lucky to be so close to one place, situated in the mountains of western North Carolina, where we lived briefly in the 1980s; there she experienced "music" at a waterfall known as Looking Glass Falls in the Pisgah National Forest. I recall standing there, wading in a clear pool, holding her close to my heart, and feeling mist from giant falls blanketing us with cool spray. The water seemed to refresh our skin—and our souls. Such a feeling evoked by the sound and sensation of water is why water has always been vital to the idea of renewal, and often used in ritual for spiritual cleansing.

Down from those mountains, much farther south in the land of the Apalachee, a magnificent waterfall once upon a time, thousands of years ago, existed in the sloping hills of north Florida. According to tales and witnesses, it was a place of splendor where the ancient Natives gathered; and perhaps over a span of many thousands of years, mothers stood there holding their own children, while delighting in the sound and sensation of falling water.

Imagine for a moment a dense hardwood forest of oak and magnolia, with tiny tributaries winding their way beneath green canopies. While you are pretending, hear, too, the sound of roaring water. There is a cascading waterfall! If someone is standing below it, they stare in awe twenty, maybe even thirty, feet upwards. At the bottom the person is then wading in a clear pool, as cool mist invigorates the body.

The "Cascades" (or Cascade), as locals in the 1800s liked calling it, was a place for folks to gather and to socialize. A few were baptized in the refreshing pool, while others set up along the stream to enjoy a picnic and to fellowship with friends. Some swam and others fished.

Rose Knox and Graham Schorb

It can be surmised that further back in time, the pool was a source of water, a place of sacred serenity for the ancient peoples. Might such a cool pool also have attracted thirsty beasts, like a saber-toothed cat, a tiny horse, or the giant creature, a mammoth?

According to Jonathan Lammers, a historian known for his comprehensive research on the Cascades, the creek once wound through the valley situated at the eastern edge of Tallahassee. Then it would flow into a ravine, which was caused by erosion. If you are ever in Tallahassee near the hillside where the capitol is today, that is where it flowed; most likely on the east side of what is currently South Monroe, where the railroad bridge is built over the road. Firsthand accounts in the early 1820s demonstrate what travelers once described when first seeing the towering waterfall. The place ". . . might be taken for a land of Fairies . . . a crystal fountain, gushing . . . sound of a beautiful cascade . . . the water is plenty and good. . . ."[2]

As the territory opened up and more pioneers poured in, the settlers soon built a mill by the stream. Changes came fast to the Cascades. The place that had gone untouched for thousands of years was being transformed. The materials to make mortar were mined; those ancient shells and fossils were dug out and used to make Florida's second capitol in 1826. If someone at that time were to look upon the waterfall, they would have seen a rock quarry beside it. Later, in the 1850s, more changes came. Men surveying, working for the railroad, determined that the "best" route over the sloping terrain of Tallahassee was to follow the valley of the St. Augustine Branch. That route would run the tracks over the exact ridge where the Cascades waterfall was located. The surveyors decided the "V" made by the waterfall would damage the rail tracks. With that concern, they "solved the problem" by filling in the natural chasm with railway ties and other debris. Their goal was to make the place level for the railway.[3]

As time slipped by, 1895 brought even more destructive changes to the Cascades. That is when the city of Tallahassee built a coal gasification plant in order to offer natural gas for local citizens. Toxic concoctions of tar and various chemicals were dumped into the once pristine St. Augustine Branch and those poisons were absorbed by the earth; toxins that remain there still. After that contamination, the Cascades' pool was polluted, so city officials deemed the area a health threat because it now seemed the "perfect environment" for mosquitoes to thrive. The once clear pool, a hallowed, beautiful place for the ancient people and beasts, was now a stagnant tarn. It soon became a popular place for area residents to dump trash.

In the 1970s a portion of land in downtown Tallahassee was named Cascades Park. At one time there was even talk of restoring the memory of the waterfall and pool by making an artificial one. A couple of architects were hired to draw a rendering of a modern-day construct that might resemble the once-natural waterfall. It would be the focal point of the park. That plan failed because the person, and the political voice of the idea, left local government to serve on a seat in Congress. But even with his help, the idea was doomed to fail because the U.S. Environmental Protection Agency, the EPA, had determined the area was still very toxic, reporting "substantial endangerment to public health."[4]

A modern-day visitor to a small area named Cascades Park will have to imagine the splendor of sound and sensation in a place once dubbed "a land for fairies" and "a crystal fountain gushing." Only in memory can a person today muse of that natural bygone wonder, forever destroyed by the exploits of what people called progress.

The lithograph is from a drawing by Comte Francis de Castelnau, and depicts the image of the once-pristine waterfall located in the Land of the Apalachee. Courtesy of the State Library and Archives of Florida 1839

Endnotes

1. Julie Hauserman, "Florida's Lost Waterfall: Cascades Park," in *Between Two Rivers: Stories from the Red Hills to the Gulf,* Susan Cerulean, Janisse Ray, and Laura Newton, eds. (Tallahassee, FL: Red Hills Writers Project, 2004).

2. Hauserman, "Florida's Lost Waterfall."

3. Hauserman, "Florida's Lost Waterfall."

4. Hauserman, "Florida's Lost Waterfall."

Rose Knox and Graham Schorb

Travel Notes

Planters of Territorial Tallahassee

"Tallahassee's existence depended upon its official status as capital of the territory and later the state. Its prosperity rested upon its merchants and the fortunes of the surrounding plantations and farms, and the labor of their slaves. By 1860 there were over 300 farms and plantations and over 9,000 slaves. The 3,000 white people of the Tallahassee country were to be outnumbered three to one by Negroes by the beginning of the Civil War."[1]

Individuals and entire caravans of planters with their families, possessions, livestock, and slaves flooded to the Tallahassee territory, hoping to establish fruitful plantations. Over the years, people with names like Call, Butler, Chaires, Brown, Gamble, Eppes, Branch, Croom, Ward, Hopkins, Randolph, Haywood, Whitfield, Williams, Cotten, Bailey, Kirksey, Carr, and many, many others would settle in the region. Some of their stories are told here, but this chronicle is merely a sketch and does mention all planters of the Tallahassee territory.

Back then, prosperity and fortunes, indeed, were to be had by a few in those sloping hills once known as the land of the Apalachee. It would be in the late 1820s that word got around that Middle Florida had some of the most fertile soil in the American South; that is when planters began preparing land for tilling and planting their cotton. As has been formerly chronicled, those lands had once been inhabited and farmed by Native Americans for thousands of years before the arrival of these planters. Some of the planters were personal friends of Andrew Jackson. One was Robert Butler and the other was Richard K. Call. Call had served previously in the Creek War of 1812 with Jackson, and he was also known as a frequent guest at Jackson's estate, the Hermitage, in Tennessee. Call would later become governor twice. The Tennesseean, Robert Butler, had likewise been with "Old Hickory" at the Battle of New Orleans and had helped Jackson capture St. Marks, taking it from Spanish control in the First Seminole War. To make an even closer connection, Butler had been wed to Mrs. Jackson's niece. Sage advice has always proclaimed, "It's not what you know, but who you know," and such was the case with Butler and Call. Both of these men were in the right place at the right time, and their close connection to Andrew Jackson gave them the privilege to acquire the choicest of land in Middle Florida.[2]

Lake Jackson was the place where General Robert Butler would ultimately build his plantation, on the southwestern shore of the lake. One of the most talked-about events of that time was called "The Feast of Roses." It was a lavish affair, a party that was considered the highlight of the year for the aristocratic class. To be included as a guest of General Butler was a great honor to an area planter. The name of the gathering was inspired by Mrs. Butler's famously known "glorious" rose garden.[3]

Richard K. Call, the other close associate of Andrew Jackson, eventually built two plantations. One was situated on Lake Jackson and was named Orchard Pond while the other, located north of the old town boundary limits of Tallahassee, was called The Grove. In time, Call would build a manor house as well.[4]

Try to picture the scene if you can: a Virginia man begins moving ever southward in the winter of 1827-'28. This man would become the future governor. Mr. Brown was, in that winter season, in charge of a caravan that included his family. Traveling with them were 140 of his slaves. The Gamble brothers came, too. And then there was Francis Eppes. He was in mourning, sorrowful over the death of his grandfather, Thomas Jefferson. He also traveled with a caravan of women and children who were riding in carriages. The men were mounted on horses, and the wagons were loaded with possessions and supplies; the slaves were in the back of the group, trudging the terrain, walking the far distance. At first Eppes was to forge into an area near the Georgia line, where he would purchase acreage on a place called Black Creek, naming that cotton plantation L'Eau Noir. When his wife died and he started to feel the real threat of potential violence caused by ever-increasing conflicts of an impending Indian War, he sold that plantation, relocating to the Tallahassee territory, where he bought land several miles from the town of Tallahassee. He would eventually grow cotton.[5]

There was, too, Frederick R. Cotten, who was the owner of thousands of acres. Records indicate he owned 274 slaves. Joseph John Williams was yet another prominent planter in antebellum Tallahassee territory. He owned five plantations which comprised 4,000 acres and were worked by 245 slaves. There was also one South Carolina planter in particular who had quite a curious background. In the 1850s a free mulatto, whose name was Dorothy O'Cane, aged fifty-nine, came to the area; she was said to have owned three houses, ten slaves, and many acres of land.[6]

All in all, these big landowners and cotton producers, establishing their plantations in the English baronial style, made Leon County the biggest cotton-producing county to rival that of the whole territory—and even the state of Florida. According to Dr. Bertram H. Groene, in his scholarly work of the period, "By 1860 they produced 12,000 of the total 16,000 cotton bale crop piled on the docks for shipment at St. Marks and Newport. This meant that three-fourths of the profits from the only major money crop in the Tallahassee country bellowed to these few." "These few," meaning about seventy-nine planters who owned and farmed over two-thirds of all of the best corn and cotton fields in the Red Hills region.[7]

The image of Robert Butler, a plantation owner in Tallahassee, Florida, depicts his likeness and was taken shortly before his death in 1860. He was a military aide to Andrew Jackson, was a Surveyor General for the territory of Florida, and did the survey of Tallahassee. He also organized the first fraternal organization in Tallahassee, Jackson Lodge #23, Masonic Lodge. Butler owned a plantation on the southwest shore of Lake Jackson, where the "Feast of Roses" annual celebration, named for Mrs. Butler's rose garden, was held. Text and image Courtesy of the State Library and Archives of Florida

Francis Wayles Eppes was a plantation owner in Tallahassee, Florida. He was a three-time mayor of Tallahassee and was the grandson of Thomas Jefferson. Eppes was born in 1801 and came to Tallahassee 1827. He later moved to Orange County in 1869. Eppes died on May 30, 1881. Text and Image Courtesy of the State Library and Archives of Florida

Rose Knox and Graham Schorb

Endnotes

1. Bertram H. Groene, *Ante-Bellum Tallahassee,* Florida Heritage Foundation, Tallahassee, 1981.

2. Groene, *Ante-Bellum Tallahassee.*

3. Groene, *Ante-Bellum Tallahassee.*

4. Groene, *Ante-Bellum Tallahassee.*

5. Groene, *Ante-Bellum Tallahassee.*

6. Groene, *Ante-Bellum Tallahassee.*

7. Groene, *Ante-Bellum Tallahassee.*

Goodwood Plantation and the
Croom Family

"The promises of Florida as a future agricultural kingdom
were touted by word of mouth, personal correspondence,
and newspaper descriptions with no less hyperbole than
descriptions of Alabama's Black Belt, Louisiana's river
bottoms, or, later, the Delta of Mississippi and Arkansas. Yet
the history of antebellum Florida's plantation region is less
well known. . . ."[1]

The story of the Croom family, and the establishment of Goodwood
Plantation and the eventual litigation that would follow, is a long and
involved one. Rogers and Clark, in their definitive work *The Croom
Family and Goodwood Plantation: Land, Litigation, and Southern
Lives*, portray a detailed story that makes an interesting chapter to
add to Leon County's antebellum history, a history that is less well
known than that of other cotton states like Louisiana, Mississippi, or
Arkansas. The authors write of Goodwood, "One of the most elegant
mansions in Florida . . . [is] one of Tallahassee's grandest historical
monuments. It was once the center of a thriving plantation founded
by the Croom family of North Carolina. . . . Hardy and Bryan Croom
developed Goodwood Plantation to over four thousand acres with
nearly two hundred slaves before Hardy along with his family were
killed in a shipwreck."[2]

How the family saga all began was with a wealthy patriarch of the
Croom family of eastern North Carolina as he made his way to Middle
Florida looking for fertile soil. William Croom would be the catalyst
and the head of the family, and he was more driven by his restless
spirit than a hungry desire for land, like the mass migration of so many
other planters of that day. Croom came from planters and politicians,
and he served in those same roles himself. Croom was born in January
1772 on his father's plantation in Dobbs (later Lenoir) County, North
Carolina. William's father, Major Croom, was the son of Daniel Croom.

Daniel came from Limerick, Ireland, around 1683. He migrated to Virginia by the early 1700s and later was endowed with a 400-acre land grant from King George II.

William Croom served in the colonial House of Commons and eventually the legislature as a senator. He was also an officer in the North Carolina state militia during the war of 1812 with a rank of major general, and he directed three brigades of militia from Lenoir and Jones Counties. After the War of 1812, William Croom retired to Newington, North Carolina, increasing his landholdings by buying several plantations, named Friendship Hall, Tower Hill, and Rountree. Territory farther south started to come open, and the propaganda of the time, publicizing that Middle Florida had ". . . fruitful soil and delightful climate . . . ," also prompted him to buy land. By the mid-1820s, William had visited, then bought, tracts of land in Gadsden County. However, in 1829 he became very sick with a serious "bilious" fever and died. Before his death, he had divided his large estate equally among his wife and children, including his daughters. Such was a practice of many wealthy, land-rich Southerners. In addition William Croom, much like other affluent planters, married more than one woman and fathered two sets of children. His first wife, Mary Bryan, bore him four children. When she died in 1807, he married, in 1809, Elizabeth "Betsy" Whitfield. Part of her dowry included slaves and land. With her, Croom had five children.[3]

Although in 1826 and 1828 William had first purchased land in Gadsden County, he never became a citizen of the Territory of Florida. Yet Bryan, a son by his first marriage, did. Richard, another son of his first marriage, bought large land tracts in Florida, and another son—again by the first marriage—Hardy Brian, established himself as a voter and signed his name to documents, listing himself as a citizen of Florida.

Accordingly, it would be Hardy and his brother Bryan who would eventually establish what came to be known as Goodwood Plantation, Hardy being the most involved. Hardy was considered a member of the upper echelon of the Southern aristocratic class, playing many important and diverse roles: aristocrat, intellectual, lawyer, scientist, writer, amateur botanist, linguist, planter, and slave owner. He was also one of only ten students in the class of 1817 at the University of North Carolina at Chapel Hill.

By 1831 Hardy was beginning to establish himself in Florida, though he divided his time, like many aristocratic planters of his day, between many places, some of which were North Carolina, New York City, and Charleston, South Carolina. But for all of his wanderings, from 1830 to 1837 he spent more time in Florida than any of those other locales. Nonetheless, there is no record that his wife or his daughters ever came to visit or to stay in Leon or Gadsden Counties. It should furthermore be noted that Hardy discovered a rare coniferous tree in Gadsden County, naming it *torreya taxifolia* after his botanist friend, Dr. John Torrey of New York City. Many years down the road, Dr. Torrey would take great pains to make sure a memorial was set up for his friend, Hardy.

By 1834 Hardy had negotiated to purchase land that encompassed some of the area of the Lafayette Grant and had begun planting there. Because Hardy traveled a great deal, he employed overseers in Leon and Gadsden Counties. These overseers were in charge of many duties, legal and civic, and they ensured that work was completed by slave labor. They also depended on others to help them. One local history book reveals, "The overseers at Goodwood ... were dependent on the judgment and skills of Fortune, a slave driver of rare talent."[4]

In the fall and winter season of 1835–'36, Hardy, according to his letters, spent time in both Leon and Gadsden counties. "Rocky Comfort" was the plantation in Gadsden, owned by Hardy's brother Bryan. Hardy also owned a cabin on Lake Lafayette, and a foreign artist once made a sketch of it.

The home, which was built on section 29 of the land grant, was first begun by Hardy and finished by Bryan. That first home faced west, positioned on a 150-foot-high hill. Breezes helped combat Florida's heat. Nearby, and located north of the home, bubbled up clear springs that offered a fresh abundance of water for the Crooms and hundreds of their slaves. This home has seen many changes over the years and is today known as the "Guest House."

Though it was well built and a comfortable structure, the home was not affluent enough for a major planter. Grand houses often served as status symbols in the antebellum South and people with money built houses in line with their financial and social status. Bryan and his wife therefore started preparations to build a house suitable to their high station. There has been a great deal of debate about exactly when Goodwood was built. Some scholars contend it was begun in the mid-1840s by a builder named Richard A. Shine. Shine was a longtime friend of Bryan's and a fellow North Carolinian. The home was completed by Hardy's brother Bryan; and Bryan and his wife Eveline lived in it. Eveline wanted a stately home. This one would be mostly Greek Revival in design with an Italianate look about it, a European-based romantic architectural movement that influenced the design of many a southern mansion in the nineteenth century.

The three-storied mansion faced south and had quite a few outstanding and lavish features. The 7,588-square-foot house included floors of heart pine; six-panel heart pine doors; silver-plated hardware on the doors; a Gothic-style window; frescoed ceilings in the north and south parlors; elaborate trim and ceiling medallions portraying the Italianate style; a ten-foot pier mirror, called a looking glass by people of that time, located in each parlor room; a thirty-inch, marble-topped console table below each mirror; and in each of the four parlors, an eight-foot-wide and six-foot-high mirror in the French rococo design hung over the mantle. Another opulent feature of the aristocratic home were sixteen sets of French doors; each room on the first two floors had a fireplace, and between the east rooms stood a grand mahogany staircase with semicircular flights that ascended to the third floor, which comprised one large room and two smaller ones. A circular wooden stair ascended farther up from the attic to the lantern. There was also a basement floor. The roomy home often accommodated guests and family members; family members were sometimes known to stay for weeks at a time.[5]

The Crooms spared no expense in furnishing the mansion, decorating it with heavy mahogany and mahogany veneer pieces, in the Empire style. The Empire design was known in England and in Savannah and Charleston as Scroll, Pillar, or Regency Style.

Though Hardy Croom played a major part in acquiring land and establishing Goodwood Plantation, his role would end abruptly when the steamboat *Home* went down on October 9, 1837. Frances Croom, their three children, and Frances's aunt all perished in the shipwreck.

Later, as more productive land was acquired by Bryan, his landholdings became so large that he decided to divide them into two plantations. Each operation was directed by its overseer and slaves. Agricultural and primary documents of the time show that the fertile soil produced numerous crops. Some were grown as food to feed the people living on the plantation. Some of those various crops included corn, peas, beans, sweet potatoes, sugarcane, rice, and, of course, the cash crop, cotton.

Bryan was a successful planter, but like many Southerners his world would come crashing down after the South fell in the Civil War. In fact, he suffered many economic tragedies after the Civil War. A man coming from generations of high social status and a station of great political and financial wealth, starting with his great-great-grandfather Daniel Croom, Bryan was to die at age seventy-five on Christmas Eve of 1875 as a mere pauper. To illustrate his low station at the end of his life, an inventory of his possessions revealed a paltry little in his possession. Those things were: "ninety-three ounces of silverware worth eighty-five cents an ounce; one pair of plated candlesticks, sixteen nut crackers, two knife rests, two salt stands, one toast rack, one egg stand, two decanter waiters on wheels, four additional single decanter waiters, one strainer, one American watch, one mahogany chest, and one sole leather trunk."[6]

A monument was eventually set in St. John's Episcopal Church in Leon County, and it memorializes Bryan's brother, Hardy Croom; the memorial is a reminder of the legacy of the Croom family of an antebellum past.

When Graham and I visited the Goodwood Plantation home in April of 2017, we marveled at the imposing appearance of the mansion, especially approaching it from the front entrance. We tried to imagine what it must have been like arriving as guests in a carriage pulled by beautiful steeds. Century oaks cast their dappled shadows over the estate, and we enjoyed reading the many historical signs dotted in certain places around the property. Visitors will get a chance to step back in time to an antebellum past, experiencing the opulent ways of the highfalutin' crowd—and of one of the richest planters in the region—when they visit the mansion and grounds at Goodwood. Graham and I also found the memorial stone for the Crooms quite interesting; that marker is located in the St. John's Episcopal Church graveyard located in Leon County.

Rose Knox and Graham Schorb

The portraits of some of the Crooms appear in the Florida Memory Project archives, and this image is listed as Nicholas Croom, Mary Croom Whitfield (1836–1867), and Richard Croom (1805–1859). Courtesy State Library and Archives of Florida

A sign in the parking lot near the Croom Mansion site will show
visitors where buildings and places of interest are situated. Courtesy
Graham Schorb

Century oaks cast their dappled shadows over the estate, and we enjoyed reading the many historical signs dotted in certain places around the property. Courtesy of Graham Schorb

The story of the Croom family and the establishment of Goodwood Plantation is a fascinating saga. A book on the family home reveals, "One of the most elegant mansions in Florida . . . [is] one of Tallahassee's grandest historical monuments. It was once the center of a thriving plantation founded by the Croom family of North Carolina. . . . Hardy and Bryan Croom developed Goodwood Plantation to over four thousand acres with nearly two hundred slaves before Hardy along with his family were killed in a shipwreck." Courtesy of Graham Schorb

When Graham and I visited the Goodwood Plantation home in April of 2017, we marveled at the imposing appearance the mansion gave off, especially approaching it from the front entrance. We tried to imagine what it must have been like arriving as guests in a carriage pulled by beautiful steeds. Courtesy of Graham Schorb

Endnotes

1. William Warren Rogers, *A Historic Sampler of Tallahassee and Leon County* (Cocoa: Florida Historical Society Press, 2005).

2. Rogers, *Historic Sampler.*

3. Rogers, *Historic Sampler.*

4. Rogers, *Historic Sampler.*

5. Rogers, *Historic Sampler.*

6. Rogers, *Historic Sampler.*

Rose Knox and Graham Schorb

Travel Notes

Federal Writers' Project: Slave Narratives and Superstition

"All I remember about the war that bring on Freedom, was that the war was going on. I remember when they couldn't get coffee, sugar, or nothing like that. You know that was a tough time to think about; we couldn't get no salt. Cut up potatoes and parch to make coffee. Boil dirt out the smokehouse and put liquor in food. Eat pokeberry for greens."[1]

Stories are the threads that keep the fabric of a people's experience alive. During the time of the Great Depression of the 1930s, several government agencies created work programs across the country in order to provide jobs for the unemployed. One of the jobs created was set aside for writers, and the Library of Congress supervised an initiative which served to collect oral narratives from former slaves. This Federal Writers Project helped to "gather the voices" of black people, and to keep for the future their experiences; what came out of it was a rich, invaluable collection of folk histories, some involving the Africans' ardent belief in the supernatural.

For the project, writers were sent out in the regional South to interview people who had once lived in slavery. Many of those ex-slaves were found and interviewed, and their stories today survive in ten thousand pages of typed manuscript that are housed in the Library of Congress. The Writers Project helped to keep the thread of the story alive, and ex-slaves' oral histories were saved, according to Hurmence, "... on a scale unprecedented at the time."[2]

In a period before tape recorders were invented, writers interviewed these former slaves using a list of questions made up specifically for the government project, and each writer meticulously wrote out the responses. The thousands of pages ended up representing about two thousand narratives, and "Vivid voices they were, too, at last having their say about that murky time 'before Freedom'"[3]

Rose Knox and Graham Schorb

The idea of slavery in the antebellum South holds great curiosity for many free Americans, both black and white, which is only one reason why these narratives are so significant. With the "peculiar institution" of that bondage now more than a century in our past—and beyond the memory of any living human being who witnessed it—that fascination still endures. In the process of collecting each narrative, the interviewer was asked to write out how the person said particular words; the special dialect and speech pattern was therefore recorded during the transcribing process. From that procedure, the authentic voices of the slaves, talking in their own speech patterns, evolved.

Later, people like Belinda Hurmence would edit the ideas for clarity, though she says she attempted to keep the speakers' meaning intact. In her volume on the experiences of South Carolina slaves, she writes, "The bucolic image of slaves living in contentment . . . has for years been labeled stereotypically. In the South Carolina narratives, we may find over and over what appears to be a reinforcement of the label. Nostalgia veils many memories for the former slaves." To illustrate, Sylvia Cannon, an ex-slave, proclaims, "Times was sure better long time ago than they be now." And Peter Clifton, from the plantation of Biggers Mobley, told an interviewer, "Yes, sir, us had a bold, driving, pushing Marster, but not a hard-hearted one."[4]

Such nostalgia may perhaps be taken with a grain of salt, however, for several reasons, Hurmence claims. Of the 284 South Carolina slaves who shared their experiences, some were around the age of ten at the time of their liberation. Others were older and a few might have been younger than ten. But they were in their eighties, nineties, and older when they were finally interviewed in the 1930s. If a person were to take the time to read the hundreds and hundreds of pages of slave narratives which were collected, there do, in fact, exist stories of terrible brutality on some plantations. This included beatings, mutilations, sexual advances by masters upon African women, and people hanged by their thumbs and flogged, among many other horrors. Such stories told about cruel masters, overseers, or the wives of the masters are quite apparent in some of the narratives that were collected by the Federal Writers Project interviewers.

Hurmence further explains that their remembrances are more than just nostalgia, a longing to go back to plantation life. She clarifies,

. . . more than nostalgia cloaks South Carolina's ex-slaves. Age, for one was a factor; all the speakers were . . . old and poor . . . a lot of them suffered the declining health that stalks old age and poverty. They also suffered the hopelessness of the Great Depression then blanketing their world. Through the scrim of the seventy intervening years, it was easy for them to view their past lives in bondage as a time of plenty, a time when pleasures were simple and their youthful energies high, a time when plantation life meant shelter, food, medical care. The American Civil War ravaged the South and took a toll on both white and black southerners.

Jake McLeod, age 83, from Timmonsville, S.C., for example, says of his experience that during slavery, 'They didn't give us no money, but had plenty to eat every day. Give us buttermilk, sweet potatoes, meat, and cornbread to eat mostly. . . . Then, they let us have a garden and extra patches of we own that we work on Saturday evenings. And we catch as much rabbits and fish as we want. Catch pikes, eels, and cats." But after the war he remembers, "All I remember about the war that bring on Freedom, was that the war was going on. I remember when they couldn't get coffee, sugar, or nothing like that. You know that was a tough time to think about; we couldn't get no salt. Cut up potatoes and parch to make coffee. Boil dirt out the smokehouse and put liquor in food. Eat pokeberry for greens."[5]

Hurmence continues,

It is useful to remember that Freedom, following the Civil War, brought virtually no improvement in the lives of the liberated. . . . They had felt safer-they had undoubtedly lived safer-in the fiefdom of their former masters. Uneducated and ignorant of the world outside the plantation, oppressed by the law, intimidated by night riders and Klansmen, few could see Freedom as a condition to be cherished."[6]

Ironically, seventy years after their emancipation, the ex-enslaved remained on or in close proximity to the plantation and existed in the 1930s in much the same way as they had lived before Freedom. The narratives of these South Carolina slaves have much in common with the story of the slaves in north Florida's plantation belt, for they mimic the same sort of life experiences before and after Freedom, and they have served to keep the thread of the narrative alive for future generations. Many of the enslaved people who were brought to northern areas of Florida came also from South Carolina.

Life on the Randolph Plantation near San Luis: Tallahassee

Interviewer J. M. Johnson from the Writers Project talked to Louis Napoleon, and details a narrative from the memories of the former enslaved individual of what life was like on a north Florida plantation:

> The slaves lived in log cabins especially built for them. They were sealed and arranged in such a manner as to retain heat in winter from the large fireplaces constructed within. Just before dawn of the day, the slaves were aroused from their slumber by a loud blast from a cow-horn that was blown by the "driver" as a signal to prepare themselves for the fields. The plantation being so expansive, those who had to go a long distance to the area where they worked were taken in wagons; those working nearby walked. They took their meals along with them and had their breakfasts and dinner in the fields. An hour was allowed for this purpose.

> The enlaved worked while they sang spirituals to break the monotony of long hours of work. At the setting of the sun with their day's work all done, they returned to their cabins and prepared their evening's meal. Having finished this, the religious among them would gather at one of the cabin doors and give thanks to God in the form of long supplications and old fashioned songs. Many of them being highly emotional would respond in shouts of hallelujahs. . . . The "wicked" slaves expended their pent up emotions in song and dance. Gathering at one of the cabin doors they would sing to tunes of a banjo, or fiddle that was played by one of their number.

> Finished with this diversion they would retire to await the dawn of a new day which indicated more work. The various plantations had white men employed as "patrols" whose duties were to see that the slaves remained on their own plantations, and [so] they were whipped with a "raw hide" by the "driver." There was an exception to this rule, however, on Sundays the religious slaves were allowed to visit other plantations where religious services were being held without having to go through the matter of having a permit.[7]

The Africans, like the Celts, brought superstitious attitudes with them to the new world. One writer recorded these words from an interview. He states, "[She] believes to this day that hogs can see the wind and that all animals talk like men on Christmas morning at a certain time."[8]

The ideas above, from a former enslaved individual of Madison County, can attest to the fact that many African slaves of the Southeast held to their superstitious beliefs. Presented here are a few stories, taken from former slaves of various states.

The following tale was told to interviewer Jules A. Frost by a former slave named Josephine Anderson. The interview was conducted on October 30, 1937, and the account illustrates the kinds of superstitions held by some of the formerly enslaved.

> Ya see brooms keeps hants away. When mean folks dies, de old debbil sometimes doan want em down dere in de bad place, so he makes witches out of em, an sends em back. One thing bout witches, dey gotta count everything for dey can get acrost it. You put a broom acrost your door at night an old witches gotta count ever straw in dat broom for she can come in . . . one night I was goin to my granny's house. It was jes comin dark, and when I got to de crick an start across on de foot-log, dere on de other end o' dat log was a man wid his haid cut off an laying plum over on his should.[9]

Eighty-two-year-old Violet Guntharpe was born a slave in Rocky Mount, North Carolina. Regarding ghosts, she told the following tale:

> I's halfway scared to death of . . . old Captain Thorn's ghost . . . you never heard about that ghost? . . . A slave boy killed his marster, old captain Thorne. He drag and throwed his body in the river . . . they catch John, the slave boy, give him a trial . . . he confess. Then, they took the broad axe, cut off his head, mount it on a pole, and stick it up on the bank where they find [body of] old Captain Thorn.
>
> That pole and head stay there till it rot down. Captain Thorn's ghost appear and disappear along that river bank ever since. My pappy tell me he see it and see the boy's ghost, too. . . . The ghost rode the minds of many colored folks. Some say that the ghost had a heap to do with deaths of that river, by drowning.[10]

Amanda McCray, a former slave in Madison County, was interviewed on December 5, 1936, by Edward Lycurgas in Jacksonville. The introduction to her story illustrates the writer's spirit of observation when he says,

> Mrs. McCray was sitting on her porch crooning softly to herself and rocking so gently that one might easily have thought the wind was swaying her chair. Her eyes were closed, her hands incredibly old and work-worn were slowly folding and unfolding on her lap. She listened quietly to the interviewer's request for some of the "high lights" of her life and finally exclaimed: "Chile why'ny you look among the living for the high lights?" There was nothing resentful in this expression, only the patient weariness of one who has been dragged through the boundaries of a yesterday from which he was inseparable and catapulted into a present with which he has nothing in common.

Regarding folktales, the writer says of McCray's experience,

> They [the children] were duly schooled in all the current superstitions and listened to the tales of ghosts and animals that talked and reasoned. . . . [She] believes to this day that hogs can see the wind and that all animals talk like men on Christmas morning at a certain time.[11]

"Aunt Memory" as she was often called, was born into slavery. When she was twenty-four years old she was taken to Tallahassee and sold to a Mr. Argyle for $800. In 1893 Aunt Memory attended the Worlds Fair, and she sold enough photographs of herself to pay for her travel expenses. Courtesy of State Library and Archives of Florida

Rose Knox and Graham Schorb

Endnotes

1. Belinda Hurmence, ed., *Before Freedom, When I Just Can Remember: Twenty-Seven Oral Histories of Former South Carolina Slaves* (Winston-Salem, NC: John F. Blair, Publisher, 1989).

2. Hurmence, *Before Freedom.*

3. Hurmence, *Before Freedom.*

4. Hurmence, *Before Freedom.*

5. Hurmence, *Before Freedom.*

6. Hurmence, *Before Freedom.*

7. *Slave Narratives: A Folk History of Slavery from Interviews with Former Slaves in the United States,* Federal Writers Project, 1936–1938, Library of Congress, Washington, D.C., Vol. 3.

8. *Slave Narratives.*

9. *Slave Narratives.*

10. *Slave Narratives.*

11. *Slave Narratives.*

The Chaires Family Plantation and the Hamlet of Chaires

"Verdura Plantation, or The Verdura Place, in its early years was quintessentially representative of the elite planter culture. The mansion home constructed in the Greek revival style was vast in size and opulent in its décor. It was a place that signaled to all comers that the owner was a very rich and important person. Sadly, Chaires may have only lived at Verdura for a few months prior to his death in 1838."[1]

Like other very wealthy planters, the Chaires first came from North Carolina. The family owned thousands of acres east of Tallahassee. Benjamin Chaires, the father, had initially settled in the frontier town of Jacksonville from 1822 until 1823, before coming to the Tallahassee territory. The Chaires were known around the region as successful planters with very large land holdings.[2]

Benjamin Chaires was born in 1786 in North Carolina; he played many influential roles in Florida's antebellum past, such as plantation owner, surveyor, and minor political figure. Members of the Chaires family line were descendants of French Huguenots and their earliest French immigrant ancestor was born in 1625. The last name was eventually Americanized, but de la Chare originally would have been pronounced "duh la Shar." Benjamin Chaires grew up in Georgia but eventually found his way to Florida. He was the son of a planter and had grown up in antebellum society. His father, Joseph, was a prosperous planter and records indicate that he had steadily increased his slave labor force between the years of 1799 and 1808.

By 1818 Benjamin, along with his brothers, Green Hill and Tom Peter, were well entrenched in plantation life, having sixty-seven slaves on land they shared.[3] Also by 1818, Benjamin had purchased his first piece of Florida land, which comprised a one-third share in a plantation located on Amelia Island. With that transaction, he became part owner of a slave force and acquired equipment and tools and canoes, along with other necessities to maintain a plantation. Ultimately, he came to own as many as 30,000 acres in Saint Johns, Duval, and Alachua Counties. Later, in the late 1820s, he settled with his family in Tallahassee and for approximately the next ten years, before his death in 1838, Chaires acquired great riches.[4]

There were many factors that helped in his success. In the middle Florida region, for instance, the growing railroad industry, banking institutions, and land speculation driven by financially lucrative contracts bestowed by the United States government were all entities in which Benjamin Chaires had involvement. In fact, he was part of an elite group of powerful people, having associations with some of the most politically influential men of the early 1800s. The wealthy men of that time were people like James Gadsen, Prince Achille Murat, and John Bellamy, among others.[5] Because of his involvement in these enterprises, which also included construction and brickmaking, he gained prosperity and was moreover involved in forming the first railroad company to serve Tallahassee.

In keeping with the tradition of big planters of the time, Chaires built a home. But before his opulent mansion was completed, it is possible that Benjamin Chaires, like many successful planters of the day, had a smaller home built for his family not far from the construction site of where the grand Verdura home would eventually be built. An archeological dig seems to confirm the first modest home. The grand mansion Chaires built was once situated about twelve miles southeast of Tallahassee and was positioned 125 feet above sea level on the edge of the Cody Escarpment. The home faced south with a glorious view of the Gulf of Mexico as seen from the home's attic. The land was purchased by Chaires in the early 1800s and the vast plot encompassed 4,560 acres. However, it is not certain if Chaires considered all of that land as part of what he named Verdura Plantation, or just the 500 acres surrounding the mansion.[6]

Chaires's great-granddaughter recalls five columns on the east and west sides (the home had ten columns in all). Each room was high-ceilinged and each had a fireplace. As with many mansions of the day, there was a detached kitchen. The magnificent home had two upper stories with a double stairway leading to the second floor. Those two stories were built upon an above-the-ground basement. On either side of the foyer were doors that, when opened, revealed an eighty-foot-long ballroom, and the floor was made of marble. Other rooms in the mansion included a spacious dining room, a sitting room, and a game and smoking room. A great-great-great-grandson recalls visiting the house when the walls were still intact and he remembers his grandfather saying that there once was a master bedroom on the second floor, with three adjoining rooms and five small bedrooms on the third floor.[7] It was once said of the home, "His home, Verdura, a few miles east of town, was an elegant Greek-revival [brick] mansion of thirteen rooms, wide verandas, and towering columns."[8] The Chaires family history reveals that the Verdura mansion was consumed by flames in 1885, but there are no newspaper articles or public papers to confirm that date.

Shields, who was part of the archeological dig at the Chaires site, writes, "Benjamin Chaires certainly used slaves to build his mansion house at Verdura, which would have included numerous construction activities, including clearing the land, cutting and milling of trees for lumber, brick and mortar production for the house, wood-workers to design and provide railings, stairway, and decorative features . . ."[9] The number of slaves Benjamin Chaires owned at Verdura plantation varied, but in 1839, the year after Chaires died, the estate owned eighty slaves. By 1840, according to that year's census, his oldest son Joseph reported owning 302. Of those slaves, 235 worked the fields while the others most likely were cooks, blacksmiths, house servants, and drivers. Shields continues, "Chaires was a cotton planter, which is borne out by his documented efforts to sell cotton at Savannah from his plantation on Amelia Island and shipping his Leon County cotton from St. Marks to ports in New York City and Liverpool, England."[10]

The hostilities of the time were to change the destiny of one of Benjamin's brothers. Green Hill and Thomas Peter had plantations that were located farther to the east and northeast of Verdura. Green's plantation was called Evergreen Hill and was positioned on the north shore of Lake Lafayette. The mid-1800s was a volatile time as violence often broke out between the Indians and settlers. Green's family was caught in the tragedy of that terrible time period. In July of 1839, the Natives attacked. In the horrendous massacre, Green's wife and children would not survive. She was shot and killed and the two children were burned alive in the home when the Natives set it ablaze. There is a small cemetery located on Old Dirt Road in Tallahassee where the remains of Green's family members were buried. The other plantation, owned by Thomas Peter, Benjamin's brother, was named Woodlawn. It was situated within today's community called Chaires. It should be noted that other large plantations in the area were also owned by the men of the Chaires family. Some of those plantation names were Fauntleroy, Southwood, Tiger Tail, Bolton, Welaunee, and Ever May, and one may have gone by the name of Paisley. Many of these large tracts of land were in operation well after the abolition of slavery.[11]

At his death at age fifty-two, Benjamin Chaires owned more than nine thousand acres and eighty slaves in Leon County, and was said by some people to have been Florida's first millionaire.[12] Clifton Paisley, in his work, *The Red Hills of Florida,* reveals that the plantation region in Leon County was located south of Lake Lafayette along Old St. Augustine Road, and there the heirs of Ben Chaires were well established. His two youngest sons—Thomas Butler, age twenty-two, and Charles Powell, age twenty—operated Verdura after Benjamin's death.[13] After their father's death those two sons continued the planter way of life, growing many crops on the plantation such as cotton, sweet potatoes, Indian corn, beans and peas.[14] There were 356 farms in all in Leon County, though many of those consisted of small acreages.[15]

Benjamin Chaires would succumb to death on October 4, 1838. The cause was believed to be yellow fever. The inscription on the monument where he is buried in the Chaires family cemetery reads:

"Sacred to the memory of Benjamin Chaires

Who died Oct 4, 1838

Aged 52 years 8 mos and 9 days

His many virtues are deeply

engraved on the hearts of

those friends from whom

death has prematurely

torn him, and by whom he

can never be forgotten.

His purest epitaph their tears.

Blessed be his spirit."

His obituary ran in the *Floridian and Journal* on October 6, in the *Apalachicola Gazette* on October 20, and in the *Florida Herald* of St. Augustine on October 25.

Today the land where the estate once was is privately owned by the St. Joseph Paper Company and is not open to the public. When I sought permission to walk around the old plantation site and the forgotten graveyard, no one from the company responded to my request. Only remnants of a once-opulent estate and operating plantation still exist in the modern era on that old estate.

The Chaires were known around the region as successful planters with very large land holdings. In fact, when Benjamin died in 1838, he died very rich; some sources indicate that he owned a 3-story brick mansion and 9,000-acres. Courtesy of the Minz family sketch and the State Library and Archives of Florida

Verdura plantation house was built in 1832 by Major Benjamin Chaires. After he and his wife died, the plantation was passed to their children. Fire destroyed Verdura and four vine-covered columns and a mound of bricks are all that remain. Text and image courtesy of the State Library and Archives of Florida and photographer, Kerce, Red (Benjamin L.), 1911-1964.

The image depicts the Benjamin Chaires grave at Verdura Plantation in Leon County, Florida, at the old estate of Benjamin Chaires, 1786–1838.3 Today the land is privately owned by the St. Joseph Paper Company and is not open to the public. Only remnants of a once-opulent estate and operating plantation still exist in the modern era on that old estate. Benjamin Chaires would succumb to death on October 4, 1838. The cause was believed to be yellow fever.

Endnotes

1. Sharyn Heiland Shields, *Whispers from Verdura: The Lost Legacy of Benjamin Chaires* (Tallahassee, FL: Sentry Press, 2016).

2. Bertram H. Groene, *Ante-Bellum Tallahassee,* Florida Heritage Foundation, Tallahassee, 1981.

3. Shields, *Whispers from Verdura.*

4. Groene, *Ante-Bellum Tallahassee.*

5. Shields, *Whispers from Verdura.*

6. Shields, *Whispers from Verdura.*

7. Shields, *Whispers from Verdura.*

8. Mary Louise Ellis and William Warren Rogers, *Favored Land, Tallahassee: A History of Tallahassee and Leon County* (Norfolk, VA: Donning Company, 1988).

9. Shields, *Whispers from Verdura.*

10. Shields, *Whispers from Verdura.*

11. Shields, *Whispers from Verdura.*

12. Ellis and Rogers, *Favored Land.*

13. Clifton Paisley, *The Red Hills of Florida 1528-1865* (Tuscaloosa: University of Alabama Press, 1989).

14. Shields, *Whispers from Verdura.*

15. Paisley, *Red Hills of Florida.*

Rose Knox and Graham Schorb

Travel Notes

Old City Cemetery

"I've been thinking about why so many of us are attracted to cemeteries full of strangers. . . . Maybe it's the stories that draw us in, the ones we get to make up as if we were children again. A particularly eloquent inscription may set us off, or a small angel holding a flower, or an embedded daguerreotype that shows us how Martha wore her hair. . . . Or maybe what brings us in is simply kinship, not the blood kind but the human kind. After all, the only difference between these people with stone names and us is that their time came but ours hasn't yet."[1] Lola Haskins

It may seem strange to some, but the place called City Cemetery in Tallahassee is quite lovely and serene. Lola Haskins might agree about the peace that seems to envelop the place. The trees inside the graveyard cast deep shade over many of the old tombs. There are cypress, oaks, dogwoods, sycamore, and a few magnificent magnolias that are said to be over one hundred years old. Once when I was walking around the tombs with Graham in May of 2017, thinking of those people and their lives, a poem from Robert Frost came to me. A verse from his "Disused Graveyard" goes like this:

"The living come with grassy tread,
   To read the gravestones on the hill,
   The graveyard draws the living still,
   But never anymore the dead."

The boneyard had indeed drawn us in!

Old City Cemetery in Leon County was originally founded in 1829. The Territorial Legislature took care of the gravesites for the first eleven years, but later that council gave the cemetery over to the city of Tallahassee, which still is managing the graveyard today.

Rose Knox and Graham Schorb

The cemetery is located just a few blocks away from the state capitol, and there are two sections to the well-shaded graveyard. Old City Cemetery is nestled in what is now a residential neighborhood. However, when it was initially established it abutted a two-hundred-foot perimeter which settlers in Tallahassee had cleared to make it easier for them to spot any attacks from Native Americans. Such an open area gave the pioneers time to defend themselves before encroaching Natives were able to get too far in. Walking around the well-kept boneyard today, most people would find it hard to believe that livestock—cattle and pigs—once traipsed freely over the tombs! Also, at that time, the graves were not well tended and were overgrown with weeds; and what a roaming cow or hog did not destroy, heavy, jostling burial carts did.

Burials back then were "crude affairs," with coffins lowered into the previously dug grave and set with ropes that would sometimes slip, dumping the corpse out on the ground. Much later, in the 1980s, acts of vandalism in the graveyard outraged local citizens, who soon raised funds to repair the damages and to make needed restorations. Later still, in the early 1990s, an iron perimeter fence was installed by skilled craftsmen, which enveloped the original cast-iron fencing already existing around some of the older plots. Like many area cemeteries, whites and blacks were not interred in the same sections. The segregated cemetery was sectioned off as east and west with white families and white individuals interred in the east, along what is today Martin Luther King Jr. Boulevard, while slaves and free men of color were buried in the west end of the cemetery.[2]

An informational kiosk at the entrance on Martin Luther King Jr. Boulevard has brochures that reveal stories of the people who are interred there. There is likewise logistical information on how to get to some of the more "interesting" gravestones. After entering the main gate from King Boulevard, a visitor might pick up a brochure. Moving left on the east side, over by the perimeter fence, are buried a number of Confederate soldiers, some of whom succumbed to injuries at the Battle of Natural Bridge. Fifty-five soldiers, some named and others unnamed, are interred there. But fifty-five markers can be somewhat deceiving, because an 1899 census shows that 186 soldiers were actually buried there; however, their memorials were most likely made of wood and have since decayed.[3]

Another gravesite of distinction is the walled area located in the northeast quadrant. Tallahassee settlers experienced many tragedies brought on by epidemics like yellow fever. In the year 1841, from May until October's end, people suffered and died because of yellow fever. What a long, enduring time those few months must have seemed to people who were watching their friends, neighbors, and loved ones die. Estimates of the death toll range from 230 to 400, though the precise count is not now known. Individuals and entire family units were affected, but there are few markers in Old City Cemetery that indicate such mass suffering of epidemic victims. Newspaper stories and obituaries kept one valid historical record, however, and reveal how members of the Scott family died. Mary Ann Scott, it was recorded, died "of bilious contagious fever on Sunday evening. Just a few days later the 3rd of July, Mrs. Rebecca Scott succumbed to congestive fever."[4] The burial record shows that there was at least one other individual buried in that walled spot.[5]

Yet another place of interest is the regimental row of Union soldiers. They repose under shades of hardwoods in the southwest quadrant and are believed to be the victims of the Civil War, killed at the Battle of Natural Bridge. Southern Leon County is where that bloody battle transpired. Confederate forces and local volunteers halted the invasion by federal troops, but by battle's end, of Union forces, twenty-one were dead, eighty-nine were wounded, and thirty-eight were recorded as missing in action. These black Union soldiers were under the command of white officers. In time some of those soldiers, originally interred at Old City Cemetery, were later exhumed, then moved to Beaufort, South Carolina, to finally rest for eternity in the National Cemetery.

One regional writer tells about that battle—how it is remembered on the first weekend in March—when he writes,

> Civil War re-enactors had come in from across the South to set up an 1860s style encampment and to fire blanks at each other. Originally, it was here at Natural Bridge that General John Newton and more than five hundred black Union soldiers tried to cross Natural Bridge in hopes of occupying the Florida capital of Tallahassee. Nearly six hundred well-entrenched Confederates, mostly old men and young cadets, repeatedly drove them back. The Yankees, charging uphill, lost 148 of their number; the Confederates only three.[6]

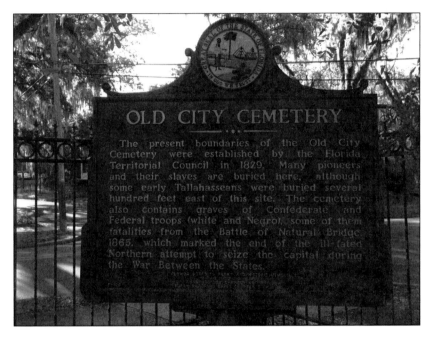

There are two sections of the well-shaded graveyard, which is located just a few blocks away from the state capitol. One is the "white" section. The other is the "black" section. Courtesy of Graham Schorb

An 1899 census shows that 186 soldiers were actually buried there—but their memorials were most likely made of wood and have since decayed. Some of these soldiers fell at the Battle of Natural Bridge. Courtesy of Graham Schorb

These are the graves of black Union soldiers, believed to have been killed at the Battle of Natural Bridge. Courtesy of Graham Schorb

THE ESCAPED SLAVE IN THE UNION ARMY.—[SEE PAGE 428.]

The image depicts a black Union Army infantryman. Courtesy of the State Library and Archives of Florida

"After all, the only difference between these people with stone names and us is that their time came but ours hasn't yet." Lola Haskins -Courtesy of Graham Schorb

The imposing monument of Elizabeth Budd Graham reveals the sort of funerary sculpture that was popular in the late nineteenth century. Such a large memorial reflects the socioeconomic status of the deceased. Many strange tales of Elizabeth have become folk legend over time; there are claims that she was a witch, and her monument faces west unlike the Christian burial tombs that face east. Courtesy of Graham Schorb

There are many citizens from the elite class buried in St. John's Episcopal Church Cemetery in Tallahassee, including Prince and Princess Murat. Courtesy Graham Schorb

Princess Catherine Willis Gray Murat was the great-grandniece of George Washington. She is buried in the St. John's Episcopal Church Cemetery. Courtesy of the State Library and Archives of Florida

Rose Knox and Graham Schorb

The image depicts the tomb of the princess located in the St. John's
Episcopal Church Cemetery. Courtesy of Graham Schorb

438

The historical sign at the cemetery chronicles some details about the life of a prince and princess. St. John's Episcopal Church Cemetery. Courtesy of Graham Schorb

Rose Knox and Graham Schorb

Endnotes

1. Lola Haskins, *Fifteen Florida Cemeteries: Strange Tales Unearthed* (Tallahassee: University Press of Florida, 2011).

2. Haskins, *Fifteen Florida Cemeteries.*

3. Haskins, *Fifteen Florida Cemeteries.*

4. Haskins, *Fifteen Florida Cemeteries.*

5. Sharyn M. Thompson, brochure: "Walking Tour of Old City Cemetery," Historic Preservation Board and City of Tallahassee.

6. Doug Alderson, "Watery Thread through Time: The St. Marks River," in *Between Two Rivers: Stories from the Red Hills to the Gulf,* Susan Cerulean, Janisse Ray, and Laura Newton, eds. (Tallahassee, FL: Heart of the Earth and the Red Hills Writers Project, 2004).

Civil War and The Capital of Tallahassee

"I made this convention to spare the blood of the gallant little army committed to me and to avoid the crime of waging hopeless war."[1] General Joseph E. Johnston

It was a pivotal day, with many more to follow, when a messenger made a way down the aisle of the St. Paul's Church in Richmond, Virginia. That episode would have direct links eventually to the fall of Tallahassee in the American Civil War. The date was April 2, 1865, and it was there that Jefferson Davis was attending spiritual services. When he received word from the messenger, Davis rose up and quietly started making his way out of the church. It was at that moment he started devising plans to leave Richmond, the capital of the Confederacy. Ironically, only two days later, Abraham Lincoln would walk down those very streets, in that same city, because the siege of Petersburg had finally been broken. On April 9 General Robert E. Lee, commander of his Army of Northern Virginia, would surrender to the Union; it was then Confederate resistance in Virginia was at last ended.[2]

But there remained three other states with their armies out fighting in the field. They were Alabama, North Carolina, and Florida. Northern forces, directed by General James Harrison Wilson and William T. Sherman, had begun to overtake two of the final resisting southern forces when, on April 12, Wilson's cavalry raiders besieged Montgomery, and by the middle of April, Sherman's troops took down Raleigh, North Carolina. One southern outpost of resistance remained, and that was Tallahassee, Florida, which was the single Confederate state capital east of the Mississippi that was still holding to the Confederate cause.[3]

General Joseph E. Johnston would be the man to carry forth the procedures for Florida's ultimate surrender. According to William Warren Rogers in his historical sampler of Tallahassee, "On April 26, 1865, at Bennett's House near Durham Station, North Carolina, a convention of surrender terms was signed between Sherman and

Johnston. . . . Since Florida was in Johnston's area of command the general wrote Florida governor A. K. Allison of his capitulation explaining, 'I made this convention to spare the blood of the gallant little army committed to me and to avoid the crime of waging hopeless war.'"[4]

Another man, Major General James H. Wilson, was the one responsible for accepting the surrender of those Florida regiments. Wilson communicated then to General Sherman that he would send Major General Emory Upton to Atlanta and Brigadier General Edward M. McCook to Tallahassee to make sure the terms were enforced. McCook was remembered as a "strong" and quite "handsome" man, and he came from a prominent Ohio family.[5]

The orders that Wilson sent with McCook were dated May 4, and McCook then traveled to Tallahassee where he was to complete the mission and to carry out the surrender orders directed at the remaining Confederate forces which were in Tallahassee and also in outlying areas. McCook was also given the responsibility of attending to the aftermath of such a high order of surrender, by trying to keep the peace and by keeping good societal order, and was given power to take into custody any outstanding "agitators" and "rebels" trying to stop the terms of surrender. Not only that, but he was to take prisoner all detachments of Johnston's or Lee's soldiers, ones not yet apprehended.[6]

In a further attempt to keep the peace, the editors of the local newspapers were also told, on McCook's command, to publish only words that would serve to promote good order and keep the peace, so as to further national unity under what he saw as the laws of the American Constitution. McCook proceeded to follow his other orders, and while in Tallahassee, he set in motion the paroling of Confederates and the taking over of their many possessions. Records of that period indicate that he paroled six to eight thousand Confederates and confiscated bounty as their conqueror, taking 40 cannon, 450 cavalry sabers, 2,500 small arms, and 1,618 bayonets, as well as some lances and pikes. Added to those confiscations were hospital supplies and quartermasters' stores that included cattle, mules, horses, and foodstuffs such as flour, salt, corn, and bacon.[7]

Some primary sources from the journals of Tallahassee were written with a tone of resentment for the Union takeover of their southern city; however, one newspaper, the *Florida Times*, published by Federal occupation forces, displayed a more cooperative attitude concerning the surrender. The words from one article read as follows: "Yankees and Rebels now mingle with each other as friendly as though they had never been arrayed against each other in hostile attitude." On May 20, 1865, in Tallahassee, the ceremony that recognized "the end of the Confederacy for all time" was conducted.[8]

Ironically, many slaves in the Confederate states were not actually freed before the ending of the war, for several practical reasons. First, most lived too far from the liberating presence of Federal troops to attempt to risk an escape. Some slaves, however, decided to stay put and to try to make the best of the situation, existing in a familiar landscape, and most continued living in much the same way as they always had, still carrying out the pre-war labor of an agrarian lifestyle.[9]

Rose Knox and Graham Schorb

Endnotes

1. William Warren Rogers, *A Historic Sampler of Tallahassee and Leon County* (Cocoa: Florida Historical Society Press, 2005).

2. Rogers, *Historic Sampler.*

3. Rogers, *Historic Sampler.*

4. Rogers, *Historic Sampler.*

5. Rogers, *Historic Sampler.*

6. Rogers, *Historic Sampler.*

7. Rogers, *Historic Sampler.*

8. Rogers, *Historic Sampler.*

9. Margaret E. Wagner, *The American Civil War: 365 Days* (New York: Harry N. Abram, 2006).

Battle of Natural Bridge and a First-Hand Account

"When the call went out for defenders, every man and boy who could bear arms volunteered to swell the thin ranks of the regular Confederate Army. Volunteers were made up of old men, a few wounded Confederate soldiers, who were home recuperating from wartime injuries, and cadets as young as 14 years of age, from West Florida Seminary."[1]

The Battle of Natural Bridge would prove a pivotal fight and was significant because the victory by Confederates held the Union forces from marching in and taking over the capital city of Tallahassee. Tallahassee was the only Confederate capital east of the Mississippi River which had not fallen to the Yankee forces.

The historical battle is commemorated each year, as men and boys dress up in uniform and bring battle-period weapons to honor the event in a reenactment. The conflict transpired on a natural land bridge near where the St. Marks River flows into the Gulf of Mexico. The river disappears and then runs through an underground cavern for about 150 feet before resurfacing, creating a natural land crossing, thus the name, "Natural Bridge."

In the winter of 1864, General Sherman was wreaking havoc. His march across Georgia had begun. Newspapers of the day spoke of Sherman's favorite line of attack, "the torch." People in Tallahassee knew also from those news reports that the general had taken every state capital in the South–that is, except for Tallahassee. A tremendous fear gripped the hearts of the people there, for they thought it was only a matter of time before their homes burned and their way of life was in ruins.

However, it was a Union general by the name of John Newton, not Sherman, who had specific plans to take over Tallahassee. Since he was already stationed in Key West, his strategic plan was to begin raiding the Gulf Coast, with the idea of first taking control of the Port of St. Marks; the port was situated fifteen miles south of the capital city. He believed from that point he could march troops into Tallahassee and the conquest of the area would be complete.

A Union fleet of boats maneuvered into the Apalachee Bay on March 1. The naval unit was manned with nine hundred soldiers. They were intent on landing at the St. Marks lighthouse and there they had plans to invade, moving northward, destroying the railroad and any Confederate surpluses. Another unit led by naval Commander William Gibson was to move his steamer up the St. Marks River in order to take over Fort Ward and Port Leon.

Days later, on March 4, the Union troops made land. On that same day, a messenger made his way in the late afternoon, proclaiming the impending encroachment by the enemy. According to one regional writer, immediate action was taken. "When the call went out for defenders, every man and boy who could bear arms volunteered to swell the thin ranks of the regular Confederate Army. Volunteers were made up of old men, a few wounded Confederate soldiers, who were home recuperating from wartime injuries, and cadets as young as 14 years of age, from West Florida Seminary."[2] (Today the school is known as Florida State University). The ragtag "regiment," led by Confederate General William Miller, took the unit, marching south to greet the encroaching invaders.

When Newton finally made it to Newport, the atmosphere was permeated with smoke from a burning bridge, and on the opposite side of the river there awaited Confederate sharpshooters. The Southerners were successful in forcing the enemy back. Newton then chose to try crossing the river a bit farther north. The location on his map called it "Natural Bridge." The Union soldiers marched down a sand road, one not often traveled, and they faced challenges offered by the landscape as they trudged through muddy hollows and pine barrens. The hard-to-travel thoroughfare must have seemed a never-ending journey. Newton soon began to second-guess himself, thinking perhaps that his guides were either not knowledgeable or they were Confederate sympathizers.

By the time Newton and his troops had marched to the crossing, Miller had strategized, predicting Newton's arrival. Newton discovered a barricade of sorts that had been hastily constructed overnight. It has been estimated that 500 to 700 Confederate defenders awaited his coming, lurking behind Confederate pickets. The Southerners at that location had a great advantage over the Yankee troops, for Confederates held an intimate knowledge of the bogs, hammocks, piney woods, and swamps of that particular area.

Newton was undaunted at first, trying to cross over the limestone bridge, but the old men and boys were able to force his troops back, retreating into a hammock. Miller's men pursued them for twelve miles, until they were certain Newton (and Weeks, who had also camped at Newport with a small unit), had boarded ships, leaving the vicinity. However, Miller was still on guard for three days, making certain the Union forces would not try another attack. After that, his ragtag unit made their way back to Tallahassee, joyous about their victory.

Visitors today will see a battlefield which is not much changed since that Confederate overthrow. The memory lives on through several historical signs and a monument with etched names of the fallen ones. Wildflowers, which were once planted by the United Daughters of the Confederacy, likewise serve as a remembrance. All help to stand as reminders of the bloody sacrifice made there by many a Union and Confederate soldier. As destiny would dictate, the Battle of Natural Bridge was the final Confederate triumph of the Civil War, because on April 9, 1865, General Lee surrendered at Appomattox.[3]

Firsthand Account at Natural Bridge

For a firsthand account of the Battle of Natural Bridge, a letter reveals one soldier's experience. The words below are derived from a work titled *Rose Cottage Chronicles*, a compilation of letters and diaries spanning two generations of the Bryant and Stephens families, "ordinary Confederate folk" whose members included secessionists, moderates, and even a few Unionists. The work depicts what many people in the Confederate states experienced in what has come to be known as "the most tragic chapter of America's history." The letters and diaries from various men and women reveal the "pathos and pain that millions experienced on a daily basis."[4]

The *Rose Cottage Chronicles* set the stage of happenings at the natural bridge, giving some more specifics of the battle. As detailed above, Federal troops about 900 strong, comprised of the Second and Ninety-Ninth United States Colored Infantry and the Second Union Florida Cavalry, were under the direction of Brigadier General John Newton. These troops were fighting against Confederate Brigadier General William Miller's force of some 1,500 boys and men. Along with G. W. Scott's Fifth Battalion Cavalry, were three companies of

Rose Knox and Graham Schorb

the Second Florida Cavalry (dismounted), Dunham's Artillery Battery, and the Cadet Corps of the West Florida Seminary, and a few battle-wounded soldiers and old men. As was also stated previously, Miller won a decisive victory. A letter from Willie, a company sergeant, states,

> Just after dinner Sunday p.m. at Lake City I was notified that I was wanted at once to get our local company together to come down here, and as I am orderly sergt., and really the head and manager, I had not appt'y to write a line before leaving that Evn'g . . . We came down to this point [railroad below Tallahassee – [Knox's addition] 4 miles from Newport, and that morning. . . were led into the fight at the "Natural Bridge. . . We at first fought across a small stream (East River) [scholars think it was probably the St. Marks] our Batty. doing all the fighting. After we got there, the Reserves having been there some hours and tired; It was a regular Indian swamp fight . . . being at close range and our men being behind trees mostly, and the Enemy behind entrenchments and logs–At about 3 o'clock p.m. the Enemy abandoned their first line near the stream, as Our fire was too hot for them, and the firing ceased almost entirely for more than ½ an hour when skirmishers were ordered to cross the Natural Bridge and find the enemy.[5]

And though Willie's accounting was off a bit, he writes,

> We only know of 35 killed, as they carried off all the white men but one, and tho' there are many negroes still scattered thro' the woods from all I can learn up to the present time, 75 will cover all prisoners, add 150 for wounded and you have an outside number of causalities—of our loss I know 3 killed, 17 wounded, and one captured with a piece of artillery at Newport. At any rate it was quite a brilliant affair. Two Deserters were hid at Newport and executed before all the troops.[6]

Willie's account was not right: Rather, historians claim 148 Federal causalities, 21 killed, 89 wounded, and 38 captured. Confederate losses–3 killed, 22 wounded–none of the young cadets were hurt.[7]

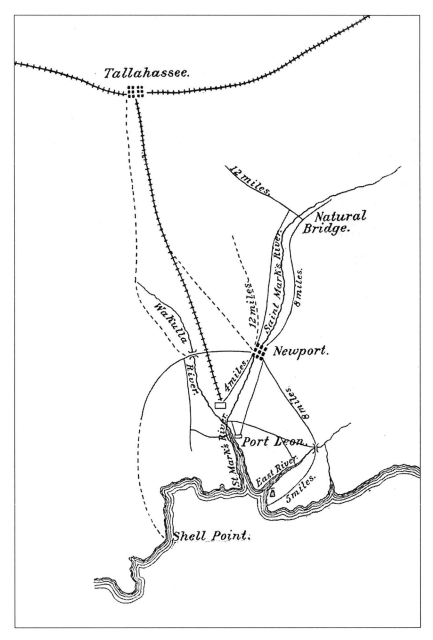

This is a map portraying the area of Natural Bridge in relation to Tallahassee and Shell Point in the year 1865, in Leon County, Florida. Courtesy of the State Library and Archives of Florida

Here is a portrait of Union Major General John Newton taken between 1860 and 1865. Newton was the Federal commander at the Battle of Natural Bridge, Florida, in early March of 1865. Courtesy of the State Library and Archives of Florida and Brady's National Photographic Portrait Galleries

The image depicts a portrait of Confederate General William Miller, Brigadier General of the defending Confederate forces at the Battle of Natural Bridge, taken between 1861 and 1865. Text and image Courtesy of the State Library and Archives of Florida

The Union soldiers marched down a sand road, one not often travelled, and they faced challenges offered by the landscape as they trudged through muddy hollows and through pine barrens. The hard-to-travel thoroughfare must have seemed a never-ending journey. Newton soon began to second-guess himself, thinking perhaps that his guides were either not knowledgeable or they were Confederate sympathizers. Courtesy of Patrick Elliott

First reenactment of the Battle of Natural Bridge at Natural Bridge Battlefield is pictured here. Courtesy of the State Library and Archives of Florida

The historic Natural Bridge battlefield is the site of the second largest Civil War battle in Florida. In 1865, during the final weeks of the Civil War, a Union flotilla landed at Apalachee Bay, planning to capture Fort Ward (San Marcos de Apalache Historic State Park) and marched north to the state capital. Volunteers from the Tallahassee area—Confederate soldiers, old men, and young boys—met the Union forces at Natural Bridge and repelled three major attacks. The Union troops were forced to retreat to the coast. The United Daughters of the Confederacy acquired the older portion of the park to erect the monument and managed the property until it became a state park in 1949. A reenactment of the battle is held at the park every March. The historic Natural Bridge Battlefield site was listed on the National Register of Historic Places in 1970 and is cited as one of the top ten endangered Civil War sites in the United States by the Civil War Preservation Trust. In February 2009, the state of Florida purchased nearly fifty-five acres of land adjacent to the original property to protect a first-magnitude spring. Text and image courtesy of the State Library and Archives of Florida

Endnotes

1. Teresa E. Stein, *Florida Cracker Tales* (Lake Placid, FL: Placid Publishing House, 1995).

2. Stein, *Florida Cracker Tales.*

3. Stein, *Florida Cracker Tales.*

4. Arch Fredric Blakey, Ann Smith Lainhart, and Winston Bryant Stephens Jr., eds., *Rose Cottage Chronicles: Civil War Letters of the Bryant-Stephens Families of North Florida* (Gainesville: University Press of Florida, 1998).

5. Blakey, Lainhart, and Stephens, *Rose Cottage Chronicles.*

6. Stein, *Florida Cracker Tales.*

7. Blakey, Lainhart, and Stephens, *Rose Cottage Chronicles.*

Rose Knox and Graham Schorb

Travel Notes

Patrick Elliott, Southern Artist: Tallahassee Resident

"When I was a little child, I drew a large snake on the walls of my home. It was a nice snake but my drawing did not go over too well with adults."[1] . . . From a visit with Robert Patrick Elliott

The image of eager, artistic hands sketching out a giant snake and drawing it on the walls of his house was a sure sign that the little boy would grow up to be a mural artist, one of the most creative, knowledgeable artists in the American South. Patrick Elliott told us his childhood story as we sat on a bench together, under the shade of grand live oak trees at the historic site called The Grove in Tallahassee. Not only is Pat a talented regional artist, but he is a history buff as well. Sitting there staring at the grandeur of Richard Keith Call's antebellum mansion, I inquired about Pat's childhood inspiration and how it all got started with him. Because I am now a grandmother, I wanted to know if Pat had any inkling of his drawing ability when he was a small child, since my own grandchild, Anna, loves to color and draw on household walls, too; even if it does not ". . . go over too well with adults," either! He has shared with me over the years how his father, his stepmother, his step-grandmother, and his own wilderness explorations led him to his ultimate passion.[2]

Elliott, a natural history aficionado, calls Tallahassee home, and today he is known around these parts as one of the most highly skilled artists in the Southeast. Among his many accomplishments, his work was displayed in Washington, D.C., during the Bicentennial event that featured various works by American artists. Pat is a fourth-generation Floridian, born in Jacksonville. Though he is a humble man, he proclaims he is "proud to be a Florida Cracker!" He grew up in Orlando years before what he calls ". . . the invasion and permanent alteration of central Florida by the theme park industry."

Pat recounts that "Over my younger years and into my older ones, I enjoyed many explorations into a diversity of wild places, whether camping for a time or visiting for a long day." These, indeed, were all settings of the sublime! He remembers, "By foot, car, RV, boat, airboat, or canoe, some of my trips included hunting and fishing." Pat also spent his fair share of time in a canoe, paddling on lazy rivers and rushing creeks, because he loves to fish. He says, "I was drawn into the wild and natural places by the beauty, complexity, and mysteries of God's creation. I was made fully aware of this cosmic and glorious fact when I met the Lord, Jesus Christ in 1970."

In his career he has depicted natural Florida ecosystems from the Panhandle down to the Keys, and has created background murals for the areas in South Carolina, Georgia, and Louisiana. In addition, he has created scenes of rural Cracker architecture, Southern mansions, Spanish fortifications, plantation sugar mills, Seminole war engagements, turpentine operations, and Confederate military sites. He also has painted planetscapes for planetarium "star shows" and produced background art for an extensive series of animated Bible features.

Pat Elliott credits several people with his early creative vision. First of all, it was his father who served as a catalyst for his reverence of wild Florida. R. B. Elliott was born in 1912. It was he who first inspired Pat and Jules, Pat's brother, to fall in love with the splendor of natural places. "Daddy" was a woodsman and an expert outdoorsman. Pat remembered, "He shared his love and wisdom of those remote places and taught Jules and me to camp, to fish, and to hunt. In that time out in nature our Daddy taught us to appreciate and to respect wild Florida." Hence, wilderness is what Pat has always sought out in his wanderings in the Big Scrub of Central Florida. Whether he was hiking, researching, working, or hunting, the isolated places were where he was most at home, and were what helped kindle his artistic spirit. In fact, that time allowed him to immerse himself in sights, sounds, scents, and wonders of the [then] wild, natural Florida landscape. Pat's deep adoration for the varied habitats of plants and animals of his native Florida, therefore, originates from his father's influence.

In his teenage years he attended Edgewater High School in Orlando. During that period Pat sought out wild creatures like snakes and alligators, and in studying them closely, he was able to practice crafting his realistic nature paintings. Spending a great deal of time exploring the Econlockhatchee River Swamp, often called the "Big Econ," as well as places of the St. Johns River basin such as "Possum Bluff," were likewise wild experiences that offered much to his burgeoning, creative vision—and gave great enjoyment to this man of nature.

He was fortunate enough to experience some of the most remote places in Florida before they were developed, as well. For some time Pat was employed as a surveyor. Those wilderness experiences had a huge impact on him. In a written piece from the Florida Ecological Arts (an ecological impact company based in Gainesville that employed him to create) back in 1976, he commented, saying, "Surveying crews are generally the first into an area scheduled for development, and they often get into places usually seen only by alligators, bullfrogs, and cottonmouths. . . ." His artistic vision teaches about a once-unspoiled Florida. Tragically, he testifies he has witnessed in his lifetime so many of these precious "God Created" wild landscapes of pine forests, river basins, coastal dunes, marshlands, and other wetlands, destroyed or transformed to make way for economic development in the form of highways, buildings, shopping centers, and resort destinations.

Pat furthermore tried to express his high regard for the outdoors to us once by saying,

> As I spent time out in forests and wetlands, sometimes on my own, and other times while working as a surveyor, I developed a technique that allowed me to see with all my senses. I call it a "looking technique." Using this method, I "drank in," absorbing with all my senses the fragility and beauty of wild Florida. Through my art, I was able to share some of those feelings—how these places were part of my heart and soul, and being out in that kind of remoteness is like getting close to God and in touch with His Creation.

When he was growing up, other encouragements came from two important women in his life; his stepmother and his step-grandmother. Leah Rader, his grandmother, was a fine artist herself, and she ". . . encouraged me to practice my art ability with discipline and with integrity." Pat asserts it was likewise through the love and encouragement of his stepmother Dorothy Elliott that he began to take his art talent seriously. And his mother and his grandmother would certainly be proud of him today.

Pat is now in his eighty-second year, and looking back at his artistic contributions over a lifetime of creating is like chronicling the fast-disappearing past, what the ancient regional environment, the old Florida landscape, used to be. Such dedicated, scholarly discipline allows Pat to depict with great accuracy the South's unique natural communities, and he likewise uses his talent to educate people about regional history, and the complexity, diversity, and fragility of natural southeastern ecosystems.

Not only is Pat a meticulous observer in those remote environments, as he seeks out serenity in forests, scrubs, dunes, marshes, creeks, and rivers, but he has also honed his academic skills. His disciplined studies have given him an intimate, intellectual knowledge of whatever person, historical event, plant, epiphyte, animal, insect, or landscape he is painting. That is why his breathtaking works appear in museums in Florida and several other southeastern states. Such a disciplined artist must take great care and planning in his procedures. Before he begins a natural history landscape, for instance, he seeks out books, articles, photographs, and paintings, and sets aside time to talk to experts like geologists, paleontologists, archeologists, anthropologists, and botanists, in order to gain knowledge to create paintings of detailed accuracy. When he creates a mural, he first produces sketches, "mock ups," and even 3-D tiny dioramas. Visiting the natural landscape and taking field sketches are also a vital part of his inventive process. While out in the wild, Pat attempts to ". . . absorb the feeling and mood of the ecosystem, taking in with the senses, the spiritual essence of the place, which God presents to me."[3]

If you have ever gazed upon one of his many landscapes, which are housed in southern museums and kiosks, you might feel you have been transported back in time. An observer might marvel, contemplating the vastness of a golden savannah. In the far, far distance a deep, ancient sea of dark blue is just visible. Across the vast wheat-colored prairie, a herd of American mastodons casually graze together, and two giant ground sloths are foraging, standing beside large fruit-laden trees. A trio of American camels and small Paleolithic horses graze for nourishment on the Cody Scarp. The mural is alive with stories from an ancient past! Stealthy creatures lurk in the golden grassland, creeping and crouching; look closely and spot a pair of dire wolves, and a saber-tooth cat hunting on the veldt. Seven- to eight-foot-tall flesh-eating birds, too, forage behind a stand of stately pines, and a giant tortoise and a rattlesnake find camouflage in the dense grassland. In the far background, an immense wildfire consumes the scrub and hammock, as a multitude of lightning bolts zigzag down to strike the Pleistocene sea. In the foreground is a large, white limestone outcropping, with clumps of green saw palmetto growing there; such a lifelike image makes an observer feel like they are standing right there in that time, with all of those creatures![4] Elliott has moreover been known to paint other ancient creatures like the short-faced bear, the tapir, the peccary, and the bison, depicting the lifelike images of a Paleolithic past; those creatures roamed in what we call today Florida. Yet in the physical world only skeletal remains from that age-old past are often discovered by archeologists in area rivers of the Red Hills.

These kinds of realistic depictions are Pat's trademark. In fact, in a feature story about the artist in the May-June 1981 issue of *Florida Wildlife* Magazine, the front cover depicts the upper St. John's River prairie and its associated hammocks and distant river swamps and shows the lifelike, untamed glory of an untouched Florida wilderness. Saw palmettos dot the scene and tall sabal palms reach skyward. One dead palm speaks of the cycle of life and death. Other plant species in the hammock are wax myrtle, sweet gum, maple, and red cedar. Feral hogs, called piney-woods rooters, are a breed that ran wild after de Soto's march in 1539; today they forage amid the broomsedge and palmettos. The swine will eat just about anything, and are nosing around for grubs, lizards, buried eggs, or carcasses. In the background an immense grey-blue sky shows low, hovering clouds. A soul can almost feel the calm before the storm and the electricity in the air. A flock of egrets is on the move to beat the approaching thunderstorm, flying in a V-formation, their white image contrasting starkly with the dark sky. Once the fury of the storm arrives, the rain will pelt the earth, the lightning will strike the hammock, and the wind will flatten the palmettos to the ground and bend the trees.

Pat's vivid scene reminds me of a story Marjorie Kinnan Rawlings penned in her work, *When the Whippoorwill*." She writes, "The roar of the wind was a train thundering nearer and nearer. The palmettos thrashed their fans in frenzy . . . ." One character, Mart, remarks "they tell the palmeeters gits flatted smack on the ground, times, like, and over in the scrub they says the trees'll done be bended." Pat Elliott depicts, too, such power and majesty of an approaching storm in his painting of the remote Florida wilderness. In yet other vivid scenes, a viewer might stare into Pat's alluring cypress swamp paintings, to encounter sunning alligators, a great blue heron, or a white-tailed deer. Flying overhead are flocks of wild geese or sandhill cranes.

To realize the many and varied creative works he has painted to present to the public in order to educate people, I asked him to write down where his works have appeared. He chronicled only a few of the accomplishments, explaining,

Because I have been doing professional work since 1955, I will tell of only a few large projects that have commissioned my pieces. I have designed and produced several exhibits for Fort Gadsden State Historic Site, Fort Foster State Historic Site, Myakka River State Park, Blue Springs State Park, Ybor City State Museum, and Constitution Convention Memorial State Museum, all in Florida.

Also, I produced wall-size background murals for wildlife habitat groups and produced paintings and drawings for exhibits on wildlife and ecology. These include several Federal museums, such as Santee National Wildlife Refuge, South Carolina; Piedmont National Wildlife Refuge, in Georgia; Tensas River N.W.R., and Sabine N.W.R., Louisiana; and St. Marks, N.W.R., Loxahatchee N.W.R. and Merritt Island N.W.R., Florida. I also produced background murals for Charleston Museum, Charleston, South Carolina and a museum at Panola Mountain State Park, Georgia.

Back in the 1960s and 70s, I was also involved in all phases of design and production on interpretative museum exhibits on Florida natural history and Florida human history and culture for a state museum in Gainesville and for Florida State Park museums and exhibits sites throughout the state, from the western panhandle to Key Biscayne. I have also in my career illustrated brochures, pamphlets, scientific papers, and other Florida state museum publications.[5]

Patrick Elliott's creations therefore depict a land of the past: of virgin cypress stands, unpolluted rivers, wild scrubs, places for creatures to forage and a safe haven of bird sanctuaries. He recollects with nostalgia and with sorrow when he says,

I fully experienced some of the richest, wildest most inaccessible places in our state before they were destroyed or irreparably altered. Many of those places are gone, replaced by shopping centers, portions of highway systems, vast amusement complexes, resort developments, subdivisions, and huge industrial complexes. How thankful I am that I was permitted to see, to enter and experience those places of rare beauty, and to absorb their loveliness into my being while they still existed."[6]

Pat is now in his eighty-second year, and looking back at his artistic
contributions over a lifetime of creating is like chronicling the fast-
disappearing past, what the ancient regional environment, the old
Florida landscape, used to be. Pat brings the fierce short-faced bear
of the Pleistocene age to life. Courtesy of Patrick Elliott

If you have ever gazed upon one of his many landscapes, which are housed in southern museums and kiosks, you might feel you have been transported back in time. The ancient long-horned bison roamed the grasslands in what is today the Florida landscape. Courtesy of Patrick Elliott

Before he begins a natural history landscape he seeks out books, articles, photographs, and paintings, and sets aside time to talk to experts like geologists, paleontologists, archeologists, anthropologists, and botanists, in order to gain knowledge to create paintings of detailed accuracy. Pat brings to life a Florida tapir of the Paleolithic past. Courtesy of Patrick Elliott

The peccary is now an extinct mammal, among many extinct creatures of the Pleistocene age. Courtesy of Patrick Elliott

A powerful ancient lion stalks its prey in the wilds of a Paleolithic past. Courtesy of Patrick Elliott

Tragically, in his lifetime he testifies he has witnessed so many of these precious "God Created" wild landscapes of pine forests, river basins, coastal dunes, marshlands, and other wetlands, destroyed or transformed to make way for economic development, in the form of highways, buildings, shopping centers, and resort destinations. Courtesy of Patrick Elliott

If you have ever gazed upon one of his many landscapes, which are housed in southern museums and kiosks, you might feel you have been transported back in time. Courtesy of Patrick Elliot

Pat told me once while visiting his Tallahassee studio, "I fully experienced some of the richest, wildest most inaccessible places in our state before they were destroyed or irreparably altered. Many of those places are gone, replaced by shopping centers, portions of highway systems, vast amusement complexes, resort developments, subdivisions, and huge industrial complexes. How thankful I am that I was permitted to see, to enter and experience those places of rare beauty, and to absorb their loveliness into my being while they still existed." Courtesy of Graham Schorb

"Over my younger years and into my older ones, I enjoyed many explorations into a diversity of wild places, whether camping for a time or visiting for a long day." These, indeed, were all settings of the sublime! Photo submitted by Patrick Elliott

Pat is a dedicated artist, and he brings the natural world and historical renderings to others. Photo submitted by Patrick Elliott

Endnotes

1. Patrick Elliott, personal interview at his studio in Tallahassee, telephone conversations, visits, and written responses, 2012–2019.

2. Elliott, interview.

3. Elliott, interview.

4. Elliott, interview.

5. Rose Knox and Graham Schorb, *Old Tales of the Forgotten South in a Georgia-Florida Swamp: Paddling Okefenokee* (Cocoa: Florida Historical Society Press, 2019).

6. Florida Ecological Arts Publication from Eco-Impact Company, Gainesville, 1976.

Rose Knox and Graham Schorb

Travel Notes

Richard Keith Call: A Pivotal Figure in Territorial Tallahassee

"The Calls became an important part of the broadcloth aristocracy that provided the territory's political, economic, and social leadership."[1]

Richard Keith Call was born in 1792 in Prince George County, Virginia. Because his father died suddenly when Richard was only a child, his mother packed up her family (she had six sons and four traveled with her), and headed to Kentucky to live and work on a small farm near Russellville. Later, in 1810, his mother died and Richard at seventeen wondered what the future would hold for him. He studied for a time at Mount Pleasant Academy in Montgomery County, Tennessee, but when conflicts between settlers and Indians increased, he left school to enlist in the army, serving as a volunteer.

His devoted service brought him to the attention of General Andrew Jackson. As time passed a friendship developed, one akin to "a parental relationship [that] profoundly affected the life of the fatherless Call."[2] He was sent southward under Jackson's orders, seeing Florida for the first time, to combat the British in Pensacola. His military service there earned him several promotions, and he became an officer on General Jackson's personal staff. By 1819 Captain Call was in Nashville, Tennessee, at the headquarters Jackson had set up at the plantation house named "The Hermitage."

Later Call, with some knowledge from his study of law, was sent back to Florida to assist in the process of transferring West Florida from Spain to the United States. The region had been under the Spanish flag for more than three hundred years. Call was also a pivotal figure in helping Jackson organize the new territory's first provisional government in 1821 at Pensacola. Call was assigned the position of acting secretary of West Florida.

Over time he opened a law firm and played a significant role in territorial decisions. In 1822 he was appointed to Florida's first Legislative Council. Then, in 1823, President Monroe appointed Call brigadier general of the Militia of West Florida, and by the time he was thirty years old, he had been elected the territory's delegate to the United States Congress. By 1824 Call had married Mary Kirkman from Nashville, Tennessee, and in the spring of 1825, they were to arrive in Tallahassee. One account reveals "The Calls became an important part of the broadcloth aristocracy that provided the territory's political, economic, and social leadership."[3]

Though many of the early pioneers were small farmers, owning only a few acres and a few slaves, a great number of planters flooding in from Kentucky, Tennessee, Maryland, Virginia, North and South Carolina, and Georgia entered the area with substantial slave forces; these planters were attracted by land offerings and fertile ground for planting. Though these aristocratic planters were a minority in the population of farmers, their tremendous influence would soon dictate political and economic issues influencing Leon and surrounding counties. Holding the position of receiver of public monies at the federal land office in Florida gave Call a golden opportunity concerning land speculation.

For instance, when land located outside of Tallahassee's city limits went up for $1.25 an acre, Call acquired a prime 640-acre parcel. To set up house, he had a cottage built as he made plans to build a more suitable residence for his wife. When they first took residence in their new home, encroachment by pioneers was still causing resentment among Native Americans, and "To protect his family from possible Indian raids, General Call cleared the land immediately surrounding the site."[4] By 1831 the couple had four girls, and the home was later named "The Grove" by two of his daughters. Finally settled in the home of their dreams, tragedy would override their joy; in August 1832 Mary Rachel, age four, died. In September 1834, during a six-day span, the epidemic of malaria took the lives of their other children, Laura Randall, Mary Jane, and baby Richard.

Only their daughter Ellen, age nine, survived, and to protect their child from the tragedy and dangers of territorial life, the Calls sent Ellen to school in Baltimore to live with relatives there. Another child, Mary, was born, but soon afterwards her mother died; her death came during a time when Call was summoned to the field to lead troops after the massacre of Major Francis Dade and his party, many of whom were women and children. Call received the news of his wife's impending death while on the St. Marks River and immediately raced forth on horseback twenty miles to offer comfort in her last moments. He made it there too late. One account of that episode reveals details of her interment, saying, "She, the first Mary Call, was buried by torch light in the family cemetery behind her beloved home and alongside her departed children. She was thirty-four years old."[5] The baby, Mary, was sent to Nashville to be nurtured by her maternal grandmother.

Finding the home he loved so empty and void of the conversation and laughter of his wife and children, Call lost all interest and motivation for its final completion. After his wife died Call never remarried, and he made sure to stay in close contact with his two daughters through correspondence and in person. At age seventeen Ellen Call came back to her childhood home in 1843. By the age of twenty-six, she was married with three children. Her father deeded The Grove and 190 acres to her, and in 1851 went to live on his property on Lake Jackson. Later, in 1862, Call died at The Grove and was buried beside his wife in the family cemetery. After her father's death, Ellen lived through the difficult time of the Civil War and its Reconstruction period. To make ends meet, Ellen rented portions of the home and sold parcels of land, as she was determined to make sure her children would have The Grove as part of the family's heritage. By the 1870s Ellen was involved in producing silk, and in 1905 she, like other family members before her, died at her beloved family home, The Grove.

The home was handed down to several subsequent generations. By the mid-1900s it had fallen into decline. Mary Call, a great-grandchild, once wrote "The house was in terrible condition, but the idea that it might be sold outside of the family and possibly commercialized worried us . . . the house seemed to ache from neglect. I had loved this house my whole life." At that time, Mary was thirty-one years old and a mother and wife. She was married to LeRoy Collins, a state senator. In time, Collins became governor. The couple, with their children, would make The Grove their home, and they gave of their time and energies to make sure it was finally restored to its original grandeur.

By 1831 the couple had four girls, and the home was later named "The Grove" by two of his daughters. Finally settled in the home of their dreams, tragedy would override their joy; in August 1832 Mary Rachel, age four, died. In September 1834, during a six-day span, the epidemic of malaria took the lives of their other children, Laura Randall, Mary Jane, and baby Richard. Richard Keith Call would soon come to rest beside his wife and children in the family grave plot, situated near the mansion. Courtesy of the State Library and Archives of Florida

Endnotes

1. Jane Aurell Menton, *The Grove: A Florida Home through Seven Generations* (Tallahassee, FL: Sentry Press, 1998).

2. Menton, *The Grove.*

3. Menton, *The Grove.*

4. Menton, *The Grove.*

5. Menton, *The Grove.*

Rose Knox and Graham Schorb

Travel Notes

The Grove: A Mansion on a Hill

"Between its sturdy walls it has experienced birth and death, success and defeat, joy and sorrow, attention and neglect. Standing resolute through struggle and triumph, The Grove is a tangible testament to civic purpose, inner strength, and family pride."[1]

Standing high on one of Tallahassee's highest points, The Grove, an example of "rustic refinement," was the home of Richard Keith and Mary Call. Like many influential people during Florida's territorial period, the Calls acquired 640 acres of rich agricultural land. The pinnacle upon a knoll located 204 feet above sea level was the perfect spot for the home; so thought Keith and Mary Call. Amid glorious moss-covered century oaks, the site was a special place. Built during the first decade after Florida became a territory in 1824, the home, though never completely finished, "expresses the early Greek Revival Style with its emphasis on balance, symmetry, and proportion."[2]

Some of the architectural aspects of the mansion include a magnificent front porch, supported by four large columns crafted from curved brick. Four smaller columns, called pilasters, repeat the larger columns, and the same sorts of columns are located closest to the exterior entryway. Impressive double-hung windows allow light in, and afford a view to the outside world, while giving the home a regal appearance. The Georgian floor plan allows for entrance through double doors, opening into a wide central hall measuring thirteen feet across. On each side of the broad hallway are positioned two expansive rooms, twenty feet wide by twenty-two feet deep. The design of twelve-foot high ceilings and the connection of yet another wide hallway through to the back of the home (and flanked also by two large rooms) allowed for ample ventilation in hot seasons. Each room was built with large windows, and each had a fireplace providing warmth in the wintertime. The first floor consisted of the library, the living room, a bedroom, and the dining room. The second floor repeats the same kind of layout, with the hallway and adjacent four large rooms; but the upstairs is six inches higher in ceiling space than the downstairs area. The two rooms on the east side of the main floor are quite decorative, showcasing ornate windows and doors and adorned with Grecian peak cornices. The fireplaces in those particular rooms still have their original marble mantles, while the fireplaces in the west side of the mansion lack the original marble because, when hard times struck, Ellen Call Long was forced to sell the marble sections.

One of the most impressive interior scenes, however, is the "graceful cantilevered" stairway with mahogany banister that connects the downstairs to the upstairs. There is also a basement that follows the physical layout of the two upper floors. Because the home represents such a significant period in Florida's history, it was "recognized in 1972 . . . listed on the National Register of Historic Places. The following year the property was zoned Historic-Cultural by the City of Tallahassee."[3] Today the home stands on a small section, not on 640 acres but on ten acres, located on First Avenue beside the Florida's Governor's Mansion, and is bordered by the hustle and bustle of Monroe Street to the east, Duval Street to the west, and Third Avenue to the north. Despite the encroachment of commerce and urban growth, the grounds and mansion remain serenely secluded and unhindered by city life. Like many mansions of the antebellum South, the home and its people experienced times of opulence and joy, and of decline and suffering. One writer put it this way: "Between its sturdy walls it has experienced birth and death, success and defeat, joy and sorrow, attention and neglect."[4]

Those stories have certainly remained alive because the house still stands today. The coffee-table book titled *The Grove: A Florida Home through Seven Generations*, written by Jane Aurell Menton, reveals a definitive history of the home. It includes many archival and modern-day pictures, and the text, photographs, and renderings tell the detailed story of a mansion in its conception, its heyday, its decline, and later its revival.

Our Field Trip to The Grove

On February 8, 2019, Graham and I and our little dog, River, traveled to Tallahassee to tour The Grove. We met our friend, the artist Pat Elliott, there. We were guided to the basement via elevator by a young woman, a history major, who told us about the original desk that Call had used to sign significant legislation. Later in time the desk was to see other significant legislation signed regarding Civil Rights, by the hand of Governor LeRoy Collins. After touring all three stories of the home and marveling at the craftsmanship of the mansion, the staircase, the fireplaces in each room, the heart pine floors, and the historical displays, we wandered the spacious grounds. We stood for a few moments at the front of the house, under sprawling oaks. In the shade of those magnificent trees, we felt the grandeur of the house as we looked up at its imposing architecture. A house of that size does evoke emotion and makes a mere human being feel miniscule. Walking down the estate's paths, we stopped to admire many kinds of plants, talking about what they were and smelling the fragrance of blooms (yes, blooms in February!) as we lingered among the grounds.

We soon found the family cemetery located about 130 yards from the back of the home. Reposing there were Richard Keith Call, his wife, and several children, among others of that family line. A stone lamb was resting at the top of one child's grave, the head of the sheep sheared off by time and erosion. We walked in silence among the tombs, thinking about the family and the times in which they had lived, until we found the path up to the mansion again.

In the parking lot of The Grove, Pat was to gift us with one of our most treasured possessions—a huge mural depicting the ancient Cody Scarp, with Paleolithic beasts of all kinds roaming the landscape. There were giant birds, tiny camels, and a herd of mastodons; in the sky flew sandhill cranes and a flock of wild geese; and in the far distance, near the ancient sea, lightning strikes were just visible. The mural once hung in the local Tallahassee museum. Someone there saved it before it was thrown in a dumpster. When Pat discovered that some unmindful soul had tried to throw the mural canvas away, he asked to keep it. One wise individual at the museum saw the travesty of trashing such an historical, artful treasure and luckily saved it before the garbage men arrived. Pat rescued his mural and gave it to us. We have it hanging today on the walls of our home.

This is the earliest known photograph of Ellen Call Long, seated in the center. Courtesy of State Library and Archives of Florida

The Grove is one of the homes on the "Tallahassee Trail" tour held each spring. The picture portrays the mansion in 1951. Courtesy of the State Library and Archives of Florida

Standing high on one of Tallahassee's highest points, The Grove, an example of "rustic refinement" was the home of Richard Keith and Mary Call. Courtesy of State Library and Archives of Florida

One of the most impressive interior scenes is the "graceful cantilevered" stairway with mahogany banister that connects the downstairs to the upstairs. Courtesy of Graham Schorb

Standing high on one of Tallahassee's highest points, The Grove, an example of "rustic refinement" was the home of Richard Keith and Mary Call. Like many influential people during Florida's territorial period, the Calls acquired 640 acres of rich agricultural land. The pinnacle upon a knoll located 204 feet above sea level was the perfect spot for the home; so thought Keith and Mary Call. There, amid glorious moss-covered century oaks, the site was a special place. Courtesy of Graham Schorb

Built during the first decade after Florida became a territory in 1824, the home, though never completely finished, "expresses the early Greek Revival Style with its emphasis on balance, symmetry, and proportion."1 Some of the architectural aspects of the mansion include a magnificent front porch, supported by four large columns crafted from curved brick. Four smaller columns, called pilasters, repeat the larger columns, and the same sorts of columns are located closest to the exterior entryway. Courtesy of Graham Schorb

We soon found the family cemetery located about 130 yards from the back of the home. Reposing there were Richard Keith Call, his wife, and several children, among others of that family line. A stone lamb was resting at the top of one child's grave, the head of the sheep sheared off by time and erosion. We walked in silence among the tombs, thinking about the family and the times in which they had lived, until we found the path up to the mansion again. Courtesy of Graham Schorb

Endnotes

1. Jane Aurell Menton, *The Grove: A Florida Home through Seven Generations* (Tallahassee, FL: Sentry Press, 1998).

2. Menton, *The Grove.*

3. Menton, *The Grove.*

4. Menton, *The Grove.*

Rose Knox and Graham Schorb

Travel Notes

Haunted Tallahassee: Town Lore

"Come let the burial rite be read and the funeral song be sung."
Tombstone Inscription

There are strange tales surrounding particular places in Leon County, and much of what survives in folklore is passed on through the oral tradition. Just like the stories that are told in Madison and Jefferson Counties, Leon County, too, is replete with strange tales. Here are only a few of them:

Goodwood Museum and Gardens, also known as the Croom Mansion site, has had some unexplained happenings over the years. Guests touring the mansion claim they have experienced a sudden drop in temperature in some areas of the home. Others say the fireplace located in the dining room emits a feeling that someone is occupying that space. Once when volunteers were taking inventory and recording items in the house, they reported particular objects which they had handled were strangely, inexplicably cold.[1]

Yet another strange happening occurred in the 1980s, when writers and artists had rented out several cottages which are situated behind the Goodwood home. The visitors reported hearing laughter and conversation emanating from the old tower that stands high over the backyard, though no one was apparently up there. In another report, back in the 1990s when a construction crew was making renovations to the main house, they claim to have heard the mysterious sound of children talking and the sound of footsteps, as if someone were running. Knowing that the owner in antebellum times, Hardy Croom, and his family perished in a shipwreck in the 1830s while traveling in a steamship (ironically named *Home*) from North Carolina to their destination, Goodwood, makes some people wonder if the children's voices are proof that some of the Croom's finally made it home—but in spirit form!

The Columns is another antebellum mansion in Tallahassee that reverberates with tales of a mourning wife. The legend concerns a young married couple and the husband's departure. The young man left her to fight for the cause of the South. She awaited word from him, but no letters ever arrived. Some people claim the forlorn wife is still roaming the home in anticipation of her Confederate soldier, her love, to return. One common episode told by several witnesses claims a spirit-woman sometimes can be seen coming and going from the big fireplace located on the first floor of the Columns.

As far as ghostly activity in a Leon County graveyard, one tale survives about Saint John's Episcopal Church Cemetery located adjacent to Old City Cemetery. According to local lore, the spirit of Princess Murat still lurks around in the mist of early dawn. It is said she can often be seen strolling among her and her husband, Prince Murat's, tombstones.

In the adjacent graveyard called Old City Cemetery, just steps away from the St. John's Episcopal Church Cemetery, one noteworthy tomb stands out. The imposing monument of Elizabeth Budd Graham reveals the sort of funerary sculpture that was popular in the late nineteenth century. Such a large memorial reflects also the socioeconomic status of the deceased. Many strange tales of Elizabeth have become folk legend; there are even claims that she was a witch. Her monument faces west, unlike many of the Christian burial traditions of placing tombs facing east. Her large monument, though, also indicates her esteemed status, contradicting the witch theory. In fact, positioning markers at the head of the tomb facing west was, at one time, a common practice, and there exist many examples of such a custom in Old City Cemetery. Though the folk tales about Elizabeth being a white witch are still being told, the religious design motif of "no cross, no crown" placed at the top of her marker reveals evidence that Mrs. Graham, indeed, enjoyed good standing in her community.[2]

Her inscription reads:

"Come let the burial rite be read and the funeral song be sung;
an anthem for the queenliest dead that ever died so young,
a dirge for her the doubly dead, in that she died so young."

Local lore sometimes claims that, as a white witch, she was capable of casting spells of love and protection; she might have even perhaps cast spells to lure a young, rich gentleman to wed her.[3]

The following tales are not part of the antebellum past, but since they concern the city of Tallahassee, I chose to include them.

There is a place called Velda Mound Park that involves supernatural stirrings. Tales of Velda Park mound surround apparitions of Native Americans. The natives have been known to gather around a campfire and they can be seen in the light given off by the flames. Other stories about the mound include a wolf that is "white and glowing," and the beast lurks in the neighborhood around Arbor Hill, within the subdivision of Killearn Estates. In fact, local residents claim that they have heard the haunting sound of howling after the sun sets and darkness descends.

Folklore surrounds the Phillips Mausoleum, which is another place of curiosity for those interested in inexplicable happenings in Tallahassee. Located in the Oakland Cemetery on Brevard Street, not far from the governor's mansion, is a large domed mausoleum. It is said to have a combination of several architectural influences, including Greek Revival, Eastern European, and Asian styles; the merging of those various architectural types gives the tomb an odd but intriguing appearance. The monument was crafted in the early 1900s solely by architect and eccentric, Calvin C. Phillips, who was known for designing various structures for the Paris Expo of 1877 and was famous as the builder of the Gothic-looking Old Clock Tower of the All Saints Neighborhood.[4]

As the story is often told, Phillips, during the construction of his mausoleum, grew weary, so he decided to take a short nap, reclining on the wooden bier platform inside of the tomb. Some onlooker happened to walk by, and he saw Phillips lying there and believed the man was dead. About that time, Phillips rose from slumber on the platform, sat up, and told the witness, "I'm just making sure it fits."[5] One version of the story posits that Phillips went into his tomb and died there. Before he went, however, he left a key in the hands of a trusted friend so the door of the crypt could be locked on the outside. People visiting the mausoleum today swear they have walked through "very cold" spots near the grave. One neighbor who lived in an apartment adjacent to the crypt claims a spirit form found her bedroom, made itself at home by sitting on her bed, and even took the time to show affection to her pet cat![6]

Rose Knox and Graham Schorb

Endnotes

1. Nicole Carlson Easley, *Hauntings in Florida's Panhandle* (Atglen, PA: Schiffer Publishing, 2009).

2. Lola Haskins, *Fifteen Florida Cemeteries: Strange Tales Unearthed* (Tallahassee: University Press of Florida, 2011).

3. Mark Hinson, "Now this Place is Downright Spooky," *Tallahassee Democrat,* October 2015, Web accessed.

4. Hinson, "Downright Spooky."

5. Hinson, "Downright Spooky."

6. Hinson, "Downright Spooky."

One More Note on Ghosts

"Is all that we see or seem, but a dream within a dream?"
Edgar Allan Poe

Over the years, in reading, listening, and taking down oral stories of the haunted South, Graham and I have noticed many similar themes in archetypal ghosts and spirit antics. The stories are usually set in ancient landscapes like Native American ceremonial mounds, or in antebellum homes, in the family burial plot in back of the house, or in old boneyards. They may involve the sound of footsteps; the creaking of pine floors; doors being swung open gently or violently; dishes falling from the wall—or flung about the room; the lingering scent of sweet cigar smoke; the tune from a piano or fiddle; the movement of furnishings; a quick gust of wind inside a house and the faint rustling of curtains; the abrupt sensation of very cold places; the sense that someone is standing in the room; shadowy images with voices, a tug at someone's clothing, or wicked hands gripping a person's neck; or the calling out of someone's name. The list goes on. Graham and I have heard some of these happenings told; after taking pictures in some ghostly places, we have seen inexplicable orbs appear in various photographs. However, we've never personally encountered a ghost in our years of wandering around the Old South in our research of the Red Hills of north Florida. (We did, however, have a strange encounter with a slamming door at an old resort hotel situated on the banks of the Suwannee River in 2006.)

Though there are all sorts of books on hauntings that take place in the southern states, we at times stumble across interesting names connected with our immediate area. For instance, in one chapter named "Hampton Plantation: Georgetown, South Carolina," the author, Alan Brown, mentions several familiar names. One historical sign near the site of Brown's story reads, "Hampton Plantation 2 mi. N.W. was established by 1730 and was one of the earliest rice plantations on the Santee River, in an area settled by Huguenots and often called "French Santee." The house was built in the 1730s for Elias Horry and passed to his granddaughter, Harriott Horry, who married Fredrick Rutledge in 1797. The plantation remained in the Rutledge family until 1971.[1] The last owner of the house was the renowned poet laureate of South Carolina, Archibald Rutledge. Today, anyone traveling around the town of Madison can ride down streets with names like Horry and Rutledge. Horry is pronounced with a European accent, Or-ee. (I spent many a childhood day bicycling down Horry Street!)

When Mr. Brown was collecting oral stories for his book, *Stories from the Haunted South*, he talked to Sarah Tyler, a tour guide working at Hampton Plantation. Tyler spoke of the year 1830 and a haunting there. She told of twenty-one-year-old John Henry Rutledge, who had fallen madly in love with the daughter of a pharmacist. The planter society rule of staying true to noble obligation dictated that the young, smitten lad should forget such a mismatched love relationship because southern etiquette demanded it. Miss Tyler put it this way, "John Henry's family were planters, and the two different classes don't mix. Both families were against them getting married or involved." As the story goes, the girl married someone else, but John Henry never got over her. He shot himself with a sawed-off shotgun in his upstairs bedroom. It was not a clean shot, however. So the young man suffered a horrendous death in the home. As years passed, rumors began to emerge about ghostly activities, supposedly witnessed by people working in the home or, later, by visitors of the plantation. Some of the things they spoke of include the following:

A servant claimed to have heard the sound of a rocking chair. When she raced upstairs, she witnessed the chair rocking on its own. Like the bloodstain mentioned in a Monticello, Florida, tale, the Hampton Plantation home allegedly has an irremovable blood spot on the floor. The stain in the Hampton mansion is located by the rocking chair. Workers say that scrubbing the stain is of no use. It refuses to disappear! And like the Smith-Wardlaw-Goza mansion in Madison, lights seem to come on when no one is in the house.

The same is true for the Hampton location, for according to tour guide, Miss Tyler, the manager claims to have witnessed something that baffled him. She recounts, "He had turned off all the lights in the house, and as he was driving away, he looked back . . . the lights were back on." When I read that tale, I remembered what the nighttime security guard at the college said to me about the Smith-Goza-Wardlaw mansion. He rejoiced, "I am so glad we sold that house!" Other rumors claim the first owner at Hampton Plantation also died a painful death from liver disease, and the haunting presence lurking there is actually his restless ghost roaming the home in South Carolina. It is also said of Hampton Plantation that George Washington visited there. Hampton Plantation is located nineteen miles south of Georgetown on U.S. Route 17.[2]

Exploring the American South is a way to get to know history in a firsthand way. Having an understanding that the Celts and the Africans had strong beliefs in the supernatural helps us to realize that the strange stories we hear in the South today are vestiges of those ancient, paranormal ideas. We hope this book will help further your interest in the lore and history of Indian mounds, mission sites, old mansions, gravesites, and historical places of the region.

Rose Knox and Graham Schorb

Endnotes

1. Historical sign, Hampton Plantation, outside Georgetown, South Carolina.
2. Hampton Plantation sign.

The Knox Family Connection: A Scot-Irish Clan in American History

> ". . . proud families had pledged themselves to starve rather than beg." Thomas Keneally

The Carolina territories of the United States were settled in great multitudes during the eighteenth century by the Presbyterian Ulster Scots. They left Ireland for reasons of religious persecution and economic deprivation. There were several mass migrations involving the Scot-Irish. The Knoxes arrived in America at various time periods, motivated to emigrate for different reasons. Billy Kennedy, in his book *The Scots-Irish in the Carolinas,* chronicles those particular migrations of the Knox clan. He writes, "This Presbyterian family of lowland Scots resided in the Ballymoney area of North Antrim from about 1750 after moving there from Scotland.

Life was harsh on the Antrim hillsides for Scottish-born James and Elizabeth Craig Knox and their family; they did not need much persuasion to take up the land grant offered by the General Assembly of South Carolina." On a vessel named the *Earl of Hillsborough* they left from Belfast headed for Charleston in March of 1767. During a perilous voyage Elizabeth was to deliver a child, but had to bury it at sea. On their arrival in Charleston, the Knoxes were allocated 450 acres of land located in what was Belfast Township or Boonesborough Township. It was situated in Chester County, one hundred miles into the Carolina up-country. The Knoxes settled there and had twelve children–six sons and six daughters.[1]

The Knoxes were to fight in the American wars. During the Revolutionary War, John, James, Robert, and Samuel Knox, sons of James and Elizabeth, fought with the South Carolina Continental Line, and were at Charleston in May of 1780 when the British attacked. The Knox men also fought at Kings Mountain. James Knox Junior was killed a year later by loyalists avenging the defeat at Kings Mountain. Captain Hugh Knox, a cousin who was born in 1755 in

Ireland, also led the militia battles at various places, including Rocky Mountain, Hanging Rock, Congaree Fort, and Kings Mountain. He was a prominent community figure, and in 1793 he served as sheriff of Chester County. James Senior was, at the age of seventy, made justice of the peace four years before his death.

When available territories opened up for pioneers in Kentucky, members of the Knox family moved there in 1788. They were traveling with other families via wagon train. There were six wagons moving together. Crab Orchard in Madison County, Kentucky, was where they settled until 1812, when they moved with another wagon train destined for Bedford County, Tennessee. The family matriarch, Elizabeth Craig Knox, was to move several times in her long life. She lived to be 103 and died in 1822.[2]

Some of the other Ulster families originally making it to the Carolinas with that Knox family migration from Ireland included the following: Anderson, Cochran, Culberton, Erwin, Hamilton, Hanvey, Hill, Hunter, Jones, Kennedy, McClurkin, McGinley, Morrison, Porter, Reid, Richey/Ritches, Seawright, Sherad, Speer, and Wallace.[3]

Another migration took place motivated out of hunger. Billy Kennedy explains of that later migration, "The horrendous potato famine of the 1840s in Ireland forced a number of Presbyterian families in the small East Antrim village of Raloo near Larne to emigrate."[4] Most of them made their way to the area of Abbeville in South Carolina. The region was previously called "Old 96." Jeanette (Jenny) Moore Knox migrated to America with eleven of her twelve children after her blacksmith husband died in 1840. She had endured great trials inflicted by the famine, but the Knox family held high hopes of a bright future in this new land. They journeyed to Abbeville and the sons and daughters dispersed to various areas with their families, but Jenny continued to live near Abbeville village with her younger children. Making the voyage with the Knox clan on that journey were also the Blair, Crawford, and Evans families. They arrived in 1844, sailing into Charleston. Then they journeyed by train to Augusta, Georgia, finally reaching the South Carolina back country of Abbeville traveling in covered wagons. The influence that these families had in this region of South Carolina over the past 150 years was quite considerable.[5]

To illustrate why the Irish were compelled to move, Thomas Keneally mentions many hardships as he writes, ". . . the population of Ireland, between the census of 1841 and the census of 1881, declined to a level barely above half of what it had been—a catastrophe unique in

Europe." He continues by saying, ". . . just under 850,000 Irish would enter the United States via the port of New York in the years between 1847 and 1851." In one chapter named "A Fond Farewell to the White Potatoes," Keneally tells in grisly fashion what plight the Irish were to suffer because of the rotting potato crop. The staple food "rotted before their eyes," and it was a frightful certainty of an "approaching famine." By 1845 ". . . peasants were starving in Ireland and in parts of the Highlands of Scotland. It came to be known as the 'Great Hunger.'"

At the same time thousands upon thousands of people were shuffling around, and roadsides and ditches were filling up with those who had collapsed and died. Ironically, many of them were on their way to work programs that had been set up by the British government. The journalists of the day recorded that Irish men, women, and children showed up in droves to work, looking much like scarecrows or walking skeletons. During this same period, the British government was shipping exports of corn and other foodstuffs in great amounts out of the country. Such exports enraged the starving people, but they were too weak and too sick to complain. Political movements that might have bettered the Irish situation all but dried up during the famine as survival was the main focus for millions.[6]

In addition, with corpses piling up like cordwood and bodies scattered in roadways, typhus or black fever also furthered the terrible suffering of thousands. Infected lice communicated the disease. Keneally illustrates the serious, contagious nature of the illness writing, "The mere squashing of an infected louse on the skin permitted invasion of the minute bacteria." Yellow fever, likewise transmitted by lice, spread. ". . . proud families had pledged themselves to starve rather than beg. Hundreds of thousands waited for typhus to 'deliver' them from the gripping horror of want."[7] To further illustrate the desperation that famine brought on, Keneally says,

> A Wicklow farmer saw groups of men cornering cattle, to cut a vein in the neck of a beast and pour . . . blood into a jar. They would repair the incision with a pin and a swatch of hair cut from the animal's tail. The blood would be salted and fried in a pan. . . . When the fish in the Ow River in Wicklow had all been caught, people ate the pencil-thick worms from the bottom of the stream. . . . Rats which had eaten of the dead were fair game.[8]

By the summer of 1847, nearly three million Irelanders, half of the population of the country, were being fed by relief committee kitchens. Such scenes illustrate why so many chose to leave hearth and homeland. In the desperate exodus from the country, many starving and very sick people boarded overcrowded ships and ". . . fever and other diseases had come on board with them."[9] And if they survived the adversities of the voyage–the fleets holding immigrants were called "coffin ships"–they met with great resistance. Keneally writes, "The look of the ragged, hungry verminous Famine immigrants unleashed much anti-Irish hysteria, as from New York to Baltimore Irishmen and women were suddenly begging on the icy streets of the eastern United States."[10] But it was hope for a better life that drove the Knoxes and others to America.

In that second migration, the Knox men served as soldiers in this new land. The Mexican War was on and James Jeanette (Jenny) Moore, Knox's oldest son, went off to fight. He never came home and was presumed dead. Of the other children, the author Kennedy writes, "David, married to Nancy Blair, and William married to Rachel Russell, followed their father's trade as blacksmiths, while Nathaniel and Samuel ended up as Confederate soldiers in the Civil War, Nathaniel dying at the Battle of Gaines Mill and Samuel at the Battle of Malvern Hill, both on Virginia soil." Also, David Crawford Knox, the oldest son of David and Nancy Blair Knox, fought in the Civil War as a rifleman. He was wounded and later was to become a blacksmith following the tradition of the family. He lived in South Carolina and Georgia. As for their religious roots, these Knox Ulster immigrants had been members of Larne and Kilwaughter Presbyterian Churches in Ireland. In Abbeville they became members of Lebanon Presbyterian Church.[11]

In October 1848 a letter from Nancy Blair Knox's mother and father, Esther and Samuel Blair, makes mention of their hardship back in Ballyvallough, near Larne, in Co. Antrim saying, "The potato rot has visited us again . . . money scarce, trade bad . . . but may God Almighty protect you and your family." In that same letter there is also mention of a burning house and the allusion to the institution of slavery. "Be thankful of your children was not burned with the blanket and be kind to the black man who saved the children. Although his skin is black, he is one of God's creations as well as you. Although he is now in bondage, death will set him free."[12]

The settlers of the Carolinas comprised three types of Scottish people. There were the Lowland Scots from Scotland proper; the Ulster-Scots, like the Knoxes, from Ireland; and the Highland Scots; they drifted in great numbers mostly to North Carolina. Some Scots had been deported by English authorities after the Jacobite rebellions of 1715 and 1745. But the majority of the Scots migrated by their own desire to better their financial lot; times were indeed hard in the late seventeenth and eighteenth centuries in both Scotland and Ulster. Some Scots had money to work with and so were able to acquire large tracts of land, while others were very poor, having only the means to purchase the ocean fare and needed supplies for the voyage. Others still were forced to indenture themselves for a ten-year term to fund their voyage to America. But no matter how they ended up in America, they were to make significant contributions to the settlement of the back country of South Carolina, even though they were "famous" for their contentious, clannish ways and had a hard time assimilating with other groups.[13]

David & Nancy (Blair) Knox

No matter how they ended up in America, they were to make significant contributions to the settlement of the back country of South Carolina, though they were "famous" for their contentious, clannish ways and had a hard time assimilating with other groups. Courtesy of an online image

Endnotes

1. Billy Kennedy, *The Scots-Irish in the Carolinas* (Greenville, SC: Causeway Press, 1997).

2. Kennedy, *The Scots-Irish.*

3. Kennedy, *The Scots-Irish.*

4. Kennedy, *The Scots-Irish.*

5. Kennedy, *The Scots-Irish.*

6. Thomas Keneally, *The Great Shame: And the Triumph of the Irish in the English-Speaking World* (New York: Anchor Books, 1998).

7. Keneally, *The Great Shame.*

8. Keneally, *The Great Shame.*

9. Keneally, *The Great Shame.*

10. Keneally, *The Great Shame.*

11. Kennedy, *The Scots-Irish.*

12. Kennedy, *The Scots-Irish.*

13. Kennedy, *The Scots-Irish.*

Rose Knox and Graham Schorb

Travel Notes

Voices Rising Up: Epilogue

As one can see, the Red Hills of rural Florida is a special place, indeed! The soil of the region and the abundant springs—and later rivers—are what ultimately attracted people to what are today Madison, Jefferson, and Leon Counties. It was the unique topography of the area, the result of melting ice caps during the last Ice Age, which created a special geographical location of rolling hills, with some of the richest farming soil to be had in the world. Some claim it was much like that of the Black Belt of the Mississippi Delta.

I grew up listening to those stories, and in my own backyard was a rich history of people, places, and happenings. In fact, just a hop, skip, and a jump from my childhood neighborhood in Madison County, I remember talk of diving archaeologists who brought up an intact mastodon tusk from the dark depths of the Aucilla River. Not far from that location, looming ceremonial mounds from the Woodland period tower over the landscape near Lake Miccosukee, their presence telling a silent story of ancient spiritual and burial practices of the indigenous tribes. What a wonderful place to have a picnic and to think of those long-ago times! It is therefore my hope that you have enjoyed this sketchbook about many people and places: ancient hunters pursuing Paleolithic beasts; the later Indian Confederations and their early farming communities; later still, the Spanish conquests and the mission period; the British army's destruction of Spanish missions; encroaching settlers and their conflicts and wars with the Seminole Nation; aristocratic planters; slave narratives; and the music coming out of the African tradition.

I hope, too, you were enthralled with the tale of an escaping Confederate war general, a haunted mansion where thirty-one Civil War soldiers died, and those cemeteries supposedly full of spooks. You might in the future be compelled to walk around in these same places to relive the history. And just perhaps you learned something of how superstitious beliefs crept into Southern folklore, emerging first out of the old belief systems and fears of the Celt and the African traditions.

Those beliefs were later transmogrified into what has become known as the Southern Gothic lore of haints that involves inexplicable, paranormal happenings.

Also, I hope you have enjoyed the visual journey through the Red Hills, with the help of archival photographs from the State Library and Archives of Florida, and with paintings of Native Americans from talented artists like Patrick Elliott and Theodore Morris. Those artists brought the ancients back to life, helping modern-day people relive a story; the tales they portrayed on canvas might perhaps remind folks of the racing heartbeat of a Paleolithic hunter downing a mastodon or giant sloth; and to think that these human beings and enormous creatures lived and walked among the Red Hills!

As a keen listener, maybe you can still hear the sound of hundreds of marching, armed Spanish soldiers and the laments of a defeated Indian Confederation of mound builders; or still imagine the mass migrations of African slaves traveling with their aristocratic masters in wagon trains pulled by oxen, as they flooded into territorial Florida. You might still be able to envision the look on one old man's face as he brought up an old mission bell from the muddy embankments of Lake Sampala; or feel the exuberance of archeological students when they, along with their mentor B. Calvin Jones, the state's archeologist, discovered a graveyard full of Christianized Indians in Madison County; the stories remain in these sloping hills.

Listen closely to hear the terrifying victory cry from Seminole braves when they took vengeance upon wealthy hunters at Clifton plantation; or watch in fascination a medieval joust in the streets of Monticello, and afterwards partake in a bountiful feast, dining with the ultra-wealthy planters of the day; then you might have heard the faint music and danced to waltzes like "Auf Wiedersehen" and the "Blue Danube" with Southern aristocrats, the women twirling in elaborate dresses and the men in their finest fitted suits. While you are imagining, you might pretend to step up a finely crafted Charleston staircase in a mansion called Whitehall, and listen to the cries of thirty-one battle-wounded Rebels and Yankees, dying in that makeshift Civil War hospital; or you might attempt to get a glimpse of the life of the slave and the master on plantations named El Destino, Casa Bianca, Pinetucky, The Cedars, and Lyndhurst.

On a lazy afternoon you might choose, like my family once did, to stroll through several boneyards where whole families are buried in mass graves—victims of yellow fever—and to think on those hard times.

If you are in Tallahassee near St. John's Episcopal Church Cemetery, and have some time to kill, try standing over two tombs where a European prince and princess are resting side by side for all eternity amid the hustle and bustle of the state capital in Tallahassee; some say the princess still lurks in spirit amid the fog of early mornings. While there, just steps away from St. John's is also Old City Cemetery where you can also meander and where black and white Civil War soldiers repose, just a few yards from one another; but be warned and make sure to stay watchful for signs of those roaming, restless spirits of an antebellum past, which folklore reveals still appear on lazy afternoons, misty mornings, or moonlit nights!

It is my hope and prayer that you will listen to the voices rising up and think of times past in these Red Hills, the realm I love, and the place that is my home!

Rose Knox

Graham's Biography

Graham Schorb is a native Floridian, and his many contributions have helped make this history book a reality. He assisted in searching out directions, finding historical locations, and working with his wife, Rose, on this, their third historical compilation. A few of the places in northern Florida he sought out and helped navigate to were the following: places of interest on the Aucilla and Suwannee Rivers; ancient ceremonial mounds; former Spanish mission sites and cemeteries; pioneer cemeteries; and antebellum mansion locations of the Red Hills.

Graham attended Pinellas Vocational Technical Institute in the 1980s, earning a certificate in Horticultural Studies. He comes from a noteworthy line of people, some of them Scot-Irish and Germanic. One aspect of his family history is that his great-great-great-grandfather, John R. Schorb, was known as America's first traveling photographer. He walked through many states, chronicling the lives of people, including some of the Catawba Indians. A museum collection at Winthrop University in Rock Hill, South Carolina, is devoted to his grandfather's photographic contributions. Not surprisingly, many of the images that show up in this book were taken by Graham. Much like Henry David Thoreau, Graham wanted little to do with the modern world, with its many distractions. In 1980 he was drawn to rural northern Florida. He went into the woods, and there he constructed his own small cabin. Preserving the history of the Red Hills would have been difficult without his knowledge and guidance.

All of the books produced by Rose Knox and Graham Schorb were published by the Florida Historical Society. Each work may be found online at the Florida Historical Society site, myfloridahistory.org.

Graham Schorb

Rose's Biography

Rose Knox grew up listening to stories about the Red Hills of northern Florida. In her "own backyard," an old, dilapidated antebellum mansion and one of the oldest pioneer cemeteries in the state of Florida were pivotal places of intrigue during her childhood. The Florida Historical Society has published several of her regional books. Those titles are *Canoeing and Camping on the Historic Suwannee River: A Paddler's Guide* and *Old Tales of the Forgotten South in a Georgia-Florida Swamp: Paddling Okefenokee*. Both works were compiled in collaboration with Graham Schorb, her husband, an outdoor guide. Her profile pieces have been featured in *Florida Wildlife* Magazine and in Florida newspapers. Rose is a teacher at a rural college in the Red Hills and is a native Floridian.

Bibliography

Alderson, Doug. "Watery Thread Through Time: The St. Marks River." In *Between Two Rivers: Stories from the Red Hills to the Gulf.* Edited by Susan Cerulean, Janisse Ray, and Laura Newton. Tallahassee: Heart of the Earth and the Red Hills Writers Project, 2004.

Aleman, Lazaro. *Monticello News & The Jefferson Journal.* ECB Publishing, Inc. January 10, 2017.

American Agriculturist 10 (1851). New York: Saxton and Miles, 1850–1859: 148.

Balfour, R. C., III. *In Search of the Aucilla.* Valdosta: Colson Printing Company, 2002.

Ball, Edward. *Slaves in the Family.* New York: Ballantine Books, 1998.

Balm, Catherine Miller. *Fun and Festival from Africa.* New York, 1935.

Bardoe, Cheryl. *Mammoths and Mastodons: Titans of the Ice Age.* New York: Abrams Books, in association with the Field Museum, Chicago, 2010.

Bartram, William. *Travels.* New Haven, CT: Yale University Press, 1958.

Blakey, Arch Fredric, Ann Smith Lainhart, and Winston Bryant Stephens Jr., eds. *Rose Cottage Chronicles: Civil War Letters of the Bryant-Stephens Families of North Florida.* Gainesville: University Press of Florida, 1998.

Brown, Alan. *Stories from the Haunted South.* Jackson: University Press of Mississippi, 2004.

Browning, Edwin, Jr. "Ellaville Stood by Confederacy." *Tallahassee Democrat,* 25 June.

Campbell, Joseph. "Folkloristic Commentary." In *The Complete Grimm's Fairy Tales.* New York: Pantheon, 1944.

Campbell, Joseph. *The Power of Myth with Bill Moyers.* Edited by Betty Sue Flowers. New York: Doubleday, 1988.

Rose Knox and Graham Schorb

Civil War Letters of the Bryant-Stephens Families of North Florida. Gainesville: University Press of Florida, 1998.

Cooke, Wythe. *Geology of Florida.* Tallahassee: State of Florida, Department of Conservation, 1945.

Counts, Derylene Delp. *Familiar Faces and Quiet Places: A Pictorial and Narrative History of Jefferson County, Florida.* Virginia Beach, VA: Donning Publishing Company, 2005.

Covington, James W. *The Seminoles of Florida.* Gainesville: University Press of Florida, 1993.

Davidson, Michelle. *Florida's Haunted Hospitality.* Atglen, PA: Schiffer Publishing Ltd., 2013.

Dillard, Annie. *An American Childhood.* New York: Harper-Perennial, 1987.

Douglas, Marjory Stoneman. *The Everglades: River of Grass.* 50th anniv.ed. Sarasota, FL: Pineapple Press, 1998.

Easley, Nicole Carlson. *Hauntings in Florida's Panhandle.* Atglen, PA: Schiffer Publishing Ltd., 2009.

Ellis, Mary Louise, and William Warren Rogers. *Favored Land, Tallahassee: A History of Tallahassee and Leon County.* Virginia Beach, VA: Donning Company, 1988.

Ervin, William R. *Let Us Alone.* W and S Ervin Publishing Company, 1983.

Ewen, Charles R., and John H. Hann. *Hernando de Soto among the Apalachee: The Archaeology of the First Winter Encampment.* Gainesville: University Press of Florida, 1998.

Fisher, Miles Mark. *Negro Slave Songs in the United States.* New York: Citadel Press, 1963.

Giblin, James Cross. *The Mystery of the Mammoth Bones.* New York: Harper-Collins, 1999.

Groene, Bertram H. *Ante-Bellum Tallahassee.* Tallahassee: Florida Heritage Foundation, 1981.

Guerreo, Gavira, and Peter Frances, sr. eds. *Prehistoric Life: The Definitive Visual History of Life on Earth.* Great Britain: Darling Kindersley, 2009.

Gunter, Herman. "Once Roamed Land of Sunshine." *Florida Highways.* August 1941, p. 13, 35.

Haley, Alex. *Roots: The Saga of an American Family*. New York: Doubleday, 1976.

Hann, John H., and Bonnie G. McEwan. *The Apalachee Indians and Mission San Luis*. A Florida Heritage Publication. Gainesville: University Press of Florida, 1998.

Harden, John. *Tar Heel Ghosts*. Chapel Hill: University of North Carolina Press, 1954.

Haskins, Lola. *Fifteen Florida Cemeteries: Strange Tales Unearthed.* Tallahassee: University Press of Florida, 2011.

Hauserman, Julie. "Florida's Lost Waterfall: Cascades Park." In *Between Two Rivers: Stories from the Red Hills to the Gulf*. Edited by Susan Cerulean, Janisse Ray, and Laura Newton. Tallahassee, FL: Red Hills Writers Project, 2004.

Hinson, Mark. "Now this Place is Downright Spooky." *Tallahassee Democrat*, October 2015. Web accessed.

Howell, Clark F. *Early Man*. New York: Time Life Books, 1965.

Hurmence, Belinda, ed. *Before Freedom, When I Just Can Remember: Twenty-Seven Oral Histories of Former South Carolina Slaves.* Winston-Salem, NC: John F. Blair, 1989.

———. *My Folks Don't Want Me to Talk about Slavery: Twenty-One Oral Histories of Former North Carolina Slaves.* Winston-Salem, NC: John F. Blair, 1984.

Johns, John E. *Florida during the Civil War*. Gainesville: University of Florida Press, 1963.

Johnson, Claudia Hunter. "The Monarchs of Eden." In *Between Two Rivers: Stories from the Red Hills to the Gulf*. Edited by Susan Cerulean, Janisse Ray, and Laura Newton. Tallahassee, FL: Heart of the Earth and the Red Hills Writers Project, 2004.

Jones, B. Calvin. 1972. *Spanish Mission Sites Located and Test Excavated.* Archives and History News 3(6): 1-2.

Keneally, Thomas. *The Great Shame: And the Triumph of the Irish in the English-Speaking World.* New York: Anchor Books, 1998.

Kennedy, Billy. *The Scots-Irish in the Carolinas.* Greenville, SC: Causeway Press, 1997.

Knight, Steve. *Madison County: From Sea to Secession.* Written history about oral stories of Madison, Florida, with added research, 1950s.

Knox, Leslie Rose, and Graham Schorb. *Canoeing and Camping on the Historic Suwannee River: A Paddler's Guide.* Cocoa: Florida Historical Society Press, 2012.

———. *Old Tales of the Forgotten South in a Georgia-Florida Swamp: Paddling Okefenokee.* Cocoa: Florida Historical Society Press, 2018.

Landenberg, Kathleen. "The Quest for Florida's Lost Volcano." In *Between Two Rivers: Stories from the Red Hills to the Gulf.* Edited by Susan Cerulean, Janisse Ray, and Laura Newton. Tallahassee, FL: Red Hills Writers Project, 2004.

Lange, Ian M. *Ice Age Mammals of North America: A Guide to the Big, Hairy, and the Bizarre.* Missoula, MT: Mountain Press, 2002.

Lanier, Florida: Its Scenery Climate. *Tallahassee Floridian and Journal,* 25 May 1850.

Lister, Adrian, and Paul Bahn. *Mammoths: Giants of the Ice Age.* London: Marshall Publishing, 2000.

Long, Karen Haymon. "Madison Mansion Given to UF." *Orlando Sentinel,* Saturday, February 18, 1984.

Mason, Ronald J. (1970). "Hopewell Middle Woodland and the Laurel Culture: A Problem of Archaeological Classification." *American Anthropologist* 72, no. 4: 802-15.

Matrana, Marc R. *Lost Plantations of the South.* Jackson: University Press of Mississippi, 2009.

McEwan, Bonnie G. "The Spiritual Conquest of La Florida." *American Anthropologist* 103, no. 3 (Sept., 2001): 633-44.

McEwan, Bonnie G., ed. *Spanish Missions of La Florida, The.* Gainesville: University Press of Florida, 1993.

McRory, Mary Oakley, and Edith Clarke Barrows. *History of Jefferson County, Florida.* Monticello, FL: Published under the auspices of the Kiwanis Club, 1958.

Menton, Jane Aurell. *The Grove: A Florida Home through Seven Generations.* Tallahassee, FL: Sentry Press, 1998.

Milanich, Jerald T. *Florida Indians and the Invasion from Europe.* Gainesville: University Press of Florida, 1995.

———. *Laboring in the Fields of the Lord: Spanish Missions and Southeastern Indians.* Gainesville: University Press of Florida, 2006.

Milner, George R. *The Mound Builders: Ancient Peoples of Eastern North America.* London: Thames & Hudson Ltd., 2004.

Morris, Theodore. *Florida's Lost Tribes.* Gainesville: University Press of Florida, 2004.

Musgrove, Eric. *Reflections of Suwannee County.* 150th anniv. ed. 1858-2008. Live Oak: North Florida Printing, 2008.

Nulty, William H. *Confederate Florida.* Tuscaloosa: University of Alabama Press, 1990.

Osborne, Mary Pope, and Natalie Pope Boyce. *The Saber Tooth and the Ice Age.* New York: Random House, 2005.

Paisley, Clifton. *The Red Hills of Florida 1528–1865.* Tuscaloosa: University of Alabama Press, 1989.

Pluckhahn, Thomas J. "Woodland Period: Overview." *New Georgia Encyclopedia* 03. August 2015. Web, 10 February 2017.

Revels, Tracy J. *Florida's Civil War: Terrible Sacrifices.* Macon, GA: Mercer University Press, 2016.

Rivers, Larry Eugene. *Slavery in Florida: Territorial Days to Emancipation.* Gainesville: University Press of Florida, 2000.

Rogers, William Warren. *A Historic Sampler of Tallahassee and Leon County.* Cocoa: Florida Historical Society Press, 2005.

Ross, Anne. *The Folklore of the Scottish Highlands.* New York: Barnes and Noble Books, 1976.

Rutledge, Archibald. *Deep River: The Complete Poems of Archibald Rutledge.* Columbia, SC: R. L. Bryan Company, 1960.

Shetterly, Susan Hand. *Settled in the Wild: Notes from the Edge of Town.* Chapel Hill, NC: Algonquin Books, 2010.

Shields, Sharyn Heiland. *Whispers from Verdura: The Lost Legacy of Benjamin Chaires.* Tallahassee, FL: Sentry Press, 2016.

Shofner, Jerrell H. *History of Jefferson County.* Tallahassee, FL: Sentry Press, 1976.

Sims, Elizabeth, et al. *A History of Madison County, Florida.* Madison, FL: Jimbob Printing Inc., 1986.

Slave Narratives: A Folk History of Slavery from Interviews with Former Slaves in the United States. Vol 3. Federal Writers Project, 1936–1938. Washington, D. C.: Library of Congress.

Smith, Julia Floyd. *Slavery and Plantation Growth in Antebellum Florida: 1821–1860.* Gainesville: University of Florida Press, 1973.

Southall, Richard. *Haunted Plantations of the South.* Woodbury, MN: Llewellyn Publications, 2015.

Ste. Claire, Dana. *Cracker: The Cracker Culture in Florida History.* Gainesville: University Press of Florida, 1998.

Stein, Teresa E. *Florida Cracker Tales.* Lake Placid, FL: Placid Publishing House, 1995.

Thompson, Edgar T. "The Plantation as a Social System." In *Plantation Systems of the New World: Papers and Discussion Summaries.* Volume 7. p. 29.

WPA Florida Writers Project. *Spanish Missions of Florida.* New Smyrna Beach, FL: Luthers, 1940.

Wagner, Margaret E. *The American Civil War: 365 Days.* Edited by Vincent Virga. New York: Abrams, 2006.

Ward, Peter D. *The Call of Distant Mammoths: Why the Ice Age Mammals Disappeared.* New York: Springer-Verlog, 1997.

Webb, David S. "Aucilla River: Time Machine." In *Between Two Rivers: Stories from the Red Hills to the Gulf.* Edited by Susan Cerulean, Janisse Ray, and Laura Newton. Tallahassee, FL: Red Hills Writers Project, 2004.

Welty, Eudora. *One Writer's Beginnings.* Cambridge, MA: Harvard University Press, 1984.

Whitaker, John O., Jr.. *National Audubon Society Field Guide to North American Mammals.* New York: Chanticleer Press, 1980.

Worth, John E. *Timucuan Chiefdoms of Spanish Florida.* Vol. 1: *Assimilation.* Gainesville: University Press of Florida, 1998.

Wright, Louis B. *South Carolina: A History.* New York: W. W. Norton, 1976.

Yonge, C. Julien, ed., and Emma Rochelle Williams, asst. ed. "The Bell of a Florida Spanish Mission." *Florida Historical Quarterly* 5, no. 3 (January 1972). Gainesville, FL: Pepper Printing Company.

Zeiger-McPherson, Christina A., Betty Davis, and Big Bend Ghost Trackers. *Haunted Monticello, Florida.* Charleston, SC: History Press, 2011.

Interviews

David Cook, personal interview, St. Marks Wildlife Refuge, Nov. 3, 2008.

Robert Patrick Elliott, telephone conversations, formal visits, and informal conversations, Tallahassee, Florida, 2012 to 2019.

Edward Jonas, email communication: "Mission at San Luis Art and Excavation," April 2012.

Theodore Morris, telephone conversation and follow-up visit to his Aviles Street studio in Saint Augustine, Florida, Oct. and Nov. 2015.

Jim Smith and Peggy, Zet, "How Our Mother, June Smith, Saved the Home: and Other Memories." Interview in Wardlaw-Smith-Goza Mansion, Madison, Florida, 2011. Transcribed by Rosanna Hughes.

Jason Welch, interview at the Treasures Museum in Madison, Florida, Spring 2016.

Rose Knox and Graham Schorb

Speeches/Presentations

Ferris, William R. "1966 Speech to the Commonwealth Club of San Francisco." *Humanities* 19, no. 1 (January/February 1998).

Harper, Charles, and Daniel M. Seinfeld. "Woodland Period Settlement Patterns at Letchworth." Presented at the Society for American Archaeology 81st Annual Meeting, Orlando, Florida, April 6-10, 2016.

"Mounds, Jefferson County, Florida." In the 81st Annual Meeting of the Society for American Archaeology, 2016.

Smith, Jim, and Zet Smith. The story of their mother, June Smith, and her fight against a powerful man. Presented to the Madison County Historical Society, April 26, 2009.

Oral Stories and Conversations

Reichert, Jhan. Conversation: Haunted Monticello, North Florida Community College Library, Madison, Florida, March 2017.

Sanders, Frances Morrow. Oral stories about area mansions and Mosely Hall Region, Madison, Florida, 1975-1976.

Historical Signs

City Cemetery, Tallahassee, Florida.

Four Freedoms Park, Madison, Florida.

Hampton Plantation, outside of Georgetown, South Carolina.

Oakland Cemetery, Madison, Florida.

Oak Ridge Cemetery, Madison, Florida.

Brochures and Pamphlets

"Lake Jackson Mounds Archaeological State Park." Florida State Parks, Florida Department of Environmental Protection. Brochure, October 2015.

"Spanish Missions: Early Encounters between the Christian and the "'Noble Savage.'" Georgia Historical Society. Brochure.

"Jefferson County: Monticello Section." Jefferson Business League. Pamphlet.

Thompson, Sharyn M. "Walking Tour of Old City Cemetery." Historic Preservation Board and City of Tallahassee. Brochure.

Wardlaw-Smith-Goza-Conference Center, Historic Florida Landmark. Brochure.

Videos/Films

Creativity with Bill Moyers: Maya Angelou. Films Media Group, 1982.

Desoto & the Mississippi Valley/1539 (500 Nations: The Story of Native Americans), published by PANGA, YouTube video, November 7, 2017.

Census Records

United States Census 1830–1860.

Diary Entries

Diary of Robert Raymond Reid, 1833, 1835.

Websites

Florida Museum of Natural History. Gainesville, Florida. www.flmnh.ufl.edu/butterflies/

Saint Marks Wildlife Refuge. www.fws.gov/saintmarks/

Index

A

Africa xvii, 2, 3, 7, 17, 27, 31, 48, 59, 61–64, 96, 110, 126, 132, 150, 153, 198, 271–273, 278, 297–299, 301, 303, 350, 409, 410, 412, 499, 509

African American cemetery 428, 429

African elephant 24

Akerman, Joe , viii

alligator 30, 94, 99, 110, 376, 381, 458, 459, 461

Amelia Island 244, 417, 419

American mastodon 17, 23, 27, 253, 460

ancient Indians 233, 252

Andrew Jackson 95, 259, 260, 307, 391, 392, 394, 475

antebellum , xviii, 2, 3, 7, 8, 61, 65, 70, 73, 77, 102, 107, 108, 111, 116, 125–127, 141, 142, 144, 147, 149, 151, 157, 169, 186, 198, 200, 202, 204, 209, 215, 271, 272, 275–277, 285, 307, 318, 392, 397, 399, 401, 410, 417, 457, 482, 493–496, 497, 511, 513, viii

anthropologist 12, 233, 237, 365, 375, 377, 460, 465

Antrim 501, 502, 504

Apalachee Indians 2, 30, 36, 38, 39, 43, 45, 54, 83, 226, 227, 242, 349–352, 353–358, 365

archeologist xviii, 12, 13, 30, 48, 239, 241–243, 254, 360, 460, 461, 465, 510

Archibald Rutledge 264, 498

architecture 125, 131, 141, 142, 150, 154, 284, 287, 293, 366, 370, 458, 483

Arctic 253

aristocrat 2, 7, 61, 62, 67–72, 128, 150, 160, 281, 292, 307, 315, 392, 398–400, 476, 509, 510

B

Rose Knox and Graham Schorb

de Soto, Hernando 36, 43–46, 127, 198, 226, 354, 359–364, 461

de Vega, Garcilaso 354

diaries 36, 43, 47, 54, 101, 226, 241, 242, 316, 360, 365, 376, 447

Dickinson, Rufus 94

dig site 83, 241–243

dire wolves 11, 251, 257, 460

disease 1, 18, 31, 48, 127, 334, 340, 349, 361, 498, 503, 504

diver, underwater 127, 251, 252, 254, 256, 257

doctrina 226

Doric 126, 132, 149

Drew, Farnell 92

Dulce Domum, plantation "Sweet Home" 282, 307

Dunbar, Lisa (Senior Curator) , vii

E

East Lafayette Street 361

Econfina River 93

economy 8, 59, 61, 68, 103, 272

El Destino, plantation 276, 283, 287, 288, 305, 510

elephant 11, 17, 18, 23, 24, 253

Elliott, Patrick 12, 14, 27, 85, 99, 113, 204, 206, 375, 381, 452, 457–474

English colony 38, 365

enslaved 2, 3, 39, 62, 64, 272, 273, 277–279, 299, 300, 365, 411–413

Europe 1, 27, 44, 60, 83, 127, 213, 219, 241, 272, 281, 292, 294, 350, 351, 353, 400, 495, 498, 503

Europeans 2, 30, 31, 35, 37, 48, 127, 198, 228, 229, 243, 281, 284, 291, 349, 350, 372, 373, 511

evil mole 253

Rose Knox and Graham Schorb

Rose Knox and Graham Schorb

Spanish , 1, 2, 7, 29, 31, 35–42, 43–46, 47–52, 53–55, 84, 105, 129, 149, 197, 198, 231, 232, 241, 242, 267, 321, 325, 349, 353–355, 360, 365–367, 370, 371, 376, 391, 458, 475, 509, 510, vii

Spanish moss xvii, 7, 29, 31, 129, 149, 181, 190, 481, 488

spirit 17, 24, 61, 148, 160, 215, 219, 242, 244, 323, 333, 334, 336, 339, 341, 397, 420, 458, 493, 495, 497, 511

spiritual belief system 1, 30, 36, 37, 227, 244, 277, 350, 368, 385, 509

starvation 31, 317, 350

St. Augustine , 2, 37, 48, 93, 198, 227, 291, 365, 366, 386, vii

Steinhatchee River 91, 94, 95, 99

St. John's Day, December 27 354

St. Marks National Wildlife Refuge 325

St. Marks River 225, 228, 353, 445, 446, 477

storyteller v, xviii, 297, 331

St. Petersburg 244, 357

succession 129, 149, 173

Susan Goza 177, 182

Suwannee River 39, 44, 59, 61, 67, 68, 97, 127, 128, 157, 158, 197–208, 251, 271, 365, 371, 497, 513, 515

swamp 2, 3, 39, 67, 88–90, 94, 96, 97, 99, 163, 197, 228, 267–269, 300, 316, 325, 447, 448, 458, 461

T

Tallahassee 2, 13, 18, 25, 31, 37, 43, 53, 54, 56, 59, 83, 142, 193, 198, 199, 201, 225, 226, 236, 244, 254, 268, 269, 281, 287, 288, 291–294, 305, 316, 322, 350, 353–358, 361, 363, 366, 370, 375, 381, 386, 387, 391–396, 397–408, 412, 415, 417–419, 427–440, 441–444, 445, 448, 449, 454, 457–474, 475–480, 481–483, 485, 486, 488, 493–496, 511

Tampa Bay 30, 43, 353

tapir 251, 461, 465

teeth 17, 23, 26, 253, 256

W

Y